D1457894

The
Ethics of
Commercial
Surrogate
Motherhood

The
Ethics of
Commercial
Surrogate
Motherhood

Brave New Families?

Scott B. Rae

Westport, Connecticut
London

Library of Congress Cataloging-in-Publication Data

Rae, Scott B.
   The ethics of commercial surrogate motherhood : brave new
families? / Scott B. Rae.
      p.   cm.
   Includes bibliographical references and index.
   ISBN 0-275-94679-7 (alk. paper)
   1. Surrogate mothers—Legal status, laws, etc.—United States.
2. Parent and child (Law)—United States.   3. Surrogate motherhood—
Moral and ethical aspects.   I. Title.
   KF540.R34   1994
   346.7301 '7—dc20
   [347.30617]   93-17667

British Library Cataloguing in Publication Data is available.

Library of Congress Catalog Card Number: 93-17667
ISBN: 0-275-94679-7

First published in 1994

Praeger Publishers, 88 Post Road West, Westport, CT 06881
An imprint of Greenwood Publishing Group, Inc.

Printed in the United States of America

The paper used in this book complies with the
Permanent Paper Standard issued by the National
Information Standards Organization (Z39.48-1984).

10 9 8 7 6 5 4 3 2

Copyright Acknowledgments

The author and publisher gratefully acknowledge permission to use
materials from the following:

Andrea Stumpf, ''Redefining Mother: A Legal Matrix for New
Reproductive Technologies,'' *The Yale Law Journal* 96 (1986): 187-208.
Reprinted by permission of The Yale Law Journal Company and Fred B.
Rothman & Company.

CONTENTS

ACKNOWLEDGMENTS

Special thanks go to numerous people who made this work possible. Their contributions were all significant, and I would be remiss not to recognize them. My colleagues at Talbot School of Theology and Biola University, particularly Dr. J.P. Moreland, Dr. Walt Russell and Dr. Klaus Issler, have been a constant source of encouragement all along the way. Their prodding to finish the book has been invaluable. The dean at Talbot School of Theology, Dr. Dennis Dirks, and his predecessor, Dr. Bing Hunter, and my department chair during most of this time, Dr. Boyd Luter, provided me with enormous flexibility in my academic schedule to enable me to complete the work.

The feedback that I received from my mentors at the University of Southern California School of Religion was extremely helpful. In particular, Dr. William W. May provided the great majority of the feedback. His contribution was immense and invaluable. Dr. John P. Crossley, Jr., also contributed to the overall style and emphasis of the book and provided some badly needed encouragement at several points in the process. Professor Charles E. Curran, who was a visiting Professor at USC during my time of study there, also provided something very valuable: his belief in me that I was capable of making a contribution that would be worth publishing. The editors at Praeger provided very helpful input to clarify numerous places that were unclear and thus made the book more readable. My assistant, Carolyn Crawford, was indispensible in putting all the necesssary finishing touches on the book. All of these people share the credit for the book, though any errors are entirely my responsibility.

Finally, my family deserves special mention. My parents contributed to our financial support, enabling me to complete the book, and I am very thankful to them for that support. My wife, Sally, and our two boys, Taylor and Cameron, bore most of the cost that writing this book involved. Without their patience and understanding, this project would never have been completed. It is gratefully dedicated to them.

The
Ethics of
Commercial
Surrogate
Motherhood

INTRODUCTION

With the advent of new reproductive technologies, surrogate motherhood has become both a highly visible and ethically complex issue. Cases such as the *Baby M* case in New Jersey illustrate the widespread publicity that surrogacy has attracted due to the non-traditional way in which motherhood occurs. For many infertile couples, surrogacy represents their last hope for having a child to whom at least one of the parents is genetically related. When a pregnancy is successfully completed and the child is turned over to the contracting couple, it seems that everyone in the arrangement walks away satisfied. The couple has the child that they so desperately desire and the surrogate has the satisfaction of having given this couple the "gift of life." In many cases, the surrogate has also increased her income with money that the contracting couple was happy to pay to achieve their goal of having a genetically related child.

However, the *Baby M* case also portrays the complex issues involved in surrogacy. For example, the payment of a fee to the surrogate raises questions about children and women becoming commodities. The introduction of market terminology into the sphere of reproduction has been the subject of great debate. Furthermore, the way in which the contract was enforced against the will of the surrogate, with police literally taking the child from her by force, raises complicated questions of parental rights and the appropriateness of using contract law to govern reproduction.

The *Johnson v. Calvert* case, recently decided by the California Supreme Court, further illustrates the complexity of issues involved in surrogacy, particularly since it is a case of gestational surrogacy, in which the surrogate has no genetic connection to the child she carried. Here motherhood is being redefined, as reproductive technologies enable society to separate the genetic and gestational aspects of motherhood. Of course, the biological and social aspects of parenthood have been separated for some time in adoption. But there is an additional complication in surrogacy, since now the genetic contributor and the person who raises the child may be the same person, even though someone else has given birth to the child. Now that the genetic and gestational aspects of motherhood can be separated, the question of what makes someone a mother is more complex, there is an urgent need to clarify the definition of motherhood since the custody of a child is at stake. In addition, the commercial aspect of surrogacy makes it a potentially very profitable business, not only for surrogates but also for the brokers who facilitate the arrangements. This raises the question of whether and to what extent for-profit commerce should be allowed to become a part of the process of the conception of children.

STATE OF THE DISCUSSION ON SURROGACY

Throughout this work, there will be interaction with some of the key proponents of contrasting positions on surrogacy. For example, some advocate both the commercial aspects and the enforceability of surrogacy contracts, essentially asserting that the parameters of contract law should govern surrogacy.[1] Others, however, advocate allowing a fee to the surrogate beyond reasonable expenses, but either do not allow the contract to be enforced or do not address the enforceability of the contract.[2] Still others favor a more contract-based approach to surrogacy, but approach it with a different set of parameters for identifying the mother. Using the prenatal intent to parent as the deciding factor in determining the mother, some proponents of surrogacy see the contracting couple as the rightful possessors of parental rights to the child.[3] Implied in their position is the legitimacy of the fee to the surrogate.[4] These alternative positions will be analyzed, and, finally, rejected in favor of a view that prohibits both the fee and the enforceability of the contract.

NEED FOR THE STUDY

With the increasing demand for surrogacy contracts to deal with the growing problem of female infertility,[5] and in order to avoid lengthy court disputes (some of the well-publicized cases are as yet unresolved and still in the courts), there is a need for legislation in this area that addresses the complexities involved in surrogacy.

However, legislation is not all that is needed. There is a significant moral component to the discussion of surrogacy that undergirds much of the legal discussion. With this moral element there is often a theological aspect, as theologians from various faith traditions seek to relate their theology to this moral dimension. For many people reproduction has unmistakable moral overtones, since a person's identity and personal fulfillment are partially dependent upon the experience of having a family. In addition, the area of reproduction is heavily value laden. One's views on reproduction are an integral part of the larger debate over the family. Thus, there is a critical moral aspect to the new reproductive technologies in general, and to the most debated of these, surrogacy. Moral principles are regularly introduced into this debate, and both proponents and opponents of the practice appeal to values such as individual procreative liberty, on the one hand, and the sanctity of the family, on the other. Since there are moral considerations at the heart of the issue, it makes sense to engage in moral analysis of surrogacy prior to drafting legislation that addresses the practice.

The two most contested issues in surrogacy are its commercial element, namely payment of a fee to the surrogate, and the assignment of parental rights to the child born of the arrangement. Both of these areas contain the above-mentioned moral overtones, as widely held principles are brought to bear on surrogacy from both advocates and opponents. Since the commercial aspect and parental rights are consistently the most intensely debated and central issues in the surrogacy debate, the moral analysis should be focused on them. Chapters two and three will take up these two important issues.

Though there are only a handful of full-length treatments of surrogacy, there has been a great deal written on the subject. However, the majority of these writings either treat surrogacy generally and from a legal perspective (though bringing in moral considerations), or they are focused on some of the most widely publicized court cases. Many treat either the commercial aspect or the parental rights issue, but the latter do not most often analyze the definition of motherhood. This is particularly important in the more recent gestational surrogacy cases, in which the genetic and gestational aspects of motherhood have been separated. The goal of this work is to undertake a moral analysis of the two most important issues in surrogacy. The resulting moral evaluation of surrogacy will then be applied to the precedent-setting court cases, state laws, and international laws. The work will conclude with a legislative proposal that is directly tied to the preceding moral analysis.

OVERVIEW OF THE ARGUMENT

The thesis of this work is that commercial, contractually enforced surrogate motherhood is inconsistent with widely accepted moral principles and should be legally prohibited. Though the tradition of procreative liberty makes room for altruistic surrogacy, there are cautions about encouraging even non-commercial surrogacy. Enforcing a prohibition on altruistic surrogacy would likely be intolerably invasive and difficult to accomplish.

The focus of the work is on the commercial element of surrogacy and on the enforceability of the contract necessary to complete any surrogacy arrangement to the satisfaction of the contracting couple. The commercial aspect conflicts with the fundamental rights of a child not to be the object of barter. Thus, the surrogate should be reimbursed only for reasonable expenses incurred in the process of conception, pregnancy, and birth. In addition, enforcing the contract against the will of the surrogate conflicts with the surrogate's right to associate with and raise her child if she so chooses. No contract that contains such an enforcement provision should be considered valid and enforceable.

In chapter one, "The Legal Tradition of Procreative Liberty," the legal landscape for surrogacy is surveyed and analyzed. Any legislation dealing with surrogacy must be set in the broader context of procreative freedom implicit in the right to privacy. Surrogacy proponents argue that the right to privacy supports both altruistic and commercial surrogacy. However, there are limits on this freedom, and aspects of the exercise of this freedom about which society should be cautious. This chapter makes the argument that even though the tradition of procreative liberty opens the door to non-commercial surrogacy, that tradition does not justify commercial surrogacy.

Chapter two takes up the practice of surrogacy in which the surrogate is paid a fee beyond reasonable her expenses. I argue in this chapter that commercial surrogacy is the equivalent of child selling and should not be allowed. Proponents of commercial surrogacy argue that the fee is for services only, not the sale of a child, and that even if surrogacy does involve child selling, the practice is quite different from black market adoptions, which the laws against child selling were designed to prohibit. I will show that both of these arguments fail, that the fee paid to the surrogate is indeed for the sale of her child, and that the differences between surrogacy and black market adoptions are either overstated or not relevant to the issue at hand.

There are other arguments attempting to justify commercial surrogacy that also fail. These include the parallel between artificial insemination by donor sperm (AID) and surrogacy, that a restriction on the fee means an unconstitutional restriction on procreative liberty, that children are not treated as commodities, and that money does sometimes properly change hands when parental rights are transferred in adoption settings.

I argue against commercial surrogacy by showing that it involves a commodification of children and of women's bodies and reproductive services, and the potential for exploitation of the surrogate. I conclude that surrogacy does indeed involve the commodification of children and women's reproductive services, and that the potential for exploitation is very real, though the empirical data do not clearly indicate the degree to which that potential has been realized thus far. It is not clear that commercial surrogacy necessarily involves the sale of women's bodies, assuming that there is no coercion of the surrogate to be involved in that role.

In contrast to the moral conclusions of chapter two, some states have chosen to allow commercial surrogacy.[6] For the surrogacy arrangement to be completed, the surrogate must transfer parental rights to the child to which she has given birth. Should the surrogate change her mind about giving up the child, the contracting couple normally seeks to enforce the terms of the contract, and to take custody of the child by force of law. Most of the court cases that have received media attention have involved this aspect of surrogacy. The issue of parental rights is complicated even further in some cases when the surrogate is not genetically related to the child she is carrying. Even if commercial surrogacy is prohibited, there will still be altruistic surrogacy, and there may arise occasions in which there is a dispute over parental rights and custody of the child born out of the arrangement.

Chapter three addresses the definition of motherhood and the issue of parental rights in surrogacy. Given the ability of specialists in reproductive technology to perform in vitro fertilization (IVF) with greater success than ever before, the prospect of a surrogate not being genetically related to the child she is carrying is more likely. In most surrogacy cases, the surrogate provides both the egg and womb, but now gestational surrogacy is a reality with which bioethics and the law must deal. I examine the case for genetics, gestation, and prenatal intent to parent as the determinants of motherhood, and argue that gestation should be the determining factor in assigning parental rights.

Once the mother is determined to be the woman who gives birth to the child, she, not the woman contracting for her to bear the child, is the one with parental rights. The surrogate can waive parental rights, as can any birth mother in adoption. This section of the chapter argues that the right of a mother to raise and otherwise associate with her child is a fundamental right that cannot be taken from her against her will. Thus, any surrogacy contract that contains a pre-birth waiver of maternal rights is voidable and cannot be enforced should the surrogate express a desire to retain maternal rights to the child. Should she desire to keep the child, this will set up a custody battle between her and the natural father. These disputes should be decided based on a dual standard. First, the best interests of the child standard should be applied to see if it indicates a clear preference for one parent over another. Should the best interests standard not be conclusive, a comparison of the strength of the competing parental claims would be made. I will argue that in most cases, the comparison would result in custody being awarded to the surrogate. In conclusion, this chapter suggests that adoption law is a more appropriate guideline for surrogacy than contract law.

Chapter four takes the moral conclusions of the preceding three chapters and applies them to current surrogacy law. This application is in three parts. First is an analysis of the precedent-setting court cases through the lenses of the preceding moral analysis of surrogacy. Second, fifteen states have passed laws that prohibit or regulate surrogacy in some form. These are discussed from the perspective of the moral analysis of this work. Finally, I survey international law and comment on the degree to which nations around the world have formulated laws that adhere to the moral conclusions of this work. In conclusion, I discuss surrogacy as viewed through the framework of existing adoption and AID laws to help complete a survey of the legal landscape in this area.

The conclusion to the work is a legislative proposal, drafted in keeping with the moral analysis of this work and consistent with most state adoption law. The thrust of this sample statute is to prohibit commercial surrogacy while allowing for altruistic surrogacy. In both types of surrogacy, the contract is voidable and unenforceable should the surrogate change her mind in the process and decide to keep the child.

NOTES

1. See for example, John Robertson, "Embryos, Families and Procreative Liberty: The Legal Structure of the New Reproduction," *Southern California Law Review* 59, no. 5 (July 1986): 939-1041; Lori Andrews, "Surrogate Motherhood: An Ethical Perspective," *Law, Medicine and Health Care* 16, nos. 1-2 (1988): 73-91; and William Handel, "An Argument for Surrogate Parenting," *Daily Journal Report* 88, no. 6 (1 April 1988): 9-16.

2. See for example, Thomas Bradley, "Prohibiting Payments to Surrogate Mothers: Love's Labor Lost and the Constitutional Right to Privacy," *John Marshall Law Review* 20 (1987): 715-45; Avi Katz, "Surrogate Motherhood and the Baby Selling Laws," *Columbia Journal of Law and Social Problems* 20 (1986): 1-53; Karen Marie Sly, "Baby-Sitting Consideration: Surrogate Mother's Right to Rent Her Womb for a Fee," *Gonzaga Law Review* 18 (1982/83): 539-65; and William M. Laufer, "Can Surrogacy Co-Exist with New Jersey's Adoption Laws?" *Seton Hall Law Review* 18 (1988): 890-95.

3. See for example Edgar Page, "Donation, Surrogacy and Adoption," *Journal of Applied Philosophy* 2 (October 1985): 161-72; Marjorie Maguire Schultz, "Reproductive Technology and Intent-Based Parenthood: An Opportunity for Gender Neutrality," *Wisconsin Law Review* 1990, no. 2 (1990): 297-398; and Andrea Stumpf, "Redefining Mother: A Legal Matrix for the New Reproductive Technologies," *Yale Law Journal* 96 (1986): 187-208. In all of these discussions, the end result of a surrogacy contract is very similar to the approach of those who advocate a contract law-based approach. These three articles are all addressed in chapter three in connection with the questions of parental rights and the definition of motherhood.

4. Neither Stumpf nor Schultz directly addresses the issue of the fee, though with their overall encouragement of surrogacy, it may be reasonably assumed that they find the fee legitimate. Page does address the fee, and considers it legitimate.

5. The Center for Surrogate Parenting in Beverly Hills, California reports that one in six couples are considered infertile. The center reports a consistently increasing demand for their services in arranging surrogacy contracts. "California may sanction paid surrogate pregnancies," *Medical Ethics Advisor* 8, no. 5 (May 1992): 56-58.

6. Fifteen states have passed surrogacy laws. A survey of these laws and some comment on the degree to which they adhere to the moral analysis of this work appear in chapter four.

1

THE LEGAL TRADITION OF PROCREATIVE LIBERTY

INTRODUCTION

The discussion of surrogate motherhood is set against the backdrop of a long-standing tradition of procreative liberty in the United States. Any legislative proposal that does not take this tradition into account will face significant obstacles in the process of being enacted into law and withstanding Constitutional challenge once enacted. The thesis of this chapter is that this tradition allows at a minimum for non-commercial, or altruistic, surrogacy. That is, the freedom to engage a third party in reproduction properly falls under the heading of procreative liberty. But when it comes to contractual, commercial surrogacy, in which the surrogate is paid a fee to conceive, gestate, and bear a child and to relinquish all parental rights, that is a different issue altogether. Procreative liberty alone does not give the surrogate the freedom to sell the child produced by the surrogacy arrangement.[1] Nor does it allow for the terms of the arrangement to be enforced against the wishes of a surrogate who desires to keep the child and share custody with the natural father.[2] There are other issues besides procreative liberty that must be resolved before commercial, contractually enforced surrogacy can be justified.

The chapter will proceed as follows:

1. *The Legal Precedent*. The key Supreme Court cases that have formed the fabric of procreative freedom will be discussed, with attention given to the moral arguments that underlie the legal verdicts. These cases form a significant part of a developing moral consensus supporting procreative liberty.

2. *Analysis of Procreative Liberty*. The conclusion that the tradition allows for third party participation in the reproductive process will be explored and defended. This section will defend the notion that procreative liberty applied to coital forms of reproduction can be extended to non-coital forms.

3. *Limits on Procreative Liberty.* Various cautions are urged in the exercise of third party procreative liberty. A further limit involves commercial surrogacy, prohibited on other moral grounds discussed in chapter two. Even though procreative liberty opens the door to altruistic surrogacy, there are other aspects of the practice that may be cause for concern.

The point of this chapter is not to make a moral argument for the right to reproduce in general or for altruistic surrogacy in particular. Rather, this chapter examines the legal and moral background to the notion of procreative liberty which might include altruistic surrogacy. One of the goals of this work is to present a proposal for a surrogacy statute that might be enacted into law. The proposed statute must be consistent with the legal and moral traditions of procreative liberty if it is to have much chance of becoming law and being upheld as Constitutional. I conclude that altruistic surrogacy is morally allowable as an extension of procreative liberty, but that commercial surrogacy should be prohibited.

THE LEGAL PRECEDENT

As the legal precedent for procreative liberty developed, the focus of the cases shifted from general concerns about family life to a more narrow concentration on contraception. The cases that dealt with contraception were based on the reasoning that came out of the earlier, more general cases. Though the earlier cases may not appear at first glance to apply to surrogacy, they are important in that they lay the foundation upon which the edifice of procreative liberty is built.

Given the centrality of abortion to the discussion of procreative liberty in general, the absence of the key abortion cases from this discussion may appear curious.[3] As important as these cases are to the general debate over procreative liberty, they are not essential to the debate over surrogacy. A significant part of the surrogacy discussion revolves around the freedom to conceive a child using non-coital methods and third parties in the conception/gestation process, putting the method of reproduction outside the parameters set by the traditional family. The issues in surrogacy and procreative liberty center on conception, not abortion. Procreative liberty issues are at stake prior to any point at which abortion would be contemplated. Most agree that once the child is conceived, a surrogacy contract cannot limit the abortion rights of the surrogate. Thus the key abortion cases are not discussed because they are not directly relevant to the procreative liberty issues that are specific to surrogacy.

Meyer v. Nebraska (1923)[4]

In the first of the cases in which the United States Supreme Court established the tradition of procreative liberty, the Court continued to broaden the scope of the liberties protected by the Fourteenth Amendment. Though the Constitution does not specifically recognize the right to privacy, the Court has continually expanded the notion of liberty to include various zones of privacy inherent in the due process clause.

In *Meyer v. Nebraska*, the Court affirmed that the protected Constitutional liberties include the freedom for an individual "to marry, establish a home and bring up children."[5] The state cannot interfere with one's decision to establish a family. Though non-coital means of reproduction were not in view in this case, some have argued that the freedom for coital reproduction extends by implication to methods that use some of the new reproductive technologies, such as IVF and AID.[6] However, the decision here clearly confined procreative liberty to married couples, and the Court appeared to assume that children (conceived by normal means) are to be brought up in a home occupied by a heterosexual married couple.

Pierce v. Society of Sisters (1925)[7]

Though this case did not deal with conception, the decision affirmed the liberty of parents to raise their children in the manner in which they see fit. It clearly limited the power of the state to interfere in the realm of family matters. This is a foundational decision that was later applied more specifically to privacy relating to contraception and abortion. Though it does not address procreative liberty per se, this decision was instrumental in beginning to define the zones of privacy that were later specified to include procreation as chief among them.

Here the Court made the phrase in the Meyer decision more precise, that an individual has the freedom to "bring up children." Assuming that the way in which that is done does not harm the child in a way that the state could readily prevent, the state does not have the authority to mandate how parents should raise their children. "It is an unreasonable interference with the liberty of parents and guardians to direct to upbringing of the children, and in that respect violates the Fourteenth Amendment."[8] The state of Oregon in this case was prevented from mandating that parents send their children to public schools until the age of sixteen.

Skinner v. Oklahoma (1942)[9]

The Court in this case struck down a mandatory sterilization law for habitual criminals, particularly those guilty of "felonies involving moral turpitude." The defendant was convicted of robbery on three different occasions, and facing sterilization, he sued, charging that the statute violated the equal protection clause of the Fourteenth Amendment.

The Court ruled that the law was discriminatory, "laying an unequal hand on those who have committed intrinsically the same quality of offense and sterilizes one and not the other [the law mandated sterilization for robbery but not for embezzlement], it has made as invidious a discrimination as if it had selected a particular race or nationality for oppressive treatment."[10]

In addition, the Court ruled that the law denied an essential civil liberty, and the language suggested that the right to procreate was so basic as to be inalienable. "We are dealing here with legislation which involves one of the basic civil rights of man. Marriage and procreation are fundamental to the very existence and survival of the race. [When sterilized] He is forever deprived of a basic liberty."[11] Thus, the right to marry and start a family established in *Meyer* cannot be forfeited by any criminal behavior.

Griswold v. Connecticut (1965)[12]

In this landmark case, the Court struck down a Connecticut law forbidding the use of contraceptives, and in doing so, affirmed the right of marital privacy. Though the Constitution does not specifically mention many of the rights that are now clearly recognized as consistent with it, the Court recognized that the right of privacy in marriage is within the penumbra of specific guarantees made by the Bill of Rights.

The Court here established the notion of peripheral rights.[13] Among these are the right to privacy.[14] "This case, then, concerns a relationship lying within the zone of privacy created by several fundamental constitutional guarantees. We deal with a right of privacy older than the Bill of Rights."[15] Here the Court affirmed the notion of substantive due process, that within the structure of the Fourteenth Amendment certain liberties exist irrespective of their specific mention in the Constitution. These unwritten liberties were identified by the Court in keeping with the spirit of those liberties protected by the Bill of Rights.[16] Clearly the Court placed the decision not to procreate within the zones of privacy, consistent with earlier decisions that affirmed the freedom to procreate.

Eisenstadt v. Baird (1972)[17]

This case broadened the right to use contraception recognized by *Griswold* to include unmarried individuals as well as married couples. The Massachusetts law in question made it a felony for anyone except a licensed physician or pharmacist, at a physician's direction to distribute contraceptives. The law provided that they could only distribute them to married couples. It was struck down by the appeals court as a violation of the equal protection clause of the Fourteenth Amendment, and that decision was affirmed by the Supreme Court.

The Court rejected the state's claim that the law was grounded in a concern for public health, concluding that it was only a mask for its real purpose of preventing premarital sexual activity.[18] In doing so, the Court affirmed the direction set in *Griswold* that keeps the government from intruding into the private realm of the bedroom.[19]

In the majority opinion, Justice Brennan clarified the right to procreative privacy.

If under *Griswold* the distribution of contraceptives to married persons cannot be prohibited, a ban on distribution to unmarried persons would be equally impermissible. It is true that in *Griswold* the right to privacy in question inhered in the marital relationship. Yet the marital couple is not an independent entity with a mind and heart of its own, but an association of two individuals each with a separate intellectual and emotional makeup. If the right of privacy means anything, it is the right of the individual, married or single, to be free from unwarranted governmental intrusion into matters so fundamentally affecting a person as the decision whether to bear or beget a child.[20]

The Court affirmed a fundamental privacy right in decisions to prevent conception. These decisions are so fundamental to an individual's goals, aims, and happiness in life that decisions in this area are to be left to the individual, assuming that no harm comes to the parties to the decision or others affected by it.

This case thus marked an important shift in the way procreative privacy rights are recognized. The *Griswold* decision assumed that a marriage constituted a separate entity that should not be subject to intervention by the state. It only protected married couples from such intervention. *Eisenstadt*, however, affirmed the individuality of the people within the marriage relationship. Thus the right of privacy was extended beyond the marital couple as a unit to the individuals that make it up. In this way, *Griswold* now can apply to individuals irrespective of their marital status.[21]

Stanley v. Illinois (1972)[22]

In a case that has important implications not only for procreative liberty but also for parental rights, the Court reversed a decision by the Illinois Supreme

Court that denied Stanley a hearing to determine his fitness as a parent prior to the state placing his children for adoption. The Illinois law in question held that upon the death of a single mother, the children were to be declared wards of the state and placed in guardianship, irrespective of the unwed father's claim to parental rights. Stanley was thus denied a hearing to determine his parental fitness and he charged that he was being denied his rights under the Due Process Clause of the Fourteenth Amendment. The Court recognized a fundamental right of parents to associate with and raise their children:

The private interest here, that of a man in the children he has sired and raised, undeniably warrants deference and, absent a powerful countervailing interest, protection. It is plain that the interest of a parent in the companionship, care and custody of his children comes to this Court with a momentum for respect lacking when appeal is made to liberties which derive merely from shifting economic arrangements.[23]

However, the Court went further and made broad statements about the significance of the family and the fundamental rights that derive from recognition of it. "The Court has frequently emphasized the importance of the family. The rights to conceive and to raise one's own children have been deemed 'essential,' 'basic civil rights of man,' and 'rights far more precious than property rights.' The integrity of the family unit has found protection in the Due Process Clause and the Equal Protection Clause of the Fourteenth Amendment."[24]

Though this case does not address procreative liberty but parental rights, clearly both sets of rights are consistent with the broad notion of liberty recognized by the Court. Decisions concerning both begetting and raising children are to be left to parents unless there is a compelling state interest that justifies intervention.

Moore v. City of East Cleveland (1977)[25]

This case reversed an appeals court decision that upheld a city housing ordinance that limited occupancy of single family homes to nuclear families. In this case, that definition excluded a family in which a grandmother chose to live with her son and two grandsons. The law was struck down as an arbitrary limit on the due process clause.

Two important points were made in the concurring opinion of Justice Marshall. First, the city cannot define a family in the way it did, restricting it to the nuclear family. This definition effectively excluded the notion of the extended family living together under the same roof, which the Court recognized has a long history and plays an important role when the nuclear family faces economic hardship or loss of one of the parents. Second, classifying families in this way "unconstitutionally abridges the 'freedom of personal choice in matters of family life [that] is one of the liberties protected by the Due Process Clause of the Fourteenth Amendment.'"[26] The family and family-related decisions, such as marriage, having children, and the manner in which they are raised are within a zone of privacy protected by the penumbra of rights guaranteed by the Constitution. This is an example of the Court's tendency to defend a narrow privacy right with broad language about the overriding right to privacy. Though the Court has yet to hear a surrogacy case, one could argue that the reasoning in this case surely supports procreative decisions that involve different definitions of family and non-coital means of reproduction that involve third party participants.

Carey v. Population Services International (1977)[27]

The Court affirmed a lower court decision that struck down a New York law that (1) restricted the sale of contraceptives to minors, (2) only allowed contraceptives to be purchased from a licensed pharmacist and, (3) prohibited anyone from advertising contraceptives. The Court ruled that the restrictions were not sufficiently narrowly drawn and thus unnecessarily burdened procreative liberty.[28] In addition, the Court held that minors have procreative liberty as well as adults and thus the law discriminated against them. Here the Court held that procreative freedom takes precedence over the state's concern to deter increasing sexual activity by minors. Finally, the prohibition against advertising violated the freedom of expression clause of the First Amendment.

The language of the decision goes beyond the narrow issue of contraception and the right to prevent conception. If that were the only aspect of procreative liberty being protected here, then one could possibly argue that the decision only protects the right not to become pregnant, and the application to surrogacy would have to be made by implication or analogy. But the decision here explicitly protects the right to achieve pregnancy. After the Court cited the long precedent for privacy in family matters,[29] it applied the *Griswold* decision to this case. "The decision to bear or beget a child is at the very heart of this cluster of constitutionally protected choices. That decision holds a particularly important place in the history of the right to privacy. Decisions whether *to accomplish or prevent conception* are among the most private and sensitive."[30] The Court's summarized by stating, "Read in light of its progeny, the teaching of *Griswold* is that the Constitution protects individual decisions in matters of *childbearing* from unjustified intrusion by the State."[31] Thus, the Court specified that procreative liberty concerns not only decisions to use contraceptives, but also not to use them. Whether the language is broad enough to include surrogacy is open to debate, but it appears that the full range of procreative decisions is in view, even though the Court had not contemplated any of the future reproductive technologies at that time. The reasoning in this case creates an opening for surrogacy arrangements, and on the surface, legitimate payment of a fee to the surrogate. To counter the extension of the reasoning to surrogacy arrangements, one would need to establish an argument for compelling state interests which could properly restrict such arrangements. Arguments for limits on the commercial aspects of surrogacy and limits on enforceability of the surrogacy contract will be addressed in the next two chapters.

ANALYSIS OF PROCREATIVE LIBERTY

Apart from the *Skinner* sterilization case, which affirmed that not even habitual criminal activity is a sufficiently compelling state interest to strip someone of the right to reproduce,[32] the procreative liberty cases fall into two principal categories. The first set of cases protects the liberty not to procreate, that is, the right not to conceive, or once conceived, the freedom not to complete a pregnancy.[33] This set includes the abortion and contraception cases. The second set of cases encompasses the right of parents to rear a child already brought into the world, and protects families from state intervention that would dictate by whom and how those children are to be raised.[34] This set of cases includes the family rights cases, such as *Meyer, Pierce* and *Moore*. The Court in these cases assumes coital means of reproduction within the context of the traditional family setting. Clearly none of these cases directly addresses questions raised by surrogacy, or reproductive technologies such as IVF and embryo transfer. Though the second set of cases provides the broad language of freedom in family-related matters, the first is more directly relevant to procreative liberty, since these cases deal with the specific decision about whether to bear children.

The cases affirm the freedom to engage in sexual relations without a reproductive intent, and to take the necessary precautions to insure that conception and birth do not occur. However, the critical question for the discussion of surrogacy is whether that freedom can be extended to protect the freedom to engage in reproduction without sexual relations.[35] In other words, does procreative liberty include the freedom to separate aspects of procreation and recombine them, even in collaboration with others?[36] This is the key extension of the Court's precedent that will be the subject of the remainder of this chapter. Though the Court has not specifically recognized these rights, are they logical extensions of liberties that have already been recognized? In addition, what, if any, are the limits on the use of these freedoms?

One helpful distinction that will limit the discussion in this area is that between the freedom *to* procreate and freedom *in* procreation.[37] The former deals with the decision to conceive, gestate, and/or rear a child. With the exception of adoption decisions that are made during the pregnancy or after birth of the child, these are decisions that are made prior to conception. Thus, in some cases the decision about rearing the child is not made prior to conception, though in most planned pregnancies, the decisions to conceive, gestate and rear a child are all made before the woman involved becomes pregnant.

Freedom in procreation concerns pregnancy management decisions, that is, the freedom to control the various aspects of pregnancy, including the decision to terminate it.[38] The freedom to procreate includes the freedom to decide when, with whom, and by what means one will procreate, and the decision to involve a third party comes under this heading.

Given the Court's tendency to use the broad language of procreative freedom in addressing more limited issues such as contraception and abortion, the precedent for recognizing other reproductive freedoms seems well within the Court's intent. For instance, in *Carey*, the Court appeared to justify not only decisions about contraception, but also decisions about whether to bear or beget a child. *Carey* specified the principle that was inherent in both the *Griswold* and *Eisenstadt* decisions, that the individual, married or unmarried, is to be free from state intervention in the general area of procreative decisions,[39] not only to prevent but also to achieve conception. Thus, the language of these key decisions provides a basis for extending the narrow range of specific constitutionally recognized procreative liberties. Thus, one can argue that coital procreative liberties, clearly assumed in the above decisions, should be extended to include non-coital means of reproduction as consistent with the established legal precedent.

Actually, non-coital means to deal with male infertility such as AID (which involve a third party) are already legally recognized, and the law has been formulated to protect children born out of these arrangements from illegitimacy and provide for their support needs. Though the Supreme Court has not ruled on a case involving such third party arrangements, it would appear to be a consistent extension from arrangements to relieve male infertility to those that relieve female infertility. This would involve the use of a surrogate mother[40] to replace the infertile female as opposed to a sperm donor replacing the infertile male in AID situations. To deny protection to surrogacy while allowing it for AID would discriminate against infertile women and would likely be found in violation of the equal protection clause of the Fourteenth Amendment.

Clearly there is a significant difference between the one-time contribution of a sperm donor and the nine-month involvement of a surrogate mother. The closer analogy to sperm donation is not surrogacy, but egg donation. This distinction is important in the later discussion of the determination of motherhood. However, the fact that surrogacy and sperm donation are not precisely analogous does not undermine the need for consistency in treating male and female infertility. Just because there are two aspects to female infertility (egg production and gestation) as opposed to one for males (sperm production) does not mean that remedies for female infertility should not be protected equally to remedies for male infertility. The point of the comparison between male and female infertility is not the inequality of contribution in sperm donation and surrogacy; it is that both are valid medical ways to alleviate infertility.

If the issue is framed as the extension of reproductive liberties for fertile couples to infertile couples,[41] again there does not seem to be a significant leap. Rather, this application involves a consistent extension of liberties already recognized. The basis for valuing procreation exists for both fertile and infertile couples, and non-coital collaborative reproduction should be protected since there may be no other way for the infertile couple to reproduce.[42] The couple's interests in reproducing (such as passing on one's genetic heritage, values, and family line) are the same, whether infertile or not. The values that are inherent in having a child (such as a feeling of family completion, and the powerful longing to love and care for one's offspring) are the same and shared, whether the couple is infertile or not. The biological effect, that of uniting sperm and egg, is the same, whether the couple is infertile or not. Thus, the interests in having a child and the biological effects involved in normal coital reproduction between a fertile husband and wife are the same as those that employ non-coital or collaborative means. In fact, the desire for a child is likely to be even stronger for infertile couples who have experienced the trauma associated with infertility. They are likely to consider the child more of a "miracle" and will appreciate the "gift" of a child more than those who have not had difficulty in reproducing. These similar interests and values are the basis for extending this freedom to include third party collaborators in the process of reproduction. The third party contributor provides the missing factor that the couple lacks due to the natural allotment of reproductive capacities. The couple is otherwise qualified to be parents and if fertile would clearly be free to reproduce. Since married and fertile couples have the freedom to beget children, married and infertile couples must also have this freedom, since to deny them this liberty would be to discriminate against them based on biological disadvantages which they did not choose and for which they are not responsible. Thus any legal distinction that is based solely on the draw from the reproductive lottery is discriminatory.

The *Eisenstadt* decision extended procreative liberty[43] to unmarried persons, and the extension of positive procreative liberties to unmarried persons is again logical based on liberties already recognized.[44] Single persons have the same desires and needs for children as married persons and similar competency to parent, and they attribute the same personal significance to reproduction as do married persons. Procreation can be as central to the life of an unmarried person as to a married couple, and the freedom of single persons to bear and rear the children they have already conceived is well established. One cannot imagine an unmarried person being forced by the state to abort or give up for adoption the child she is carrying. Thus, the shift to the freedom to conceive a child in the first place is a minor, not a major shift. State interests in preventing extramarital sex and teenage pregnancy are not involved here, nor is there any reason to suppose that single persons are inherently inferior to married persons as parents.[45] Though two-parent families are the most favorable environment, the children of single parents frequently thrive, and often there is no noticeable difference between their emotional health and that of children of two-parent families. Thus, there do not seem to be any compelling reasons to limit procreative freedom solely to married couples, though the demands placed on a single parent warrant significant caution before encouraging unmarried persons to exercise this freedom.

LIMITS ON PROCREATIVE LIBERTY

In general, procreative freedom may be limited, both by law and on moral grounds, on the same basis on which most other freedoms may be limited: the prevention of harm to the parties involved. The freedom to reproduce in general, whether using non-coital collaborative means or the traditional method may be limited if the harm to the child may result.[46] For instance, the likelihood that a severe genetic disease will be transmitted to the child may establish a moral obligation not to reproduce, depending on factors such as the disease involved, its social costs, and the risks involved. However, the risk of physical harm to the child from non-coital or collaborative means appears to be minimal, and the use of these means to prevent such transmission of disease would almost certainly be justified. In addition, if the couple, specifically the mother, were unwilling to provide proper prenatal care for the developing child, this should place moral limits on the right to reproduce. A mother's alcoholism, exposure to toxic chemicals or sexually transmitted disease during pregnancy, or drug use all place the child at great risk of being born with significant defects, and in some cases lead to premature fetal death. Unless the couple is willing to provide adequate care to a child in the womb, there is a moral obligation not to conceive. A further limit that comes out of a concern not to harm the child would be the inability of the couple to perform the functions of parenthood. These range from mental retardation to inadequate financial means to support a child.

In collaborative reproduction, protection of the collaborators from harm would also justify restrictions on procreative liberty, though the state has no responsibility to protect mature adults from the folly of their choices.[47] Such harm to the collaborators is most evident in the regret, at times severe,[48] that surrogate mothers may experience when giving up the child they have borne to the contracting couple. Yet the state is usually not justified in restricting people's freedom to undertake risky behavior that many would consider foolish, such as skydiving or employment as a stuntman. However, if there were evidence of clear harm to the parties involved in the collaborative process, restrictions on it could be justified. For instance, performing the procedures involved could justifiably be limited to licensed medical facilities.[49]

Collaborative reproduction also raises the issue of psycho-social harm to the child. Since the child is cut off from at least half of his biological lineage, and perhaps deceived by not being told about it, there is the prospect that the child will suffer from identity confusion about his or her genealogy. This confusion is compounded if the social parents make no attempt to tell the child about his or her birth circumstances (or perhaps attempt to cover them up and deceive the child), and the child does discover them, which usually occurs. Collaborative reproduction thus has the ability to separate the different aspects of parenthood, and this separation could contribute negatively to a child's sense of self-esteem.

Yet this separation between gestation and rearing occurs regularly in adoption situations, and though there are examples of children who adjust poorly to adoption and other blended family arrangements, many children thrive with adoptive parents. Though the desire to connect with one's biological lineage is undeniable and often overpowering, there is little evidence that this separation of aspects of parenthood has produced tangible harm to the adopted children. In fact, one could argue that surrogacy arrangements would be less disruptive than adoption, since in surrogacy there is usually some genetic link to the parents who are rearing the child.[50] Further, it is clear that this genetic confusion, should it occur, is not comparable to the child never having been born at all.

Yet the adoption parallel is hardly exact. Though it is undeniable that adopted children do cope, and even thrive, there is a significant difference between after-the-fact crisis management and preplanning to duplicate the same conditions.[51] Adoption is clearly a rescue operation that delivers the child from an emergency situation in which the birth mother is unable or unwilling to take on rearing responsibilities. Rescue solutions normally make for poor operating standards, and the fact that children do cope in adoption settings hardly justifies intentionally creating similar situations. However, the difference between the rescue situation of adoption and the preplanned setting of surrogacy does not by itself serve as a bar to surrogacy arrangements. It does, though, raise questions about the appropriateness of the adoption analogy as a justification for surrogacy.

One might also appeal to the adoption parallel to justify the attempt of couples to connect biologically to their future offspring through the genetic link that surrogacy provides. Just as in adoption adopted children often have a strong desire to connect back with their natural parents, so do prospective parents have a desire to connect forward to their future children. But the courts have not as yet accorded any fundamental rights to adoptees to connect to their biological lineage, even though the desire may be very strong. As Professor Joan Hollinger states, "Is it reasonable, then, to expect that an adult's claim for constitutional protection for an interest in connecting to future generations through the use of non-coital means of reproduction would be taken more seriously than the adoptee's desire to be linked back in time to his or her genetic heritage?"[52] No fundamental right to connect genetically to one's parents has been established, though one understands the intense desire to do so. Should there, then, be a right to have a genetic connection to future generations?

When assessing the potential harm to children born of surrogacy arrangements, past legal precedent has placed the burden of proof on those who would limit a freedom to show evidence of tangible harm. Yet here it is not possible to prove harm before the fact, since there has not been adequate time since the first surrogate birth to assess any kind of harm to the children. Even with children born from AID, there has not been enough long term-study to reach any conclusions about harm. As a result, the approach of those who strongly favor surrogacy is to proceed with minimal restrictions, working only from the adoption parallel. Given the current uncertainty about harm to the child, it may be more prudent to err on the side of caution than freedom. This is already the case with adoption, as the state regularly intervenes when the well-being of children is at stake. There is great care taken to insure that adoptions protect the child's best interests, illustrated by careful adoption proceedings, custody decisions, and the voluminous laws that regulate adoption. As Professor Sidney Callahan states, "Should not medical professionals be similarly responsible in carrying out the interventions which will, in essence, give a couple a baby to rear?"[53]

A similar note of caution is raised by those who see the traditional family structure at stake in surrogacy.[54] However, one cannot use the model of the traditional nuclear family to limit procreative freedom. A state's concern with maintaining the nuclear family and thus limiting surrogacy likely would not be upheld constitutionally, since the state permits activities that are contrary to the accepted values of the majority of society.[55] Even though the decline of the traditional family may have serious long-run consequences, and thus a compelling state interest would be served by preserving it, society should be careful not to place form over function, or structure over relationships, in determining which environments are best suited for children's needs.

A further note of caution in the exercise of procreative freedom comes from surrogacy's unique circumstances. In screening women to select the most ideal surrogates, one looks for the woman's ability to give up readily the child she is carrying. Normally, the less attached the surrogate is to the child, the more easily the arrangement is completed. This is hardly an ideal setting for a pregnancy. Surrogacy sanctions female detachment from the child in the womb, and fails to recognize that pregnancy is not an organically neutral experience but a time of bonding to the developing child. Not only are women separating personal responsibility from the ability to create life and isolating their identities from their reproductive capacities, but surrogacy is turning a vice into a virtue.[56] Detachment from the child the woman is carrying (and in many cases, a child to whom she has made a genetic contribution) would be discouraged in a normal pregnancy, but is encouraged in surrogacy. Further, women who would tend to attach to the child are screened out and disqualified from being surrogates.[57] Should surrogacy be widely practiced, Daniel Callahan of the Hastings Center describes what one of the results would be: "We will be forced to cultivate the services of women with the hardly desirable trait of being willing to gestate and then give up their own children, especially if paid enough to do so. There would still be the need to find women with the capacity to dissociate and distance themselves from their own child. This is not a psychological trait we should want to foster, even in the name of altruism."[58]

There is currently debate over the degree to which attachment in utero affects the developing child, but it is clear that in a healthy pregnancy, at least in non-surrogacy pregnancies, attachment to the child is a highly desirable trait. No one would imagine intentionally detaching from a child they were intending to rear, and the importance placed on this for surrogacy contracts to be completed gives cause for caution in encouraging this exercise of procreative liberty.

A final limit on procreative freedom comes from the obligation to recognize the procreative liberties of all parties involved, especially the surrogate. Both the natural father and the surrogate have procreative liberties that deserve protection. In a contract law approach to surrogacy, in which the contract is fully enforceable, the interests of the infertile couple in forming a family are the only ones considered. For example, in the *Baby M* case, the lower court in New Jersey upheld the contract, based on the freedom of the contracting couple to use non-coital means to establish a family; the interests of a third party were held not to stand in the way of this fundamental liberty.[59] As George Annas responded to that decision, "The right to procreate is determinative in this only if we assume it is exclusively a male right and not one that Mary Beth Whitehead retains."[60] There is no inherent reason to favor one person's procreative liberties over another's, and one of the limits on procreative freedom that should be imposed on surrogacy arrangements is that the right of a contracting couple to use collaborative means to form a family cannot be done at the expense of the surrogate's procreative liberty. She is, after all, procreating too, even as a surrogate, and even if she initially agreed to waive parental rights. As Judge Wilentz stated in reversing the lower court ruling, "To assert that Mr. Stern's right of procreation gives him the right to the custody of Baby M would be to assert that Mrs. Whitehead's right to procreation does not give her the right to the custody of Baby M."[61] Thus when a surrogacy contract is enforced against the will of the surrogate, the parties are in the unusual position in which one person can exercise his procreative liberties only on the condition that the other's are forfeited.[62] The constitutional freedom to procreate does not include the right to deny someone else's similar right to parent.[63] The liberty of one person to procreate does not include the right to deny another's freedom to rear and associate with the child to which that other has made a genetic and/or gestational contribution.[64] As stated by the New Jersey Supreme Court in the *Baby M* case, "There is nothing in our culture or society that even begins to suggest a fundamental right on the part of the father to the custody of the child as part of his right to procreate when opposed by the claim of the mother of the same child."[65] Thus, a conflict of procreative liberties exists in surrogacy that must be resolved if the use of collaborative reproduction is to be constitutionally consistent.

CONCLUSION

Though the long tradition of procreative liberty opens the door to surrogate arrangements, that does not mean that the liberty is absolute. There are significant limits that constitutionally can be placed on the exercise of this liberty. In addition, recognizing the right does not obligate society to provide access to the necessary means to employ it, and society is not obligated to encourage the practice.

It is important to realize that recognition of procreative liberty only justifies non-commercial, voluntary surrogacy, or the freedom to engage a third party in the reproductive process. Whether or not the surrogate may be paid a fee beyond reasonable expenses is a separate issue. Whether the state can intervene to prevent commercialization of surrogacy is not the same issue as whether the state can prevent the general practice of altruistic surrogacy. Though the cautions raised in this chapter apply to both commercial and altruistic surrogacy, the lack of clear evidence of harm is sufficient to keep the state from interfering with couples who desire to utilize a third party to produce a child. There are other issues involved besides procreative liberty that must be resolved in order to justify commercial surrogacy in which the contract is enforced.[66] Thus, procreative liberty makes room for altruistic surrogacy, though there are reservations and cautions about the non-commercial practice of surrogacy that must be taken seriously.

NOTES

1. This limit on procreative liberty as applied to surrogacy will be addressed in chapter two, where it will be established that commercial surrogacy is the purchase and sale of a child, and should be prohibited.

2. This further limit on surrogacy as an application of procreative liberty will be addressed in chapter three. It will be established that surrogacy contracts that are enforced against the will of the surrogate violate her fundamental right to associate with her child.

3. These cases include *Roe v. Wade*, 410 U.S. 113 (1973), *Doe v. Bolton* 410 U.S. 179 (1973), *Planned Parenthood of Central Missouri v. Danforth*, 428 U.S. 52 (1976), *Webster v. Reproductive Health Services*, 109 S. Ct. 3040 (1989), and *Planned Parenthood v. Casey*, a 1992 case in Pennsylvania, citation not yet available.

4. 262 U.S. 390 (1923).

5. Ibid., 399.

6. See for instance, John Robertson's statement about this and other Supreme Court decisions. He states, "In dicta, however, the Supreme Court on numerous occasions has recognized a married couple's right to procreate in language broad enough to encompass coital and most non-coital forms of reproduction." He then cites the Meyer case as one example. "Embryos, Families and Procreative Liberty: The Legal Structure of the New Reproduction," *Southern California Law Review* 59, no. 5 (July 1986): 958.

7. 268 U.S. 510 (1925).

8. Ibid., 534.

9. 316 U.S. 535 (1942).

10. Ibid., 541.

11. Ibid.

12. 381 U.S. 479 (1965).

13. Citing *NAACP v. Alabama* (357 U.S. 449), the Court ruled that the First Amendment protected freedom of assembly and privacy in one's associations. "While not expressly included in the First Amendment, its existence is necessary in making the express guarantees fully meaningful." Ibid., 483.

14. Ibid., 484.

15. Ibid., 486.

16. In his concurring opinion, Justice Goldberg stated, "I do agree that the concept of liberty protects those personal rights that are fundamental, and is not confined to the specific terms of the Bill of Rights." Ibid., 486.

17. 405 U.S. 438 (1972).

18. Ibid., 452.

19. Justice Douglas used a graphic illustration in *Griswold* to make this point. "Would we allow the police to search the sacred precincts of marital bedrooms for telltale signs of the use of contraception? The very idea is repulsive to the notions of privacy surrounding the marriage relationship." *Griswold v. Connecticut*, 381 U.S., at 485-86.

20. Ibid., 453.

21. M. Louise Graham, "Surrogate Gestation and the Protection of Choice," *Santa Clara Law Review* 22 (1982): 310-11. She states,

Eisenstadt recognized that the marital relationship was not a unity, but rather an association of two emotionally and intellectually distinct individuals. Thus the right of personal privacy belonged to individuals, rather than to the marital unit, and it extended to all adults regardless of their marital status.

Because privacy was extended from the family to the individuals that constitute the family, procreative liberty applied to more than simply family units, but to individuals. Thus, it can be said that the right to privacy goes beyond individuals within a marital unit, to individuals outside the family unit as well. Once privacy was seen as applying to individuals instead of family units, the door was open to the exercise of procreative liberty outside the normally defined family unit.

22. 405 U.S. 645 (1972).

23. Ibid., 651.

24. Ibid., 651.

25. 431 U.S. 494 (1977).

26. Justice Marshall was citing *Cleveland Board of Education v. LaFleur,* 414 U.S. 632, 639-640 (1974).

27. 431 U.S. 678 (1977).

28. This reasoning is similar to that used in *Doe v. Bolton* 410 U.S. 179 (1973), that restricting abortions to licensed hospitals unnecessarily limited a woman's access to an otherwise protected right. Cited in *Carey*, 431 U.S., at 688. However, the Court did acknowledge that "even a burdensome regulation may be validated by a sufficiently compelling state interest." Ibid., 686.

29.   "It is clear that among the decisions that an individual may make without unjustified government interference are personal decisions relating to *marriage* (*Loving v. Virginia*, 388 U.S. 1,12, 1967), *procreation* (*Skinner v. Oklahoma*, 316 U.S. 535, 541-542, 1942), *contraception* (*Eisenstadt v. Baird*, 405 U.S. 453-454, 460, 463-465), *family relationships* (*Prince v. Massachusetts*, 321 U.S. 158,166, 1944), and *child rearing and education* (*Pierce v. Society of Sisters*, 268 U.S. 510, 535, 1925; *Meyer v. Nebraska,* 262 U.S. 390, 399, 1923)." Ibid., 685.

30. Ibid., 685.

31. Ibid., 687.

32. In fact, in light of *Skinner*, it is difficult to imagine circumstances that could justify forced sterilization, if habitual criminal activity is not considered a valid basis for so doing.

33. The limit on the freedom not to carry a pregnancy to term is limited by the viability of the fetus. After viability, the right to terminate the pregnancy becomes the right not to carry or rear a child to which one could give birth.

34. The limit on this is, of course, in the case of parental unfitness, or neglect/abuse of the child.

35. See chapter four for one aspect of this latter element that is protected, the right to reproduce by artificial insemination, either by a woman's husband or by a known or unknown sperm donor.

36. This is essentially the definition of procreative liberty put forth by John A. Robertson in "Procreative Liberty and the Control of Conception, Pregnancy and Childbirth," *Virginia Law Review* 69 (April 1983): 410.

37. This distinction is made by Robertson. Ibid., 410.

38. Though abortion rights do intersect with the surrogacy question, they are not the heart of the issue. Most legal and ethical commentators on surrogacy admit that the surrogate has a right to privacy that cannot be infringed upon during the pregnancy she is experiencing for another couple. For instance, she cannot be forced against her will not to smoke or drink alcoholic beverages, even though these may harm the fetus. Further, she cannot be forced to terminate the pregnancy at the insistence of the contracting couple, nor can she be prevented from doing so if she so desires. The issue of damages due the contracting couple is separate from her right under *Roe v. Wade* to end a pregnancy until viability. Even the lower New Jersey Court that upheld the Stern-Whitehead contract ruled that the part of the contract that limited Whitehead's right to abortion was unconstitutional and therefore void.

39. As stated in the *Eisenstadt* decision, "If the right of privacy means anything, it is the right of the individual, whether married or single, to be free from unwarranted governmental intrusion into matters so fundamentally affecting a person as the decision to bear or beget a child." 405 U.S. at 453. Clearly, here, the contraception decision is couched in broader terms that validate the freedom to make procreative decisions.

40. The term surrogate mother is misleading, since in most cases, she is the actual mother of the child since she has contributed genetic material to the child. She is in reality the surrogate wife, replacing the father's wife in the childbearing function. The father's wife is the real surrogate parent, replacing the woman who bore the child in the social and relational parenting role.

41. This way of framing the issue is taken from Robertson, "Procreative Liberty," 428.

42. The rights of unmarried persons to procreate outside of marriage will be considered in the next section.

43. Even though *Eisenstadt* dealt specifically with contraception, the decision made it clear that the right to privacy included not only contraception but the right to be free from government intrusion (apart from compelling state interests) in matters of bearing or begetting a child. Thus, the reasoning behind the legitimacy of contraception also includes the positive side of reproduction, that of producing a child rather than preventing such a process.

44. See Robertson, "Procreative Liberty," 418-19. Further see John Robertson, "Embryos, Families and Procreative Liberty," 962-63.

45. Note, "Reproductive Technology and the Procreative Rights of the Unmarried," *Harvard Law Review* 98 (January 1985): 682-684.

46. Hull, Richard T., "Introduction: Claims About the Right to Assisted Reproduction," in *Ethical Issues in the New Reproductive Technologies,* ed. Richard T. Hull (Belmont, CA: Wadsworth Publishing, 1990): 16-17.

47. Robertson, "Procreative Liberty," 433-434.

48. See for instance, the anguish and extreme depression experienced by Mary Beth Whitehead following her release of Baby M to the Sterns.

49. Robertson, "Procreative Liberty," 434.

50. Robertson, "Embryos, Families and Procreative Liberty," 1000.

51. Sidney Callahan, "Lovemaking and Babymaking: Ethics and the New Reproductive Technology," *Commonweal,* 24 April 1987, 235.

52. Joan Heifetz Hollinger, "From Coitus to Commerce: Legal and Social Consequences of Non-coital Reproduction," *University of Michigan Journal of Law Reform* 18 (Summer 1985): 879-880.

53. Callahan, "Lovemaking and Babymaking," 236.

54. Callahan, for instance, rejects surrogacy out of a desire to safeguard the western ideal of the family, without the patriarchal bias. Thus, any reproductive technique that involves collaborators is unethical, since it destroys the connection between marital unity and childrearing and introduces a foreign element that skews the equal genetic contribution of parents. Ibid.

55. In its statement on procreative liberty, the Ethics Committee of the American Fertility Society stated, "The constitutional status of procreative liberty illustrates the recurring dilemma of fundamental rights in a society of limited governmental powers. Recognition of procreative rights is essential in the constitutional scheme; yet, it permits activities that may run counter to the values that a majority hold and may even lead to a transformation of those values. Even so the community may not legally prevent the exercise of those rights other than by persuasion, even if an impact on its value structure occurs." Ethics Committee of the American Fertility Society, "The Constitutional Aspects of Procreative Liberty," in Hull, *Ethical Issues in the New Reproduction,* 14.

56. Callahan, "Lovemaking and Babymaking," 238-39.

57. One notable exception to this is Mary Beth Whitehead, who was psychologically evaluated as part of the screening. The psychologist who performed the screening discovered that she was likely to form a strong attachment to the child, but the Sterns were never told this, apparently since it would have jeopardized the contract. As Judge Wilentz put it in his decision, "It is apparent that the profit motive got the better of the Infertility Center." *See In the Matter of Baby M,* 109 N.J. 396, 537 A. 2d 1227 (1988).

58. Daniel Callahan, "Surrogate Motherhood: A Bad Idea," *The New York Times* (20 January 1987): B11.

59. In re Baby M, 525 A. 2d 1128, 1164 (1987).

60. George Annas, "Baby M: Babies (and Justice) for Sale," *Hastings Center Report* 17 (June 1987): 13-14.

61. *In the Matter of Baby M,* 537 A. 2d, 1254.

62. In commenting on the *Baby M* case, in which, initially, the contract was enforced over the desire of the surrogate to keep the child, Paul Armstrong, Vice Chairman of the New Jersey Bioethics Commission, and Patrick Hill suggest that the term surrogate mother is an oxymoron. "Surrogate motherhood is a contradiction in terms," they state. If the surrogate can only perform that function by giving up her procreative rights, it is difficult to see how she can be called a mother. Paul W. Armstrong and T. Patrick Hill, "Baby M: New Beginnings and Ancient Mileposts," *Seton Hall Law Review* 18 (1988): 854.

63. That is not to say that a woman cannot agree to function as a surrogate and then voluntarily waive her parental rights. A surrogate's fundamental rights are denied only when the terms of the contract are enforced against her will, and she is denied her right to associate with the child she has borne.

64. The waiver of parental rights and the distinction between a genetic and gestational mother will be discussed in chapter three.

65. *In the Matter of Baby M,* 537 A. 2d, 1246.

66. Of course, a state may have a situation in which commercial surrogacy is allowed, but the contract is not enforceable should the surrogate desire to keep the child. The limits on procreative liberty in surrogacy revolve around payment of a fee to the surrogate beyond reasonable medical expenses and enforcing the contract when the surrogate desires to keep the child. The ethics of commercial surrogacy and the waiver of parental rights are two separate issues that will be addressed in chapters two and three respectively.

2

THE ETHICS OF COMMERCIAL SURROGACY

INTRODUCTION

In the *Baby M* case, the New Jersey Supreme Court equated surrogacy with baby selling, in violation of the state's adoption laws. The lower court had maintained that surrogacy cannot be baby selling since one of the parties involved is the natural father. The lower court ruled that the adoption laws did not contemplate surrogacy arrangements, and thus that extending them to surrogacy was invalid. The state Supreme Court sharply disagreed, defining surrogacy as inherently the sale of children, rejecting any attempts to evade what the court considered obvious.

The differences between the two decisions have helped set the parameters for the debate over the ethics of commercial surrogacy. The argument in favor of allowing payment of a fee to surrogates beyond their reasonable expenses has taken one of two forms. First, it is argued that commercial surrogacy is essentially not equivalent to baby selling. Instead, the fee is payment for gestational services rendered. Second, it is granted that surrogacy does constitute baby selling, but the argument is made on the grounds that surrogacy is qualitatively different from the types of situations that the baby selling laws were designed to prevent. This chapter will argue that commercial surrogacy is indeed the sale of children, and that the differences between surrogacy and black market adoptions do not justify allowing for payment of a fee to surrogates. Thus, commercial surrogacy should be prohibited, and consideration paid to surrogates should only be for necessary medical expenses and other expenses associated with the pregnancy.

Twenty-five states currently have laws that prohibit the exchange of consideration for adoption of a child.[1] These laws were enacted to prevent economically and emotionally vulnerable birth mothers from being coerced into giving up children for adoption that under non-coercive circumstances they would not otherwise give up. The abuses and excesses of black market adoptions were, and still are, the target of these laws. As applied to surrogacy, however, these laws have been interpreted by the courts in different ways. For example, in Michigan[2] and New Jersey,[3] the laws have been applied to prohibit any commercialization of surrogacy. But in Kentucky, the courts have ruled that surrogacy does not fall under the heading of baby selling because the natural father cannot buy back what is already his.[4]   Kentucky's interpretation of adoption statutes seems to be the exception rather than the rule, since the surrogacy laws in the states that have enacted them are generally consistent with existing adoption laws.[5]

ARGUMENTS IN FAVOR OF COMMERCIAL SURROGACY

The Fee Is for Services Rendered, Not for the Sale of a Child

Though this argument takes various forms, proponents insist that surrogacy is not inherently baby selling, since the fee that is paid to the surrogate is for her gestational services, and thus constitutes simply another expense for the contracting couple, parallel to the medical and legal expenses involved. This argument assumes sensitivity to existing adoption laws, being careful to delineate exactly the things for which the fee pays, and insuring that the transfer of parental rights is not included under that heading. Most surrogacy contracts are structured to relate the fee to the specific gestational services rendered by the surrogate, and those who frame the contracts are careful not to make any mention of surrendering parental rights as part of the services for which the fee is paid.

Among the various forms that this argument can take, William Laufer suggests that the contracting couple does not buy the child, but rather buys the woman's egg and rents her womb, emphatically denying that the couple pays for an adoption.[6] Avi Katz suggests that the fee pays for the entire process, not just the final step in it, and thus calls surrogacy contracts to bear a child, not contracts to sell a child.[7] Karen Marie Sly terms surrogacy not baby selling, but prenatal baby-sitting, and the surrogate has the right to rent her womb for a fee.[8] This definition of surrogacy is the foundation for her argument that prohibiting commercial surrogacy violates a woman's constitutional right to contract.[9] Lori Andrews draws a parallel between the fee paid to surrogates and the other payments to those involved in helping relieve infertility. She states, "Prohibiting payment to the surrogate is as much an interference with the couple's reproductive rights as passing a law which bans payment to doctors who perform in vitro fertilization or a law which bans payment to pharmacists for contraceptives."[10]

She parallels that analogy with an analogy drawn between childrearing and childbearing. It is legitimate to pay for all kinds of services involved in childrearing, from wet nurses to day care. Since childrearing, not childbearing, is the more influential element in the child's well being in the long run, if it is justifiable to pay people for childrearing, then surely it is valid to pay them for childbearing.[11] Finally, Christine Sistare insists that all the attention being paid to baby selling is a "red herring" that distracts from the real issue of a woman's autonomy and a male fear that women's reproductive capacities will no longer be available cheaply or on demand.[12]

Evaluation

The argument that the surrogacy fee is for services and not for the sale of a child fails to take into account both the nature of the surrogacy contract and the intended end of a surrogacy arrangement. Most surrogacy contracts are structured around the product, not the process or the service of surrogacy. For example, the Stern-Whitehead contract specified that only in the event that Whitehead delivered a healthy baby to the Sterns would she be paid the entire $10,000 fee. If she miscarried prior to the fifth month of pregnancy, she would receive no fee, though all medical expenses would be paid. If she miscarried after the fifth month, or if the child was stillborn, she would only receive $1,000 of the fee. The contract was oriented to delivery of the end product, not the service rendered in the process.[13] Normally, the majority of the fee (usually half), if not all of it (as was the case with the Stern-Whitehead case), is withheld until parental rights are actually waived and the custody of the child is turned over to the contracting couple. Thus, it is difficult to see how the fee can be for gestational services only when the service itself is not the final intent of the contract. Payment is made upon the surrogate fulfilling all the necessary responsibilities to insure the transfer of parental rights. Alexander M. Capron and Margaret J. Radin of the University of Southern California Law Center suggest that the claim that the fee is for gestational services alone is merely a disguise that serves to hide the true intent of the contract. They state, "The claim that the payment to the surrogate is merely for 'gestational services' is just a pretense, since payment is made 'upon surrender of custody' of the child and for 'carrying out obligations' under the agreement. These include taking all steps necessary to establish the biological father's paternity and to transfer all parental rights to the biological father and his mate."[14]

The Stern-Whitehead contract specified that, "$10,000 will be paid to MARY BETH WHITEHEAD, surrogate, *upon surrender of custody to WILLIAM STERN* (emphasis added), the natural and biological father of the child born pursuant to the provisions of this Agreement *for surrogate services and expenses in carrying out her obligations* under this agreement (emphasis added)."[15]   The fee for services includes both childbearing services and surrender of custody "services," though the surrender of custody is critical to completing the arrangement. The fee is to be paid not upon birth of the child, which would constitute completion of the childbearing services, if that were the only thing for which the fee was being paid, but on surrender of custody. In most cases, the fee is placed in an escrow account and held until the necessary legal work has been completed to insure a successful transfer of parental rights and adoption by the wife of the biological father.

The Stern-Whitehead contract goes on to describe more of the "services" to be rendered in exchange for the fee. "MARY BETH WHITEHEAD, surrogate, and RICHARD WHITEHEAD, her husband, agree to surrender custody to WILLIAM STERN, Natural Father, immediately upon birth...as well as institute and cooperate in proceedings to terminate their respective parental rights to said child. "[16]   To be sure, the contract included detailed sections about the gestational services provided, but they are not central to the main intent of the contract. The intent of surrogacy is not solely, or even primarily, to bring a child into the world, though of course that is a very important aspect. The main intent of surrogacy contracts is to effect the legal transfer of custody and parental rights, in a way virtually identical to adoption proceedings. The Stern-Whitehead contract clearly connects the intent of the contract with the willingness of the Whiteheads to do whatever is necessary to facilitate parental rights being vested solely in the Sterns. For example, continuing with the part of the contract cited above, "to terminate their parental rights to said child, and sign any and all necessary affidavits, documents and the like, in order to *further the intent and purposes of this Agreement* (emphasis added)."[17]   The intent of the contract has little do with the birth of the child. Though a necessary occurrence, it is hardly the central focus of the contract. The intent of the contract is for the surrogate to bear the child and transfer parental rights, and it is for that latter "service," that the fee is at least partially, if not entirely, being paid.

This explains why contracting couples sue for specific performance of the contract when the surrogate decides to keep the child. If the contract were for gestational services only, on what basis could the couple request the state to enforce the terms of the contract, when the surrogate breaches it by keeping the child? Under the gestational services scheme, specific performance could only refer to the surrogate's failure to maintain the pregnancy, either by abortion on her demand, or by engaging in personal behavior such as drinking, smoking or drug use that brings harm to the fetus. Specific performance could only relate to the procreative services for which the contracting couple is presumably paying. Any damages that would be awarded in lieu of specific performance, typical in service contracts, since courts are generally reluctant to enforce specific performance in service contracts, would be groundless, since the surrogate would not actually have breached the contract.

Thus, surrogacy contracts are not pure service contracts. They are mixed contracts for both a service and a product. Under a pure service contract, even if the surrogate kept the child, she would have fulfilled the contract. Yet it is clear that this is by no means a satisfactory outcome for the contracting couple. For them, the service is incidental to the product. That is, the contract, though mixed, is not primarily concerned with the service, but with the product being delivered. Law Professor Herbert T. Krimmel, in his 1987 testimony before the California Senate Committee on Health and Human Services, compares contracts in which the service and the product are primary, respectively. He states, "If I contract to have a masseur give me a back rub, it is to the service alone that my expectations lie. But if I contract to have my portrait painted, I am not satisfied that the artist performs all the necessary services well. The essence of the contract was that I wanted a picture of myself. Until that is delivered, I am not satisfied. So it is with the adopting couple in surrogate mother arrangements."[18]

Even if the fee is for the entire process, not just the final step, as Katz suggests,[19] the fee is still paying for more than simply gestational services. Katz betrays his own position when he admits that the entire fee is to be paid after the child is delivered, with only expenses paid until then. He makes this point to support his argument that commercial surrogacy is not inherently exploitative of the surrogate. He states, "No funds, beyond reasonable expenses, are advanced to her during pregnancy, and it is not until after she releases the child that she is entitled to her fee."[20] It should be clear that in a scheme like this, payment of the fee is dependent upon surrender of parental rights, and not simply as a part of the overall process. Surrender of parental rights is clearly the part of the process that matters most, and all other parts are superfluous if this one is not completed. Thus, it is difficult to maintain that this is not a "fee for parental rights" scheme, thereby constituting baby selling. The delivery of the product is the bottom line in surrogacy, and at best, only part of the fee pays for that. But it still is paying for that, and thus constitutes the exchange of money for transfer of parental rights, or baby selling.

A more sophisticated form of this argument, that the fee pays for the entire process, not simply the transfer of parental rights, rests on a particular understanding of a service. R. Jo Kornegay attempts to show that the objections to commercial surrogacy on the grounds of baby selling "rest on a spurious concept of what the services are."[21] Surrogacy represents a service that leads to a specific outcome. In reference to the *Baby M* case she states, "Mrs. Whitehead's contract was in this respect rather like an agreement whereby a lawyer receives a percentage of the settlement if s/he wins that case and nothing if s/he loses it, or whereby a plumber guarantees his or her work and receives a certain fee if s/he fixes a leaking sink but nothing for a failed attempt to stop leakage."[22]

She further compares this with a contract for an assassin in which payment for the service depends on a specified outcome, the death of the target person. "Fulfillment of the contract depends on a particular outcome," she states.[23] Thus, the services involved in surrogacy are not simply gestation and childbirth, but are a means to an end, that of giving the contracting couple a child to rear. She concludes, "Moreover, in light of reflection on what the term service means and on the intentions of the parties entering the contract, it seems more reasonable to interpret the contract as calling for payment of $10,000 for various services *as well as the transfer of custody rights* (emphasis added)."[24]

According to Kornegay's definition of service, the final intended outcome is not only the birth of the child, but clearly the transfer of parental rights. It appears that she is simply including that under the heading of various services rendered, parallel to the way in which Katz explained that payment of the fee was for the entire process, not simply the end product. She correctly focuses on the intended outcome of surrogacy, and once she does that, it is difficult to see how the fee is only for gestational services. Her clarification of the definition of a service does little to support her argument that commercial surrogacy is not baby selling, since the transfer of custody rights is admitted to be one of the various services that leads to, and actually is indispensable to, the outcome desired by the contracting couple. If the fee pays for transfer of parental rights, it is no different from paying a birth mother a fee to surrender her child in adoption proceedings. The fact that the fee pays for other services as well is irrelevant to the central fact that it does pay for the transfer of parental rights. If transferring parental rights is included as one of the various surrogacy services rendered, which it must be for any hope of a completed transaction, then it is difficult to see how this is different from the baby selling that is prohibited by adoption laws.

If one insists that the fee paid to the surrogate is for pregnancy and childbirth services only, then one must be prepared to be consistent in the way the fee is structured and paid. If the child is stillborn, the fee should be the same as if the child were born healthy, assuming that the stillbirth occurred through no fault of the surrogate. If she miscarries at some point during the pregnancy, she should be paid a fee for her services (beyond expenses, of course), prorated for the number of weeks during which she carried the pregnancy. Most importantly, if the surrogate decides to keep the child, then she is still owed the entire fee, since the service for which she contracted has been performed in full. If the fee is for services in carrying and giving birth to the child, then receipt of the fee should be dependent on her fulfilling those obligations and no others beyond them.

Given these dramatically increased risks to the contracting couple, it is unlikely that any couples except the most wealthy and most desperate to have a genetically linked child would arrange surrogacy. It is further unlikely that surrogacy would continue to be the big business it is today. Though there would certainly be exceptions to this, most surrogacy agencies would see business significantly decline if the fee structure were implemented in a way compatible with the claim that the fee is for gestational services only.[25] In short, it is unlikely that many of the participants in surrogacy would continue to participate under a consistent fee for gestational service scheme.

In light of the above evaluation, it should be clear that contrary to Laufer, a contracting couple is doing more than purchasing an egg and renting a womb.[26] There is no denying that they are buying the egg and renting the womb, or in the case of gestational surrogacy, only renting the womb. But they are also, and primarily, purchasing the parental rights to the child born out of the arrangement.

Laufer acknowledges that opponents of commercial surrogacy object to paying a fee because the surrogate provides the egg, and thus is the natural and legal mother. He states that, "Had the egg belonged to someone other than Mrs. Whitehead, a compelling argument could be made that the surrogate was merely providing the means for the birth of someone else's child. The situation is essentially the same, however, even though Mrs. Whitehead provided the egg. The Stern's bought a surrogate's services and her egg. They did not pay for an adoption."[27] Here he is assuming a parallel between gestational and genetic surrogacy. There is great debate whether those two situations are indeed analogous, and even if they are, it does not make Laufer's case. Rather, it makes the opposing one. If genetic and gestational surrogacy are parallel, then the genetic surrogate does not give up parental rights, but the gestational surrogate acquires them. Few seem willing to see the genetic surrogate as inherently not possessing parental rights. But that is not as clear with gestational surrogacy. However, if they are parallel, that gives the gestational surrogate standing to claim parental rights to the child. The parallel does not enable proponents of commercial surrogacy to strip genetic surrogates of their parental rights. It is debatable that a compelling argument can be made that a gestational surrogate is merely an incubator.[28] But even if such an argument can be made, Laufer's leap from gestational to genetic surrogacy cannot be justified. Perhaps in gestational surrogacy, womb rental is all that is taking place, and all that the fee is paying for. But one cannot say that of genetic surrogacy.[29] When the surrogate contributes the egg, the term surrogate mother is no longer accurate. She is the natural mother, and the one normally referred to as the surrogate is in reality, a surrogate wife to the natural father.[30] Thus the parallel that Laufer makes between genetic and gestational surrogacy fails to establish his point that baby selling is not occurring.

It should also be apparent that Sly's term for surrogacy, prenatal baby-sitting[31] is far from accurate. This term assumes that the contracting couple is paying for prenatal baby-sitting services only, and that they are the legal parents. Since the surrogate has signed a contract agreeing to relinquish parental rights upon birth of the child, during the nine months of pregnancy she is only doing the maternal equivalent of house-sitting for someone who is out of the country.

If the surrogate contributes the egg, then calling her contribution baby-sitting far understates the reality of what is occurring. Parents are never said to baby-sit their own children; that is a term reserved for someone who is not a parent and who is paid for a service only. Baby-sitting and parenthood simply do not fit under the same umbrella. The term baby-sitting may be appropriate for gestational surrogacy, but only for that, at most. If the traditional definition of motherhood is employed, in which the mother is the woman who gives birth to the child (and her husband is presumed to be the legal father), then it does not fit even gestational surrogacy. Even to strengthen the term and call the surrogate a prenatal foster parent is at best appropriate only for gestational surrogacy. But if she is as much a mother as the one who contributes the egg, then it is difficult to see how one can be a foster parent to one's own child. It should be clear that neither term is fitting for genetic surrogacy.[32]

Sly appears to overstate the case greatly when she confuses the fee paid to the surrogate with the expenses that can be legitimately reimbursed. For example, in arguing for a right to compensation she states, "To cut off the right to receive compensation and to rely instead on the good-heartedness of surrogates to bear children *at their expense* is unsatisfactory."[33] Later she states, "Without the *lure of expenses* and a reasonable fee, surrogate mothers will choose not to perform their 'baby-sitting' services and deprive couples of a viable childbearing alternative (emphasis added)."[34] Nowhere is it claimed that the surrogate must bear the entire expense of childbearing herself. Not even the most ardent opponents of commercial surrogacy would deny the surrogate the right to reimbursement of reasonable medical expenses incurred as well as lost wages, if applicable. Any state that prohibits the fee is not preventing an infertile couple from utilizing a surrogate, only from paying her a fee in exchange for transfer of parental rights. This hardly precludes payment for legitimate expenses, as Sly suggests.

Her argument that the surrogacy fee is payment for services is foundational to her insistence that prohibition of the fee violates a woman's constitutional right to contract. She states, "To deny the surrogate mother her right to contract for a fee, to perform this service, is to deny her choice to work and the responsibility and status such work entails. These philosophical liberties are rooted in our American society and should be upheld as long as not detrimental to the citizenry."[35] It is true that anyone is free to sell his or her services for a fee; however, this does not imply that the right to contract is absolute. Prostitution is a service that one does not have a constitutional right to sell (in most states). One cannot contract to sell himself or herself into slavery, nor can one contract to sell one's already existing child to adoptive parents. A woman does indeed have the right to contract for services, but she does not have the right to contract to sell her as yet unborn child. One may sell services, but not children.

Andrews draws the parallel between surrogacy and other medical services that help alleviate infertility. She suggests that if it is legitimate to pay physicians for performing in vitro fertilization, then it is surely legitimate to pay surrogate mothers for their role. She states, "Prohibiting payment to the surrogate is as much an interference with the couple's reproductive rights as passing a law which bans payment to doctors who perform in vitro fertilization. Yet the expenses paid by the couple in contracting a surrogate are not disproportionate to those paid by infertile couples to bring a child into their family through other means."[36]

It should be clear that the role of a surrogate in childbirth and a physician in in vitro fertilization are entirely different. Andrews is operating under the assumption that the surrogacy fee is for services only. Yet it clearly is not, and thus there is a significant difference between an infertility specialist who performs in vitro fertilization, a legitimate medical service for which he is entitled to payment, and a surrogate mother, who not only performs a service, but also becomes a parent in performing that service. The expenses paid by a couple to an infertility clinic do not purchase a child for them. They purchase a service that may enable them to have a child of their own. The fee paid to a surrogate purchases not only egg and womb, but also the parental rights to the child, much more than simply payment for services rendered.

Bradley draws on the parallel between surrogacy and a physician's services as well in arguing for commercial surrogacy. He states, "In light of these rulings [post *Roe v. Wade* decisions], the Court would undoubtedly find that a law that prevented a woman from paying a doctor to perform an abortion would unduly burden her decision whether to have a child. Laws that prevent payments to surrogates also burden a married couple's decision whether to procreate by surrogate motherhood."[37]

Again the parallel fails to make an important distinction. Prohibiting payments to surrogates on the grounds that it constitutes the sale of children is entirely different from prohibiting women from paying physicians to perform abortions, recognized by our society as a legitimate medical service (at least for now, given the possibility of *Roe v. Wade* being overturned). It is legitimate to pay someone to terminate a pregnancy because that is a medical service. However, this is quite different from paying someone to secure a child, since that involves much more than a childbearing service being rendered. It involves waiving parental rights as well, for which a fee is not allowed under adoption laws. Further, if the payment does comprise baby selling, it does not matter if it restricts infertile couples from utilizing surrogacy. In fact, a law prohibiting payment would be *designed* to restrict couples from purchasing parental rights to a child. This would be similar to adoption laws that prohibit payment of a fee to the birth mother, even though such a prohibition severely restricts the number of available children and greatly prolongs the waiting period for most couples seeking adoption.[38]

Andrews also uses the parallel between childrearing and childbearing to justify a fee for surrogates, yet again does not distinguish between the service rendered and the product delivered. She states, "Moreover, the most important part of parenting is childrearing, not childbearing. Yet it is permissible to pay all sorts of surrogate childrearers, e.g., baby sitters, nannies and day care centers. Payment to women who serve as surrogate mothers should similarly be allowed."[39]

Again this is comparing two things that are incomparable. Surely it is legitimate to pay surrogate childrearers, for they render a valuable service. But the fact that childrearing is more important than childbearing is irrelevant, and the difference between the two types of surrogacy is that in surrogate childbearing, the surrogate becomes a parent, whereas in surrogate childrearing, no parental rights are acquired that must be transferred, or to be more explicit, sold. In addition, the former is a pure service contract, whereas the latter is a mixed contract, in which the service is incidental to the product. Thus the parallel fits only if the fee does not include the sale of parental rights, an indispensable part of the contract.

Surrogacy Is Very Different from Black Market Adoptions

Proponents of commercial surrogacy argue that there are significant differences between the circumstances surrounding surrogacy and black market adoptions.[40] Not only did the adoption laws not contemplate situations such as surrogacy, but the laws should not be applied to them, because they are entirely different settings in which parental rights are transferred. Thus, even if proponents concede that the surrogacy fee pays for more than procreational services rendered, the circumstances in surrogacy are so distinct that the fact that money changes hands as parental rights are transferred is at worst benign and at best virtually irrelevant.

The differences between surrogacy and black market adoptions are numerous, and include the following:

1. *In surrogacy, the natural father of the child is also the intended social father of the child.* The adopted child is only adopted by one parent, the wife in the contracting couple. Thus, there is a biological link between the child and at least one of the parents who will raise the child.[41] Instead of the child going to strangers, he goes to the natural father, and in some cases, also to the natural

mother. This helps insure that the child's best interests are the primary consideration.

2. *Black market adoptions are rarely concerned with the child's best interests.* Normally, the only screening of the adopting couple that is done is financial, and the broker's only motive is profit, irrespective of what is best for the child. The potential parent-child relationship is thus undermined, or precluded by financial concerns. This is clearly different from surrogacy, in which there is a reasonable certainty that a healthy home for the future child exists prior even to conception.[42]

3. *Surrogacy results from a planned and often desperately desired pregnancy, not an unwanted pregnancy.* The child is conceived after much planning, and with plenty of time for the surrogate to weigh her desires, with freedom to back out of the arrangement at any time prior to insemination. Thus there is little potential for coercion of the surrogate, and no prospect for the contracting couple to pressure the surrogate. The decision to undergo insemination is solely the surrogate's, and if she refuses, she will not have an unwanted child to raise. The surrogate does not enter the arrangement in an emotionally vulnerable state, having to deal with a tragedy after the fact. Surrogacy is not the result of adverse circumstances, but of forethought and advance planning. In other words, the transfer of parental rights in surrogacy is contemplated prior to pregnancy, not after it has begun. The decision to be a surrogate is a rational one, not one made under the duress of an unwanted pregnancy that is often accompanied by abandonment by the biological father. The surrogate is not coerced to give up a child she otherwise would not have, since the option to back out is always available prior to conception.

4. *There is usually a significant difference between birth mothers in adoption cases and surrogate mothers.*[43] A surrogate mother is typically married, middle class, stable, reasonably well educated and has already had at least one child. She knows first-hand what the experience of childbirth is like, and she is aware of the bonding that occurs between mother and child and the resulting difficulty involved in giving up one's child to another. On the other hand, in the typical black market adoption situation, the birth mother is a teenager, unmarried, financially insecure, and pregnant with her first child. She is unfamiliar with childbirth and unaware of the attachment that she will develop to her child and the subsequent grief she will likely feel at giving up her offspring. These characteristics contribute significantly to the degree of coercion inherent in black market adoptions that are absent from surrogacy arrangements.

5. *The stranger has no constitutional right to adopt, but the natural father has a right to associate with his offspring.*[44] Thus the state can place obstacles, such as prohibition of a fee to birth mothers and proper screening (and denial of adoption for those who fail the screening) for parental fitness of the adoptive

parents, in the way of people attempting to adopt, without violating any of their fundamental rights. In surrogacy, since the contracting father is the biological father, a key constitutional right is being undercut by prohibiting the fee, since that would dramatically reduce the pool of available surrogates available to infertile couples. A biological father has the right to procreate and associate with his own child, and any overreaching restrictions on this right are unconstitutional. Hence narrower regulation of the practice, not prohibition of the fee, is more constitutionally consistent.

Evaluation

Though the differences between black market adoptions and surrogacy are undeniable, questions remain about the extent to which these differences are either overstated or relevant to the debate about baby selling.

Certainly having the child raised in a home in which the natural father resides is quite different from placing the child with a stranger whose only qualifications to be a parent may be the ability to pay for the child.[45] All other things being equal, one would prefer that the biological father also assume the role as the social father. However, being a biological father does not automatically or necessarily make for a better parent, nor does it enable one to assume that the bond between father and child is necessarily stronger with a natural father than with an adoptive one.

Factors brought out in two recent Supreme Court cases have a bearing on whether or not this difference is overstated. In *Quilloin v. Walcott*,[46] the Court ruled that a natural father with no relationship to the child does not have the right under the due process clause to veto the adoption of the child by the mother's husband. (She and the child's father were never married, and the father had made no attempt to establish or continue a relationship with the child.) Here the social parenting role was considered to be the determinative one, and clearly the natural father was not as fit to be the parent of the child as was the husband of the mother.

Similarly, in *Lehr v. Robertson*,[47] the biological father's rights to block an adoption were denied because "he has never established a substantial relationship with the child, [therefore] the statutes at issue did not operate to deny his due process."[48] This is not inconsistent with an earlier decision in *Caban v. Muhammed*,[49] which affirmed that a natural father who had a social role in parenting his child did have rights under the due process clause. "The mere existence of a biological link does not merit equivalent protection. If the natural father fails to grasp the opportunity to develop a relationship with his child, the Constitution will not automatically compel a State to listen to his opinion of where the child's best interest's lie."[50] Clearly it is not automatic that a natural father is the best parent for a child. These cases affirm parental rights when there is a blood link and an existing social relationship between the child and father. Thus, there is a social element to parenthood that the Court has affirmed and that is highly valued by almost every set of adoptive parents. If the difference between a biological and a social father is the only one, then it is preferable to be raised by one's biological father, because of the biological connection. But rarely is that the only difference. Thus it seems that this distinction as applied to surrogacy is somewhat overstated. Genetics alone does not necessarily make for a better home or a closer relationship.

The relevance of this distinction between biological and social parenthood for commercial surrogacy revolves around another argument that is derived from the argument that in surrogacy, the intended social father is also the natural father of the child. If the child is to be transferred to its natural father's custody, then how can surrogacy be described as a commercial transaction at all? The assumption that gives this distinction its force is that a natural father cannot buy back what is already his. This is another key argument in favor of commercial surrogacy, that it is not baby selling since the natural father cannot, by definition, buy back what is already his. This argument was foundational to two specific surrogacy cases; the Kentucky case of *Surrogate Parenting Associates, Inc. v. Kentucky*,[51] and the lower court decision in New Jersey that preceded the *Baby M* verdict by the State Supreme Court.[52] In both of these cases, the courts affirmed commercial surrogacy by finding that it is not inherently the sale of children, since the natural father is involved in the arrangement.

This argument erroneously assumes that the child for which the natural father has contracted, and for which he is paying, is *all* his. It clearly is not. Under current AID laws, the child's father is legally presumed to be the husband of the surrogate, thus giving the natural father no parental standing. Of course, that presumption is rebuttable, and in most surrogacy cases, it is assumed that the surrogate's husband, since he has consented to his wife's AID, has no parental rights. However, in the cases in which the surrogate supplies the egg,[53] the child does not belong solely to the biological father. One can easily argue that because of genetics and gestation both, the surrogate has to this point made a greater contribution to the child than has the natural father. Thus, if the biological link is the key to determining parenthood, the surrogate's claim is at least equal to, if not greater than, the father's. Unless one summarily dismisses the surrogate, there are no grounds for the natural father to claim that he has sole rights to the child.

At best, he can claim a parental equivalent to joint tenancy in a piece of property.[54] Though it is true that a man cannot buy back what is already his, he can pay a joint tenant to give up rights in property. As Alexander Capron comments on the *Baby M* case, "Looking at the contract, it is apparent that Stern planned to pay the Whiteheads the equivalent of a quit claim to their interests in the baby, who was thus treated like property."[55]   Thus, even though the contracting father is also the biological father of the child, he is still buying the rights to a child. Money is being transferred in exchange for parental rights, even though the purchaser is one of the natural parents.[56]

Another form of this argument is that in surrogacy parental rights are not transferred, but waived. In commenting on the charge that commercial surrogacy transforms the parent-child relationship into a property relationship, H. M. Malm suggests that "there is nothing in the nature of surrogate motherhood arrangements that requires that custody be transferred rather than waived."[57]   The argument is that custody only needs to be waived by the surrogate in order for the natural father to assume sole custody, thus fulfilling the surrogacy contract. Therefore, the child is not being transferred as in a property relationship; custody is only being given up by the surrogate.

However, even if custody is only being waived, it is still being waived for a fee, which still constitutes baby selling. In addition, the surrogacy arrangement is not complete until the natural father's wife is able to adopt the child. Though many surrogacy contracts skirt carefully around this aspect for fear of violating state adoption laws, it is undeniable that waiver of custody is not everything that the contracting couple desires from the surrogate. Parental rights, that is, the rights to future association with the child, not solely custody, must be waived, and this is done not only so that the contracting couple can have sole custody of the child, but so that the social mother can actually adopt the child. The importance of this is evident from the action of the lower court in the *Baby M* case. Immediately following the verdict, Judge Sorkow invited the Sterns into his chambers where Elizabeth Stern adopted *Baby M*. The parental rights were in reality being transferred from Mary Beth Whitehead to her, for a fee. To suggest that parental rights are only being waived seems not quite accurate, given the necessity of adoption to complete the arrangement. In addition, this argument fails to distinguish between custody and parental rights.

The second difference between surrogacy and black market adoptions emphasizes the priority given to the best interests of the child. Lizabeth Bitner stresses that a birth mother being coerced by financial considerations to give up her child is against the state's policy of protecting the best interests of the child.[58]   Similarly, Robert Black points out that the fitness of the adoptive parents to be parents is not a factor (except for their financial fitness), seriously compromising the child's best interests.[59]   Surrogacy is claimed to be significantly different from this situation.

However, this difference too seems to be overstated. Most of the screening done prior to signing a surrogacy contract involves the fitness of the surrogate, not the contracting parents. The fitness of the surrogate physically and psychologically is the primary concern, specifically her psychological disposition related to her tendency to bond with the child in utero and her difficulty or ease in giving up the child to the contracting couple. Rarely are the contracting parents screened for anything but their ability to pay the bills involved with surrogacy. As George Annas comments, "Surrogacy brokers need a dose of realism. They should not be permitted to hide behind the grief of infertile couples. They are not in business to help them; they are in business to make money. The primary screening brokers do is monetary; does the couple have the $25,000 fee?"[60]

Of course, this problem could be remedied with more thorough screening of the contracting couple. Yet given the financial incentives involved for the brokers, it is unlikely that they would turn away a financially qualified couple, unless there is obvious, gross unfitness to parent. In addition, some have even suggested that any screening of the contracting couple violates their right to procreate, and further opens the door to bias against the couple and abuse of the screening process.[61] Thus, there may be constitutional obstacles to more adequate screening. Even if the fitness of the contracting parents is considered, it is nowhere near as thorough as the screening done by adoption agencies, which operate under a publicly stated best interests of the child standard, and do not operate under the same system of financial incentives. It seems that the only time in which the child's best interests are guaranteed is when the surrogate changes her mind and the case goes to court for a judge's careful weighing of what will be best for the child.

One trend that is indicative of how the child's interests are placed in the background is the trend toward separate counsel for the surrogate and for the contracting couple. Yet the idea of counsel for the future child is normally not seriously considered.[62] The only interests that are taken into account are those of the contracting couple and the surrogate. Thus, to distinguish between surrogacy and black market adoptions on the basis of the best interests of the child is to misrepresent surrogacy. Though many children born out of surrogacy arrangements are given over to stable, healthy homes (in fact, the same can also be said of black market adoptions), it is misleading to suggest that surrogacy takes the best interests of the child as a top priority, while black market adoptions ignore it. The latter is clearly true, but it is not at all evident that surrogacy takes the child's best interests as high a priority as proponents suggest.

Interestingly, the arguments that support commercial surrogacy are quite similar to the arguments for a black market in babies in the way that they frame the problem.[63] Both are viewed as desirable from a utilitarian standpoint in that both increase the satisfactions of infertile couples by increasing the available quantity of the specifically desired product. The arguments made for both are generally based on the interests of the adopting, or contracting couple, and place in the background most considerations that relate to the birth mother-surrogate, her family, and the child in question. In addition, the interests of already existing homeless children that may be more difficult to adopt due to more advanced age, race or handicap are rarely taken into account in any formulation of public policy in this area.[64] This is the reason why most, if not all adoption advocacy groups such as RESOLVE have come out strongly against surrogacy.

The third and fourth distinctions (third, that surrogacy results from a planned and often desperately wanted pregnancy, not an unwanted pregnancy, and fourth, that there is usually a significant difference between birth mothers in adoption cases and surrogate mothers) focus on the coercive nature of black market adoptions as opposed to the rational environment surrounding surrogacy, as well as the potential for exploitation. Clearly the duress factor is less in surrogacy, since the surrogate contemplates giving up the child prior to conception. But to suggest that the surrogate is free from coercion again overstates the case. As the pregnancy progresses, and the surrogate becomes attached to the child she is carrying, another form of coercion can set in. Though the surrogate does not have an unwanted pregnancy, if she begins to change her mind about keeping the child, she will have a *wanted* pregnancy and an *unwanted* contract. As the pregnancy develops, then, the difference between surrogacy and black market adoptions is overstated. William Laufer maintains that the surrogacy contract is not coercive since the surrogate enters into it without the emotional and financial vulnerability that a teenager with an unwanted pregnancy does.[65] But that does not mean that the contract cannot become coercive after the pregnancy begins. As the *Baby M* case illustrates, the contract can be extremely coercive when it forces a woman to give up a child to whom she has become significantly attached. Though the incidence of surrogate retractions is relatively small compared to the number of arrangements that are completed without complications, it simply is not the case that surrogacy does not also involve coercion, even though the arrangement is initiated prior to conception. The potential for coercion exists and when it occurs, it can be overpowering to the surrogate. To suggest that black market adoptions are inherently coercive and surrogacy is inherently not coercive ignores the coercive element in surrogacy. The publicity given to the cases in which surrogacy does become coercive may increase the awareness among surrogates that they are indeed entitled to a parental claim on the child they are carrying. As this awareness increases, the potential of a wanted pregnancy and an unwanted contract clearly increases.

A further way in which duress is involved concerns not the surrogate, but the contracting couple. Normally, an infertile couple resorts to surrogacy after all other alternatives have been exhausted. Many couples who seek out surrogates are desperate to have a child and are willing to try anything to obtain a genetic connection to their child. Thus there is the potential for brokers to exploit the contracting couples because of their overwhelming desire to conceive a child. To say that the surrogacy environment is free from coercion, in contrast to black market adoptions, seems to overstate the case.

A final difference focuses on the constitutional aspects of surrogacy. As discussed in the previous chapter, there is a constitutional right to procreation that has resulted from numerous Supreme Court decisions affirming procreative privacy. On the other hand, there is no constitutional right to adopt a child. Thus, it is argued that the state is justified in placing restrictions on the latter, but not the former, since procreation is considered a fundamental right.[66]

This distinction, however, obscures the real constitutional issue. The question at hand is not the right to procreate as opposed to the right to adopt, but the right to procreate as opposed to the right of a person to buy the child produced by the surrogacy arrangement. By restricting the fee, the state is not preventing anyone from arranging surrogacy. It is true that eliminating the fee will diminish the number of available surrogates, but the state is not placing a ban on surrogate arrangements per se. One is still free to utilize third parties in collaborative reproduction. One is just not free to compensate them beyond reasonable expenses incurred. Simply because one has the right to engage in collaborative reproduction free from state interference, it does not follow that one also has the right to purchase the child born out of these collaborative efforts. A restriction on the fee to surrogates does not necessarily render the right to procreate an empty right.[67] Such a restriction makes procreative liberty empty only if one collapses the distinction between positive and negative rights. If the state has an obligation to insure that each person is able to procreate, thus making it a positive right, only then is the right empty if the fee is restricted. This would then obligate the state to use public funds for infertility treatment, for example, and very few argue that that is the responsibility of the government. However, if the right to procreate is only a negative one, as was argued in chapter one, then the state is only required to avoid actively preventing someone from utilizing a third party in reproduction. Not *providing* for someone to exercise a right is not the same thing as not *preventing* someone from exercising a right.

The Supreme Court, in affirming that privacy rights are negative rights, put it this way: "Our cases have recognized that the due process clauses [from which the right to privacy and procreative liberty are derived], generally confer no affirmative right to government aid, even where such aid may be necessary to secure life, liberty or property interests of which the government itself may not deprive the individual."[68] If this distinction between positive and negative rights is blurred, then it can be said that the right to procreate is empty if the fee is restricted. But such a blurring would create obligations that clearly lie outside the responsibility of the state. Thus, one has a negative right to procreate, but it does not follow from that right that the parties to a surrogacy arrangement have the right to buy and sell the child produced by such an arrangement. They are separate issues. If, in the protection of children from being bought and sold, other rights of adults end up being restricted, then the interests of children must be upheld, even at the expense of adults' rights. Society has rightly seen fit to give higher priority to protecting children, and has consistently given preference to children when their interests conflict with those of adults.

Thus, it appears that the differences between surrogacy and black market adoptions, though apparent, have either been overstated or are of questionable relevance for the issue of commercial surrogacy. The critical question is not whether the circumstances are different from situations in which children are clearly bought and sold. Rather, it is, "are children being bought and sold?" Though it is true that legislators who framed adoption laws did not foresee surrogacy, it is also true that they did not envision any exceptions to the laws prohibiting baby selling.[69] Even if black market adoptions placed children in good homes without coercion of the birth mothers, and were conducted by lawyers with high moral values, the adoption laws would still apply, different circumstances not withstanding. The ACLU, in its amicus curiae brief in the *Johnson v. Calvert* case suggested that "there is nothing so unique about surrogacy arrangements that they warrant making a first, judicially crafted exception to the rule that the custody of children should not be for sale to even benevolent purchasers."[70]

Parallel Between AID and Surrogate Motherhood

The fact that both semen and egg donors are legally paid for their donation suggests that the fee for surrogates should also be legal. Robert Black suggests that AID is the male parallel to surrogacy, and because it is legal, to deny paid surrogacy violates the Equal Protection Clause. In fact, the risks and "labor" involved in surrogacy more strongly warrant payment than in the parallel, and relatively simple, case of semen donation. He states, "The irony (in denying the fee to surrogates) is that the masculine counterpart to surrogate motherhood (the "surrogate fatherhood" of a sperm donor in the AID situation) is apparently lawful in all jurisdictions. Additionally, the AID concept enjoys explicit legislative recognition in some jurisdictions despite the fact that the semen is usually paid for and the sperm donor assumes none of the risks and burdens which an "ovum donor" does."[71]

The conclusion from this parallel is that one may not discriminate between sperm donors and surrogates by allowing payment for their donation in one case and not in another without denying equal protection.[72] Similarly, John Robertson argues that surrogacy and AID, since they are both essentially forms of collaborative reproduction with similar legal issues, deserve the same legal protection, since the law does not, and should not differentiate between the different reasons that couples have for employing collaborative reproduction arrangements.[73]

Evaluation

If the parallel between AID and surrogacy were more exact, this would be a powerful argument in favor of allowing for a fee to be paid to surrogates. But the counterpart to AID that does fit is egg donation, not surrogacy. Surrogacy is essentially dissimilar to sperm donation because of the risk and burden of pregnancy, the attachment that develops between mother and developing child, and the maternal contribution to fetal development. In addition, in AID, no parental rights accrue to the sperm or egg donor, thus highlighting the similarity between egg and sperm donation. These factors suggest not that the fee should be proportionately greater for surrogates (and thus that $10,000 is at the least appropriate), but that the comparison is misplaced.

There is, of course, debate over the morality of paying for donations of sperm and eggs. Even if one grants that it is legitimate to sell sperm and eggs, at best that only legitimates the surrogate's right to be paid for the gestational services rendered in donating her egg or "renting her womb." As mentioned above, those services are important, but they are not the only components of a surrogacy arrangement. The right of a woman to be compensated for services does not include the right to sell the child that she has borne. The transfer of parental rights is not a service for which she may receive a fee, making surrogacy significantly different from AID, since the sperm donor acquires no parental rights that must be transferred or may be sold. As George Annas states, "The [New Jersey Superior Court in the *Baby M* case] court's notion that if men are legally permitted to sell their sperm, women must be legally permitted to gestate children for pay, is constitutionally and biologically baseless. Equal protection may require that women be permitted to donate or sell their eggs, but it surely does not require that gestation [and parental rights, my addition] be for sale."[74]

Restriction on the Fee Means Restriction of Its Use

Another major argument in the case for permitting payment of a fee to a surrogate mother focuses on the negative impact of a restriction on fees for services. Since prohibition of the fee to surrogates will drastically reduce the pool of available women willing to serve as surrogates, this is tantamount to a prohibition of the practice itself, and thus is an unconstitutional restriction on a couple's procreative liberty. Laws restricting fundamental rights, such as the right to procreate, must be narrowly drawn to achieve a compelling state interest. An absolute restriction on any fee paid to a surrogate, rather than regulating the fee to insure that it does not become coercive or exploitative, is thus overreaching, and places a significant burden on the exercise of a fundamental right. Though there was not a financial aspect to the abortion decisions following *Roe v. Wade*, the Court, until the 1989 *Webster* decision, struck down attempts to place obstacles in the way of women attempting to procure elective abortion.[75]

In response to the 1981 Michigan decision in the *Doe v. Kelley* surrogacy case,[76] plaintiff's attorney Noel Keane argued that the court's restriction on the fee was in violation of judicial precedent set four years earlier in *Carey v. Population Services International*.[77] In that case, the Court struck down a New York law that outlawed the sale of contraceptives except through licensed pharmacists. In his decision, Justice Brennan stated that, "A total prohibition against the sale of contraceptives, for example, would intrude upon individual decisions in matters of procreation and contraception as harshly as a direct ban on their use. Indeed, in practice, a prohibition against all sales, since more easily and less offensively enforced, might have an even more devastating effect upon the freedom to choose contraceptives."[78]

As applied to surrogacy, it would appear that the argument is all the more persuasive, since the demands of surrogacy are generally considered to be too burdensome to be supplied altruistically, except perhaps by a close friend or family member. A prohibition of the fee would be much more restrictive than the restrictions on access to abortion or contraceptives, which have been struck down already as unconstitutional. Thus restrictions that significantly burden a fundamental right, in the absence of a compelling state interest, cannot be sustained, particularly when the restrictions, for all practical purposes, prohibit a practice.

Similarly, in *Grissom v. Dade County, Fla.*,[79] a Florida Superior Court ruled that an indigent woman who sought to adopt a child whose mother could not be located did not have to pay the cost of publishing notice of suit, since she did not have the means to do so. The publication fee requirement was ruled an undue restriction on her access to the courts, specifically in a matter in which a fundamental right was involved. The state cannot choose a method of meeting an important state interest that unnecessarily burdens the exercise of a fundamental right. The same reasoning is applied to surrogacy since it, too, concerns a fundamental right that the state is attempting to burden unnecessarily by prohibition of the fee.

Evaluation

There is little doubt that restriction of the fee to surrogates will reduce the number of available surrogates. Women who perform the surrogate role do so for a variety of reasons, some altruistic, out of a desire to help an infertile couple, some personal, out of the fulfillment that comes from pregnancy and childbirth, and some financial, for the standard $10,000-15,000 fee. However, it is clear that without the financial incentive, the other benefits are normally not sufficient to motivate women to bear a child for someone, especially if the couple are not close friends or family.

However, in considering the precedent set by the *Carey* case, one should recognize that there is a significant difference between the issue at hand in *Carey* and that in surrogacy. In *Carey*, what is at stake is the sale of contraceptives; in surrogacy, what is at stake is the sale of children. Though one has a fundamental right to procreate, nowhere does an individual possess the right to sell the product of procreation. The better parallel might be between *Carey* and a restriction on a fee to pay for the gestational services involved in surrogacy, though the argument that the fee pays for those services only cannot be sustained. Children and condoms are qualitatively different, and though there is a fundamental right to procreate, it does not follow that one has a fundamental right to sell children, irrespective of the circumstances in which the transaction takes place. By prohibiting the fee the state is restricting the sale of children. This restriction is not overreaching, nor is its purpose to further a compelling state interest, the same state interest that motivates the adoption laws. The rationale for the adoption laws is certainly to prevent exploitation of birth mothers and insure the best interests of the child. But it is also to prevent children from being bought and sold as commodities, consistent with the Thirteenth Amendment, and consistent with the child's best interests. Even in cases in which the circumstances of adoption are benign, and no coercion takes place, the law still restricts baby selling, because children are not inherently objects of barter. Condoms are legitimately bought and sold as commodities, and thus the restrictions on their sale in *Carey* can be termed overreaching. But that is not the case with children, since any restriction on the purchase and sale of children is not inherently overreaching. Certainly the adoption laws that restrict couples from paying birth mothers for their children drastically restrict the number of available adoptable children. But that alone hardly justifies repealing the adoption laws and allowing a black market in children to be established, since children are not to be bought and sold. Similarly, in surrogacy, though the fee reduces the number of available surrogates, that alone does not justify commercial surrogacy. The state is not prohibiting a couple from utilizing the services of a surrogate; only from her selling the child produced as a result.

The Children Born in Surrogacy Are Not Treated as Commodities

Proponents of commercial surrogacy suggest that their opponents are overly focused on the technicality of baby selling, and missing the more important consideration: are these children actually being treated as tradable commodities? Rather than treating the children as commodities, the reverse actually happens. Clearly surrogacy brings desperately wanted children into loving homes. The child that is brought home from the hospital is treasured for the priceless gift that he or she is. Since the average couple who arranges surrogacy has been infertile for some time and has likely exhausted every other avenue to have a child, the child born to the surrogate is the answer to years of yearning and dreams. These are hardly the circumstances in which a child would be treated as a thing, whose worth is determined only by its market value.

Thus, the notion that surrogate children are turned into commodities as money changes hands in connection with them is a piece of legal and philosophical theorizing with little foundation in reality. Law professor Michael Shapiro, in the Minority Report to the California Legislature, stated, "There is simply no evidence that children born of surrogate parenting arrangements are *in any sense* viewed by anyone as things manipulable at will, fungible or disposable. The idea that surrogacy is transmogrifying children into "things" is simply a theoretical concept without factual foundation."[80]   This is further supported by the Majority Report's admission that their fears about children being treated as commodities have largely been allayed by the way that surrogate children are successfully integrated into their nuclear families.[81]

Shapiro and the other minority members of the committee use a medical parallel to establish this point, suggesting that the money used on infertility treatments and the fee paid to the surrogate are both means used to obtain a child. The fact that money goes to a physician in one case and to a surrogate mother in the other is irrelevant, since both involve the outflow of money to achieve the birth of a child. Since no one would consider the child born as a result of in vitro fertilization or some other sophisticated procedure to alleviate infertility as commodified, neither should one so consider the child born out of surrogacy. Shapiro states, "By this theory (that commercial surrogacy is baby selling) any and every child is an "object" if money is paid to achieve his birth. This would include, of course, the child born as a result of infertility treatments in which medical professionals are paid (perhaps $20,000 or more) and adoption proceedings in which attorneys and others are paid (perhaps $10,000 to $15,000 or more). Just as with surrogacy, in both of these examples the prospective parents are paying money to obtain the child. There is no difference."[82]

Evaluation

The most persuasive part of this argument is the empirical experience of children born out of surrogacy. Clearly, they are not being treated as commodities by the parents who receive them into their homes. It is true that they are desperately wanted children who are normally placed into loving stable homes. However, the fact remains that children are still being bought and sold, something that is inherently immoral and in violation of the Thirteenth Amendment, irrespective of the surrounding circumstances.

Though slavery in the South during the Civil War era was not a benign experience, there were undoubtedly instances in which slaves were treated humanely, without having to suffer the indignities that were forced upon many other slaves. But that did not change the fact that they were still slaves. They were still objects of barter that could be bought and sold, even if they were bought and sold into environments in which they were not treated as slaves. One doubts that proponents of this argument would suggest that the treatment slaves received was the important aspect of the slavery question. Once slaves were freed, owning slaves per se violated the Thirteenth Amendment, irrespective of how they were treated.

The same parallel can be drawn with present-day adoption laws. Though many children placed through black market adoptions are placed into healthy, loving homes, that is irrelevant in determining whether state adoption laws have been violated. Adoption laws were enacted only in part to avoid the negative circumstances involved with the black market in children (a slippery slope argument). They were also passed for deontological reasons: because children are not intrinsically commodities. Thus the setting into which a child is sold is not the determining factor. The fact remains that a child has been bought and sold for a set price. Children, like adults under slavery, are not to be objects of barter, since by nature they are not things, but people of infinite value. Child selling, like slavery, is inherently objectionable, whether or not it is accompanied by objectionable circumstances.

As was the case with Andrews's argument, the use of the payment for medical services parallel does not fit. Proponents of commercial surrogacy such as the authors of the Minority Report to the California Legislature insist that in treating infertility, money is paid to a physician in the same way that money is paid to a surrogate in order to produce a child for the contracting couple. To make the parallel appropriate, the Minority Report must be assuming that the surrogacy fee is for services only. Yet, as has been shown, that assumption cannot be sustained, and thus the parallel fails to prove its point. Infertility specialists and adoption attorneys are rightly paid their respective fees for their medical and legal expertise. But unlike the service of surrogacy, exercise of their expertise does not acquire parental rights for them to the child created by their part in alleviating infertility or arranging surrogacy. In her "work," the surrogate becomes a parent,[83] and though she is paid for her pregnancy and childbirth services, she is also paid for her willingness to transfer parental rights. Thus, in surrogacy the payment is actually for the rights to the child. Though clearly in IVF, for example, the physician's fees are paid to obtain a child, they are not paid to the physician to obtain a child that rightly belongs to him. The child that is born out of the physician's expertise has no relationship to the physician, and the physician has no claim to any parental rights. Likewise, the adoption attorney is being paid so that a couple can obtain a child. But it is not the attorney's child that they are obtaining. This is not the case with surrogacy. The child for which the money is being paid is the legal child of the surrogate, and the fee is paying for much more than simply gestational services.[84] The parallel employed in the Minority Report fails to recognize this critical distinction between the fee to the surrogate, which purchases parental rights, and other expenses for legitimate professional services that have nothing to do with the parental rights of the one who accepts the fee. To suggest that simply because money changes hands in the process of relieving infertility and procuring a child for a childless couple, irrespective of the recipient of such money, obscures a critical difference between infertility services and surrogacy. The surrogate sells parental rights along with her gestational services, whereas the medical or legal professional simply sells services that do not require him or her to relinquish parental rights in the process of providing those services. Part of the surrogate's service involves baby selling, which is objectionable irrespective of the circumstances into which the child is placed.

Money Does Change Hands When Parental Rights Are Transferred

Though adoption laws prohibit the exchange of consideration for the transfer of parental rights, there are cases where exceptions to the general rule have been made when parental rights are transferred between family members. Thus, there is precedent for something like commercial surrogacy, particularly since the cases involved family members, the adoptive parents were not unfit, and the child's best interests were apparently served by the arrangements.

Two specific cases provide this precedent. In *Reimche v. First National Bank of Nevada*,[85] the court affirmed an agreement in which the natural father provided adequately for the natural mother in his will in exchange for her consent prior to birth to allow him to have sole custody of the child. Similarly, in *In re Shirk's Estate*,[86] the Kansas Supreme Court enforced an agreement in which the decedent agreed to give up one-third of her estate in exchange for her daughter's consent to allow her daughter to be adopted. In both of these cases, the exchange was between existing family members and involves existing children, with clear indications that the child's best interest is being given high priority. These circumstances roughly parallel those of surrogacy, in which the child is being given up by one family member to another, without any conflict with the child's best interests.

Evaluation

Some states' adoption laws contain an exception clause that exempts children transferred between parents from the baby selling. sections of the law. For example, in Washington, the relevant segment of the adoption laws states, "A transaction shall not be a purchase or sale under subsection (1) [which states, "It is unlawful for any person to sell or purchase a minor child,"] if any of the following exists: (a) the transaction is between parents of a minor child."[87] Thus, under Washington law, it would appear that surrogacy would not violate existing adoption law, and would be consistent with legal precedent set in Nevada and Kansas.

However, there is also legal precedent that does not allow any consideration to be exchanged for parental rights to a child. In *Willey v. Lawton*,[88] an Illinois appeals court ruled that an agreement between natural parents to forgive a child support debt in exchange for consent to adoption was unenforceable as contrary to the state's public policy. In this case, a former husband of a woman who had since remarried who was behind in his child support payments agreed to allow her second husband to adopt the child born to them during their marriage in exchange for releasing him from the delinquent child support and $5,000 in cash. The court ruled that to allow bartering of children "tends to the destruction of one of the finest relations of human life."[89] The court did not mention the circumstances into which the child would be adopted, clearly a good home. Nor did it mention any economic distress that likely motivated the natural father to consider consenting to adoption. Rather, the court held to the inherent objectionable nature of bartering children for money, irrespective of the type of financial exchange that is being made. Nor did it matter that it was between already existing parents.

Even if one grants that the exchange of consideration is morally legitimate when it involves two already existing parents, that does not justify it in surrogacy. The difference between the two precedent-setting cases and surrogacy is that the child was already existing at the time of the arrangement, and the two parents had previously been married and now were divorced. In other words, they were a distinct family unit at the time of the child's birth. That is quite different from surrogacy, in which the two natural parents to be are, in most cases, total strangers at the time the arrangement is made. Though most of the fee will be paid when they have become parents, surrogacy is not similar to the above situations in which the arrangements were made between two existing family members. A child is in effect being bartered between strangers, a situation that the baby selling laws are designed to prohibit. In addition, in the one case (*Willey v. Lawton*) in which straight cash was exchanged, as is the case with surrogacy, the Court considered the agreement invalid, since it clearly involved the sale of a child.

ARGUMENTS AGAINST COMMERCIAL SURROGACY

The focus of this chapter so far has been on the arguments in favor of commercial surrogacy. Proponents argue that surrogacy does not constitute baby selling as contemplated by many states' adoption laws that prohibit black market adoptions. The evaluation of each of the specific arguments has attempted to establish that surrogacy is indeed the sale of children and should be prohibited as a violation of the Thirteenth Amendment and state adoption laws. Thus, the main objection to commercial surrogacy still remains: it is the sale of children. However, there are other arguments against commercial surrogacy that must be considered. These are as follows: (1) surrogacy involves the sale of women's bodies, (2) surrogacy involves a potential for exploitation of the surrogate, and (3) surrogacy involves commodification of children. This last argument is an expansion of the initial argument that surrogacy constitutes baby selling, to which proponents of commercial surrogacy are responding as they attempt to make their case in favor of the practice. The inherent moral objections to child selling will be addressed in greater detail in this section.

Commercial Surrogacy Involves the Sale of Women's Bodies

A principal argument against commercial surrogacy focuses on the surrogate, not the child,[90] and objects to the commodification of the woman's reproductive services. Beyond the argument that surrogacy can be exploitive of poor women, the question is raised about the appropriateness of women selling their reproductive capacities, parallel to the questions that emerge in considerations about prostitution.

Philosopher Sara Ann Ketchum argues strongly for this view, based on the Kantian maxim that people are to be treated as ends, not means, and that there are some activities that are such a significant part of one's personhood that participation in those activities inherently violates one's dignity as a person. Thus, there is a substantial difference between selling one's labor in most other areas and selling one's reproductive capacities. Though the right to contract clearly gives one the right to sell one's services, there are certain services that cannot be for sale without violating human dignity. For example, a contract that allowed one to be sold into slavery would not be valid or enforceable. Neither would a contract to conduct a duel, even assuming that it was entered into without coercion by consenting adults. Prostitution is treated in like manner in most states, and organ sale contracts, even if uncoerced, would be similarly void.

Ketchum argues from the case of rape, in which an assault on a woman's body is inherently an assault on her person. It is treating another person's body as part of one's personal domain, as a thing to be used to advance one's interests, and in effect is a denial that the person exists as a person.[91] This is then extended to apply to the sale of persons. Ketchum states, "To make a person or a person's body an object of commerce is to treat the person as part of another person's domain, particularly if the sale of A to B gives B rights to A or to A's body. What is objectionable is a claim--whether based on welfare or contract-- to a right to another person such that that person is part of my domain. The assertion of such a right is morally objectionable even without the use of force."[92] Thus, any market in women's bodies, in literal prostitution or in reproductive prostitution, as Ketchum terms it, though it gives women freedom to enter the marketplace and profit financially from it, is an ironic freedom. They enter the market not as persons but as commodities, and partial evidence for this is that the brokers (whom she terms "reproductive pimps") make the majority of the profit from the surrogacy arrangement. She then uses a slippery slope argument that is drawn from the connection between prostitution and rape. If women's bodies are viewed as things to be bought and sold, then what is to prevent them from being viewed as objects to be stolen, and used against their will?[93]

Evaluation

Ketchum's argument fails to take into account the difference between paying people for their labor and actually acquiring rights over them in the process. In critique of this argument, H. M. Malm suggests that there is a distinction between "(a) my paying you for *me* to use your body in a way that benefits me and (b) my paying you for *you* to use your body in a way that benefits me."[94] One can pay for labor without necessarily acquiring any rights over the one who has been hired. Malm cites as an example the case of one who hires out his services to do yardwork and owns his own lawnmower.[95] It is one thing for me to pay him to use the lawnmower to mow the lawn myself, thus renting the mower, and acquiring limited rights to it for the time in which I have rented it. It is quite another matter if I pay him for him to use his lawnmower to cut my grass, thus paying for his services that involve the use of his lawnmower. In this latter case, I do not acquire any rights to the lawnmower. At best I have the right to expect that he does with his lawnmower that for which I am paying him, and that to which he has agreed. Thus, in surrogacy, the contracting couple is purchasing the service that the surrogate performs with the use of her body, not any rights over her body itself.

This, of course, assumes that the surrogacy contract does not contain any provisions that give the contracting couple the right to mandate the surrogate's lifestyle while she is pregnant or force medical treatment decisions on her against her will. Malm states it this way: "the woman is being paid for *her* to use *her* body in a way that benefits him (the natural father)--she is being compensated for her services. But that does not treat her body as an object of commerce--any more than does my paying a surgeon to perform an operation, a cabby to drive a car or a model to pose for a drawing."[96]

A surrogate agreeing to use her reproductive capacities in this way does not surrender her rights to the contracting couple, nor does she necessarily allow the purchasers domain over her. Thus, it is not clear that surrogacy involves the kind of morally objectionable commodification of women's reproductive services that Ketchum envisions. Consistent with the overall thrust of this chapter, the act of commerce that makes surrogacy objectionable is the sale of children that results from the arrangement, not necessarily the sale or rental of a woman's capacity to reproduce. This, of course, assumes that such a sale is free from coercion or the potential for exploitation. A second argument against commercial surrogacy is that it includes just such a potential.

Commercial Surrogacy Involves Potential for Exploitation of the Surrogate[97]

There seems to be little doubt about the possibility for commercial surrogacy to be exploitive. The combination of desperate infertile couples and middlemen with varying degrees of moral scruples expands the possibilities for abuse beyond the surrogate herself being exploited. Numerous critics have constructed the scenario in which middle to upper-class women hire poor women to bear their children for them. They insist that the fee paid to surrogates constitutes an undue inducement to get them to do something they ordinarily would not do.[98] However, the fee functions in this way for most surrogates, since most, except perhaps close friends or family members, would not undergo surrogacy voluntarily. The fee thus provides effective incentive for an otherwise altruistic action. Such an incentive is not necessarily an undue inducement, though it can function as such.

Interestingly, feminists are divided about this potential for exploitation. For example, Janice Raymond of the University of Massachusetts, Amherst, has argued that even altruistic surrogacy is exploitive, in that it continues to set women apart as the caregiver and breeder class.[99] She further points out that surrogacy can be coercive even without the fee, as family members could easily put enormous pressure on a physically qualified relative to act as a surrogate for an infertile family couple. But other feminists, such as Lori Andrews, warn society of acting paternistically toward women, specifically about the assumption that poor women are incapable of acting in their best interests in this area and are driven by their poverty to act in ways that they would otherwise reject.[100] This too, they claim, is reinforcing a negative stereotype of women and encouraging paternalism toward them as a class. Ruth Macklin, of the Albert Einstein College of Medicine, is similarly concerned about exploitation, but only toward poor women, not women in general.[101] She admits that the fee is an undue inducement for a woman to do something she would not normally do. But surrogacy is something that most surrogates would not do apart from the incentive of the standard $10,000-15,000 fee, and her argument assumes that poor women are not capable of assessing their own interests.

Those who suggest that the fee is not exploitive argue that people have a right to compensation for the services they render.[102] As was discussed earlier, this widely recognized right applies to surrogacy only if the service does not include the waiver or sale of parental rights. In addition, lower classes frequently provide services for hire for the upper classes, and that alone does not make it exploitative. In fact, much of our economy is built on this phenomenon, and though there are occasionally objections to the overt forms of exploitation, such as occurs with migrant agricultural workers, for instance, there does not seem to be anything inherently exploitive about it. It does raise the potential for abuse, but it takes more than simply a lower class person being hired by an upper class person to make it exploitive.

Statistics on the approximately six hundred known surrogacy arrangements made to date indicate that this potential for exploitation has not materialized. Most surrogates are financially much like Mary Beth Whitehead, women of moderate means. The average annual income of the family of the surrogate is around $25,000.[103] They are clearly not destitute, but they are just as clearly motivated by the money. Except in rare altruistic cases, the money is the principal motivation, irrespective of the surrogate's financial status, and the potential for exploitation, though real and a danger to be taken seriously, has yet to be realized on a widespread scale.

However, this does not mean that one should dismiss the potential for abuse in the long run. Should surrogacy become more socially acceptable, and if more states pass laws permitting commercial surrogacy, it is not difficult to imagine the various ways in which brokers would attempt to keep costs down, thereby maximizing their profit in each arrangement. One of the most attractive ways in which this could be done would be to recruit surrogate mothers actively from among the poor in this country, and particularly in the Third World.

The statistics on the average income of the surrogates cited above are somewhat misleading, since they only take into account the women who were actually chosen to be surrogates. They do not reveal anything about the living standard of women who applied to be surrogates and who were rejected. In his 1983 study psychiatrist Philip Parker found that more than 40 percent of the applicants for surrogacy services were either unemployed or receiving some kind of financial assistance.[104] Similarly, in the initial applications for surrogate positions in Australia in the early 1980s, close to half of the applicants were divorced or single and ranged from being financially reasonably comfortable to penniless widows and wives with husbands having terminal diseases.[105] Some even believe that those with financial need make the best candidates for surrogacy, assuming they have the physical capacities, since they are, for financial reasons, the least likely to keep the child. As Dr. Howard Adelman, staff psychologist for Surrogate Mothering, Ltd. in Philadelphia put it, "I believe candidates with an element of financial need are the safest. If a woman is on unemployment and has children to care for, she is not likely to change her mind and want to keep the baby she is being paid to have for somebody else.[106] Similarly, attorney Noel Keane admitted that women for whom money is not a factor are not likely to serve as surrogates. In his attempts to recruit surrogates from around the country, the vast majority of women who answered his ads stated that the principal reason for volunteering was that they needed the money. The need ranged from moderate to desperate.[107]

Some are further suggesting that women be recruited from the Third World to serve as surrogates. For instance, John Stehura, president of the Bionetics Foundation, revealed that his firm was planning to move into international circles, particularly Asian countries such as Thailand, Korea, and Malaysia, to obtain candidates for surrogacy.[108] The rationale for such recruitment is that it dramatically decreases the expenses involved in surrogacy. Stehura stated that the surrogates from these countries would only receive travel expenses and basic necessities. Perhaps unknowingly revealing a strongly exploitive bias, he stated, "Often they're looking for a survival situation--something to do to pay for the rent and food. They come from underdeveloped countries where food is a serious issue." But he added, "they know how to take care of children, obviously it's a perfect match."[109] Now that embryo transfer is technologically more of a viable option, Stehura suggests that the use of Third World women could expand even further, and bring the price of surrogacy down even more. He speculates that perhaps one-tenth of the fee could be paid to some of these women, and it would not even matter if they had some other health problems, as long as they had an adequate diet and no problems that would affect the developing child.[110] It is not difficult to see the potential for crass exploitation of poor women in statements like these, a potential that is already being seriously considered by brokers in the industry. It is not clear the degree to which these statements are representative of the entire surrogacy industry, but with the profit motive being the primary factor in these arrangements, it does not take much imagination to see the potential for women to be exploited.

Commercial Surrogacy Involves Commodification of Children

The stronger argument against commercial surrogacy is based on the violation of human dignity that occurs when any human being is an object of barter. Since commercial surrogacy clearly involves the sale of children, it is prohibited on deontological grounds: that human beings, and particularly the most vulnerable human beings, children, must not be put up for sale, even to benevolent buyers, because people have inherent worth that places them above the vicissitudes of the market. In the West, this has been ultimately grounded theologically in the dignity and value of the individual who possesses the image of God, and thus cannot be for sale. It is also grounded constitutionally in the Thirteenth Amendment that prohibited slavery, principally on the grounds that human beings, irrespective of race or color, are not fungible items that can be traded for financial consideration. It is further grounded in the virtually universally accepted Kantian maxim that people are ends, not means, and should be treated as such. There are also consequential reasons for prohibiting the sale of human beings, especially children, such as to prevent exploitation of the mother and the contracting couple, to safeguard the best interests of the child from the profit motive, to prevent lack of counseling and screening of the contracting couple, and to insure that predictable human suffering is prevented. But there is also a deontological reason that human beings should not be bought and sold, that the purchase and sale of people inherently violates personal integrity and dignity, by regarding people as something they intrinsically are not.

The laws against slavery, the adoption laws in many states, and perhaps even laws against enforcing specific performance of service contracts (since that has parallels to a form of slavery), preclude the purchase of persons both on consequential and deontological grounds. Yet even if slavery were acceptable on overwhelming utilitarian grounds, it is unimaginable that it would ever be reinstituted, because of the strong deontological ground that puts the sale of human beings outside our moral parameters. The New Jersey Supreme Court recognized that baby selling was problematic outside of its potential for exploitation. Appealing to the inherent worth of persons, they stated, "There are, in a civilized society, some things that money cannot buy. There are values that society deems more important than granting to wealth whatever it can buy, be it labor, love or life."[111] The court rightly pointed out that with the use of the contract to circumvent the adoption laws against baby selling, the broker or middleman has been introduced.[112] As a result, in the words of the court, "the profit motive predominates, permeates and ultimately governs the transaction."[113] The sale of children, which inevitably results from a surrogacy transaction, is inherently problematic, irrespective of the benefits that emerge, in the same way that slavery is inherently morally troubling, because human beings are not objects that are for sale.

Of course, surrogacy itself is not slavery. But there are certainly strong parallels between enforcing the surrogacy contract and slavery, particularly in the forced breakup of the family that results as mothers are forcibly separated from their children.[114] As George Annas states, "Selling children conjures up the indignity and degradation of selling any human being; but more than that, specifically enforcing contracts that lead to the involuntary breakup of a family unit is at the heart of what many Americans found most repulsive about slavery prior to the Civil War."[115] He further points out that the way in which advocates of commercial surrogacy mask baby selling as well as the forcible removal of children from their mothers under specific performance of a contract, "indicates our preference for dealing with fairy tale versions of surrogacy."[116] There is no doubt that advocates are sensitive to this charge and they attempt to show that surrogacy is not baby selling, or that if it is, it is so different from slavery or black market adoptions that commercial surrogacy can be justified. There seems to be a widespread consensus on deontological grounds that persons should not be for sale, and the above attempts to skirt a problem that cannot be avoided reflect this same conviction.

Thus, it seems that deontological reasoning is both appropriate and helpful in regard to surrogacy. Advocates of commercial surrogacy resist the analogy to slavery, and would likely invoke deontological arguments to object to slavery in general. Yet their acceptance of surrogacy is based principally on utilitarian grounds, specifically that there is no evidence of clear harm to the child, and that in most cases, all parties to the arrangement benefit. The way the issue is framed is largely in these consequentialist terms. Since one of the suggested weaknesses of utilitarianism is its failure to offer a principled rejection of slavery, as philosopher Sara Ann Ketchum points out, "it is hardly surprising that utilitarians will find it difficult to discover within that theory an argument against selling babies."[117] Thus it would be very difficult for advocates to justify slavery on the same grounds on which they accept surrogacy.

The sale of human beings falls under the heading of what Professor Michael Walzer calls "blocked exchanges."[118] In any given society, there is the sphere of money and the domain of rights, in which rights prevent the sphere of money from dominating the entire range of social interactions. That is, there are some things that are outside the realm of the market. Rights thus put limits on those things that can be bought and sold.[119] This is society's way of distributing its goods and protecting its rights by means other than money. Examples of blocked exchanges include the sale of human beings, protecting the right to life and liberty, political power, criminal justice, freedom of speech, press, assembly, and religion, marriage and procreation, and freedom to leave the political community. The principal blocked exchange, fundamental to all the others, is that human beings cannot be bought or sold. This is more than a prohibition on an exchange born out of desperation.[120] It reflects a fundamental way of viewing human beings as inherently not commodities and thus not for sale.

The reason that the sale of human beings is a blocked exchange is that there are things that are so close to one's personhood and individual self-fulfillment that they cannot be objects of barter without denigrating personhood. They are what Professor M. J. Radin calls "market inalienable."[121] Rejecting both universal commodification and non-commodification, she insists that there should be some things that should not be for sale, without rejecting the entire market mechanism for distributing society's goods. Things that are market inalienable are those things that are essential to an appropriate concept of human flourishing and personhood.

Personhood has three principal overlapping aspects.[122] The first is freedom, or the power to choose for oneself; that is, the person is an autonomous individual who is able to act for himself through the exercise of his own free will. The second aspect of personhood is contextuality, or the necessity of relationships with the social and natural world. The third aspect is that of identity, that the person has a self that is integrated with the integrity and continuity necessary for successful individuation. Universal commodification undermines all of the above aspects of personhood, since conceiving of personal things and attributes as commodities does violence to personhood.

When a monetary price is put on a human being or an attribute of personhood, this creates an alienation by separating the person from the thing that has been commodified. As Radin states,

Universal commodification undermines personal identity by conceiving of personal attributes, relationships and philosophical and moral commitments as monetizable and alienable from the self. A better view of personhood should understand many kinds of particulars--one's politics, work, religion, family, love, sexuality, friendship, altruism, experiences, wisdom, moral commitments and personal attributes, as integral to the self.[123] To understand any of these as monetizable or completely detachable from the person--to think, for example that the value of one person's moral commitments is commensurate or fungible with those of another, or that the "same" person remains when her moral commitments are subtracted--is to do violence to our deepest understanding of what it is to be human.[124]

Thus, in order to determine what is market inalienable, one must be able to relate that attribute to an accepted concept of human flourishing.[125] Even if there is debate over the specifics of what should appropriately be market inalienable, it seems clear that the person himself or herself falls under this heading, since persons cannot be bought or sold with violating the freedom aspect of personhood, or without conceiving of persons in terms of market rhetoric.

This refusal to allow human beings to be bought or sold reflects the Kantian maxim concerning persons, that they should not be used as means, but treated as ends in themselves. This maxim underlies the widely accepted moral principle of respect for persons that is ultimately grounded in the biblical notion of persons being created in the image of God. As a result, each individual, as God's unique creation, has inherent immeasurable worth. Thus, persons are not inherently commodities whose value can be quantified or exchanged in a free market. The commodification of individuals in market rhetoric is not consistent with a view of persons as unique creations who are to be treated as ends, not means.

Commodification further tends to undermine altruism, reducing gifts to disguised sales, as opposed to appropriate expressions of relationships between the self and others.[126] This in turn increases the sense of separateness between the individual and the other members of the human community. This point was initially made in the now well-known debate about donating blood. Richard Titmuss, in *The Gift Relationship: From Human Blood to Social Policy*,[127] suggests that in commodifying blood, society actually ends up limiting freedom, specifically the freedom to be altruistic to strangers. The monetary motivation of the market is inconsistent with the freedom to give to strangers. Though one cannot legitimately claim a right to someone's blood, it does not follow that the person does not have some moral responsibility to consider the other's need. It is not clear why the individual has exclusive control over the resources necessary to help someone in grave need. Commodification of body parts, not to mention persons, minimizes the place of gifts in a society.

As applied to adoption, Radin suggests that the reason society finds adoption acceptable and baby selling unacceptable is that market rhetoric surrounds the sale of babies.[128] Irrespective of any of what she calls the "domino effect," that is, the fear of the slippery slope of market domination of a sphere that should be market inalienable, the availability of children for sale at all is a "good" that should not be, given the inherent worth of children. That is not to say that some children should not be given up for adoption in order to prevent them from being treated in ways that are deleterious to their personhood. But as Radin states, "Conceiving of any child in market rhetoric wrongs personhood. In addition, we fear, based on our assessment of current social norms, that the market value of babies would be decided in ways injurious to their personhood and to the personhood of those who buy and sell on this basis, exacerbating class, race and gender divisions. Conceiving of children in market rhetoric would foster an inferior conception of human flourishing, one that commodifies every personal attribute that might be valued by people in other people."[129]

Commercial Surrogacy Involves the Commodification of Women's Reproductive Services

Not only does surrogacy address children in market rhetoric, it does the same for a woman's reproductive capacities. Commercial surrogacy creates what Radin calls a "double bind" for women, in that it empowers and disempowers women at the same time.[130] Though the new range of reproductive service choices can be seen as liberating for women, particularly because of the additional income that accompanies it, it can also be enslaving, since it reinforces traditional gender stereotypes about women as the breeder class, carrying the genetic seed of the man.[131] Women's reproductive abilities are now products available for purchase to satisfy the male need to carry his seed and prolong his line.

In the *Baby M* case, the contract gave the Sterns control over Mary Beth Whitehead's lifestyle in areas related to the health of the fetus she was carrying. She would have to undergo amniocentesis on demand to insure that the fetus was genetically healthy, and on demand of Stern, she would have to terminate the pregnancy if some genetic defect was discovered. She could not terminate the pregnancy on her own volition, apart from Stern's approval, unless her physical life was endangered by continuing to carry the child. This is a further example of the double bind of surrogacy, liberating and limiting at the same time, particularly limiting the woman by making her subject to the contractual demands of the man, the contracting natural father.

Further, in the *Baby M* case, the lower court judge referred to surrogacy as a "viable vehicle" to help alleviate the difficulties the Sterns would have had in carrying a child to term.[132] Similarly, one of the expert witnesses who testified in the case referred to Whitehead as a "surrogate uterus."[133] George Annas suggests that surrogacy entails a powerful deception that must be sold to surrogates, that they are simply containers for someone else's child.[134] Numerous surrogates testify to their belief from the start of the pregnancy that the child they are carrying is not theirs, but that they are "baby-sitting" the child for the contracting couple. For instance, the first well-publicized surrogate, Elizabeth Kane, stated, "It's not my baby, it's the father's; I'm just growing it for him."[135] Thus the service that surrogates perform, particularly if the surrogate contributes the egg, involves a misconception about her role as the child's mother, and treats the woman as a reproductive vessel, carrying the precious genetic cargo of the man.[136]

CONCLUSION

This chapter has attempted to show that commercial surrogacy is indeed baby selling and should be prohibited. Given the long tradition in the United States against the sale of human beings, as with slavery and with children through adoption laws, the burden is on the advocates of commercial surrogacy to show either that it does not involve the sale of children or that it is an acceptable form of it. Most of the arguments in favor of commercial surrogacy are sensitive to the charge of baby selling, and supporters go to considerable lengths to show that it is not, or that if it is, it is benign in its effects.

The purpose of this chapter has been to analyze the arguments on both sides of the issue. However, the focus of this discussion has been on evaluating the arguments in favor of commercial surrogacy. The reason for giving so much attention to these arguments is that they constitute the heart of the debate. There is not much controversy in American society concerning the morality of selling children. Most agree that children should not be objects of barter, both for utilitarian and deontological reasons. The real debate in surrogacy is whether the practice does indeed constitute the sale of children, and if it does, whether this makes a morally significant difference. The conclusion of this chapter is that surrogacy is the equivalent of selling children, and does not constitute an acceptable form of baby selling.

The first argument made by proponents of commercial surrogacy is that the fee paid to the surrogate is payment for gestational services, not for the sale of a child. Yet upon closer examination, a substantial portion of the fee pays for the willingness of the surrogate to waive parental rights to the child she is carrying. Many surrogacy contracts include provisions that the balance of the fee, if not all of it, will be held in escrow until the arrangement is completed, that is, until the child is turned over to the contracting couple and adopted by the natural father's wife. These contracts also often include provisions that the surrogate will receive less of the fee should she miscarry or give birth to a stillborn child. The contract and payment schedule are oriented to the product of the arrangement, not to the process. If it were process oriented, the surrogate would receive the same fee whether she turned over the child or not, a situation inconceivable to surrogacy brokers. Thus, the way the fee is paid indicates that it is indeed for the waiver of parental rights, precisely the thing that adoption laws were written to preclude, since such a waiver for a fee constitutes baby selling.

A second argument attempts to distance surrogacy from the practice that the adoption laws were written to discourage, black market adoptions. Proponents suggest that there are major differences between the two practices. Yet as these were examined in greater detail, there turned out to be more similarities than differences. The differences were either overstated or not relevant to the discussion of surrogacy. For example, one major difference is that the adopting father is the child's natural father, as opposed to a stranger. However, genetics alone does not necessarily make for a better parent, and simply because the natural father is involved in the transaction does not make it any less of a transaction. He is not the sole owner of the child, but a joint tenant with the surrogate. He is in effect, buying out the surrogate's rights to the child with the fee. A further difference is that surrogacy is concerned with the child's best interests as opposed to black market adoptions which are solely financially driven. Yet this overstates the difference, since the only psychological screening done in surrogacy is on the surrogate, and normally the only screening done on the contracting couple is financial. A third difference is that in surrogacy, coercion of the surrogate cannot take place since the agreement is entered into prior to the onset of pregnancy. Thus there is no unwanted pregnancy that might coerce a young unwed mother, for example, to give her child up when she would not do so under less coercive circumstances. But to suggest that surrogacy is free from coercion overstates the case, since once the pregnancy begins and the surrogate decides she wants to keep the child, she may have a wanted pregnancy and an unwanted contract that will force her to give up the child she is carrying.

A third argument attempts to draw a parallel between AID and surrogacy. Proponents of commercial surrogacy insist that since AID is legitimate, and men can be paid a nominal amount for sperm donation, women should also be able to engage in surrogacy for a fee. But the more appropriate parallel to AID is not surrogacy, but egg donation. Equal protection only requires that women be able to donate their eggs for a small fee in the same way that men donate their sperm.

A fourth argument was drawn from Supreme Court decisions (principally the *Carey* decision) that struck down laws that restricted the sale of contraceptives, insisting that a restriction of the fee for surrogacy constituted an overreaching restriction on a couple's constitutionally protected procreative liberty. Though it is undeniable that a ban on the fee beyond reasonable medical expenses will dramatically reduce the pool of available surrogates, the issues of procreative liberty and the right to sell the children produced out of the exercise of that liberty are quite separate. *Carey* protected the sale of contraceptives, commodities which are qualitatively different from children. Although one cannot constitutionally restrict the sale of a commodity such as condoms, it does not follow that the state cannot restrict the surrogacy fee, since payment of it constitutes the sale of children. Further, if the state restricts the fee, it is not interfering with a couple's right to arrange a third party procreative agreement: it is only restricting the right of the third party to sell the child produced by the agreement.

Further arguments include the fact that children are not treated as commodities in surrogacy and that money changes hands in some adoption proceedings. It is true that the majority of children born to surrogates are well treated by their new families. But the fact remains that they are still being bought and sold. Even though there were certainly slaves who were treated well, that hardly justifies the sale of human beings. In response to the concept of money changing hands in some adoption proceedings, the permitted exchange of money in adoption occurs between two already existing parents, not between two people who have been strangers prior to the surrogacy arrangement being organized. Further, the exchange of cash, as in surrogacy, has been banned even between already existing family members. The consideration being exchanged in the cases being used to support this argument was forgiveness of a debt or a child support obligation, not a cash deal as is the case in surrogacy.

The most obvious argument against commercial surrogacy is that it constitutes the sale of children, violating adoption laws in many states as well as the Thirteenth Amendment. Commercial Surrogacy is prohibited because it involves the commodification of children, that is, it is one of the blocked exchanges, blocked because of society's desire to protect certain areas of social life from the realm of the market. Baby selling is blocked because babies are market inalienable, that is, because human beings cannot be bought and sold without doing violence to an essential aspect of personhood.

Further arguments against commercial surrogacy include the notions that women's reproductive capacities should not be subject to the dictates of the market. However, it is not clear that surrogacy involves a morally objectionable market transaction: only the sale of the child that results from the agreement is inherently morally objectionable. What makes the commodification of women's reproductive services argument more compelling is the potential for exploitation of the surrogate. Although such exploitation has not materialized so far, there is evidence of surrogacy brokers marketing surrogacy among poor women, particularly those in the Third World, and thus the potential for exploiting women is real.

The main objection to commercial surrogacy is that it is the equivalent of baby selling, a practice that is inherently morally objectionable, because human beings are not objects of barter or commerce. Any attempt to show that surrogacy does not constitute child selling fails to account for the realities of the surrogacy contract. Thus, public policy should be formulated to prohibit a fee to surrogates beyond reasonable medical expenses and perhaps lost wages due to the pregnancy. Any fee to surrogacy brokers to set up a commercial surrogacy arrangement should likewise be prohibited.

NOTES

1. States which have such laws include Alabama (Ala. Code 26-10-8, 1977), Arizona (Ariz. Rev. Stat. Ann. 8-126 (c), 1974), California (Cal. Penal Code 273 (a) West 1970), Colorado (Colo. Rev. Stat. 19-4-115, 1973), Delaware (Del. Code title 13, 928, 1981), Florida (Fla. Stat. Ann. 63.212(1)(b), West Supp. 1983), Georgia (Ga. Code Ann. 74-418,

Supp. 1984), Idaho (Idaho Code 18-1511, 1979), Illinois (Ill. Rev. Stat. chapter 40, 1526, 1701, 1702, 1981), Indiana (Ind. Code Ann. 35-46-1-9, West Supp. 1984-85), Iowa (Iowa Code Ann. 600.9, 1981), Kentucky (Ky. Rev. Stat. 199.590(2), Supp. 1986), Maryland (Md. Ann. Code 5-327, 1984), Massachusetts (Mass. Ann. Laws chapter 210, 11A, Michie Law Coop. 1981), Michigan (Mich. Comp. Laws Ann. 710.54, West Supp. 1983-84), Nevada (Nev. Rev. Stat. 127.290, 1983), New Jersey (N.J. Stat. Ann. 9:3-54, West Supp. 1984-85), New York (N.Y. Soc. Serv. Law 374(6), McKinney 1983), North Carolina (N.C. Gen. Stat. 48-37, 1984), Ohio (Ohio Rev. Code Ann. 3017.10(A), Baldwin 1983), South Dakota (S.D. Codified Laws Ann. 25-6-4.2, 1984), Tennessee (Tenn. Code Ann. 36-1-135, 1984), Utah (Utah Code Ann. 76-7-203, 1978), and Wisconsin (Wisc. Stat. Ann. 946.716, West 1982). Some states, such as Arizona, California, and Florida, exempt stepparents from such laws. Approximately half of the states impose criminal sanctions ranging from simple misdemeanor to felony. Some further will not grant a final disposition of the adoption proceedings until a list of expenses incurred in connection with the adoption has been submitted to the court (Arizona, Delaware, Iowa, Michigan, New Jersey, and Ohio).

2. See *Doe v. Kelley*, 106 Mich App. 169, 307 N.W. 438 (1981), and the discussion of this case in chapter four.

3. See *In the matter of Baby M*, 109 N.J. 196, 537 A. 2d 1227, and discussion of this case in chapter four.

4. See *Surrogate Parenting Associates, Inc. v. Kentucky* (704 S.W. 2d 209 (1986). Capron comments on this case, "The decision is curious because the court rested its finding that surrogacy was not baby selling on the ground that surrogacy cannot involve adoption because the biological father already has a legal relationship with the child. But that begs the question: may the state forbid a man's wife to pay another woman to transfer the latter's parental rights to her without violating the "privacy" rights of the parties?" See Alexander Morgan Capron, "Alternative Birth Technologies: Legal Challenges," *University of California, Davis Law Review* 20 (1987): 696, n. 47. This argument that surrogacy is not baby selling since a natural father cannot buy back what is already his was a key aspect of the lower court decision in the *Baby M* case, and will be addressed later in this chapter.

A further argument made by the Kentucky Court was that the state's adoption laws did not apply to surrogacy since there was no child prior to the agreement. The court held that since "the agreement to bear the child was entered into *before* conception," the laws prohibiting money for adoption did not apply (at 211-212); cited in William M. Laufer, "Can Surrogacy Co-Exist With New Jersey's Adoption Laws?" *Seton Hall Law Review* 18 (1988): 892. Thus, when the contract was signed, there was no child in existence, so there could not be a payment for adoption scheme. However, this seems to be an attempt to obscure the obvious, since a child will result from the arrangement, and it is irrelevant when the child under consideration actually appears on the scene. Bonnie Steinbock, for example, has labeled surrogacy as "prenatal adoption," which seems consistent with the realities of surrogacy (though she holds that the fee to the surrogate is for services rendered, not the sale of a child). See Bonnie Steinbock, "Surrogate Motherhood as Prenatal Adoption," *Law, Medicine and Health Care* 16, nos. 1-2 (1988): 44-50.

5. That is, no fee is allowed beyond reasonable expenses, and a recission period in which the surrogate is allowed to change her mind should she desire to keep the child. This latter point will be addressed in detail in chapter three.

6. He applied this to the *Baby M* case. See Laufer, "Can Surrogacy Co-Exist, 891-92.

7. Avi Katz, "Surrogate Motherhood and the Baby Selling Laws," *Columbia Journal of Law and Social Problems* 20 (1986): 24.

8. Karen Marie Sly, "Baby-Sitting Consideration: Surrogate Mother's Right to Rent Her Womb for a Fee," *Gonzaga Law Review* 18 (1982/83): 549-51.

9. Ibid., 561-63.

10. Lori Andrews, "Control and Compensation: Laws Governing Extracorporeal Generative Materials," *Journal of Medicine and Philosophy* 14 (October 1989): 541-60, 550. The latter example of selling contraceptives will be addressed later in this chapter.

11. She states, "Moreover, the most important part of parenting is childrearing, not childbearing. Yet it is permissible to pay all sorts of surrogate childrearers. Payment to women who serve as surrogate mothers should similarly be allowed." Ibid., 551.

12. Christine Sistare, "Reproductive Freedom and Women's Freedom: Surrogacy and Autonomy," *Philosophical Forum* 19 (Summer 1988): 237.

13. William F. May suggests that Judge Sorkow's distinction in the lower court Baby M decision between the process and product of surrogacy "flies in the face of the facts." He states, "Let no one doubt that the contract points toward the delivery of a product. And when the mother delivers that child, she must relinquish her rights as its genetic mother, her presumptive rights of custody over an already extant child. It is baby selling." "Surrogate Motherhood and the Marketplace," *Second Opinion* 9 (1987): 135.

14. Alexander Morgan Capron and Margaret J. Radin, "Choosing Family Law over Contract Law as a Paradigm for Surrogate Motherhood," *Law Medicine and Health Care* 16, nos.1-2 (1988): 37.

15. Cited in Capron and Radin, "Choosing Family Law over Contract Law ," 37.

16. Ibid.

17. Ibid.

18. Herbert T. Krimmel, "Surrogate Motherhood Arrangements from the Perspective of the Child," *Logos (USA)* 9 (1988): 107, n. 9. He also cites the helpful example of the opposite situation from surrogacy, in which the product is incidental to the service performed. "An example of a mixed contract where the sale of a product is incidental to the service would abe where you employ a doctor to sew up a wound that entails the sale of stitches. Quite a different case [from surrogacy]." Ibid.

19. Avi Katz, "Surrogate Motherhood and the Baby Selling Laws," 23-24.

20. Ibid., 21.

21. R. Jo Kornegay, "Is Commercial Surrogacy Babyselling?" *Journal of Applied Philosophy* 7 (1990): 48-50.

22. Ibid., 48.

23. Ibid. She insists that the nature of a contract implies that the one who contracts somehow must benefit from the arrangement for which he or she is paying. Thus a pregnancy that did not result in a birth, such as a miscarriage or stillbirth, would not benefit the contracting couple in any way, and a service would not have been rendered to them.

24. Ibid., 49.

25. One exception recently noted is the Beverly Hills, California office of William Handel, the Center for Surrogate Parenting of Los Angeles, where payment is made to the surrogate regardless of her consent to adoption or her relinquishment of custody. Whether it is the full amount of the fee that she would be paid if she did not surrender custody is unclear, but this appears to be an attempt at making the fee structure consistent with the claim about the services for which it pays. This is included in the Minority Report to the California Legislature. See Joint Legislative Committee on Surrogate Parenting, *Commercial and Non-commercial Surrogate Parenting* (Sacramento: Joint Publications Office, November 1990): M36.

26. William Laufer, "Can Surrogacy Co-Exist?," 891-92.

27. Ibid.

28. This will be addressed in more detail in the following chapter on parental rights under the heading of "Definition of Mother."

29. There is the possibility of in utero egg donation by the surrogate herself, with the egg then being fertilized and the embryo gestated in her own womb. This is the position of British philosopher Edgar Page, in his attempt to justify commercial surrogacy. His position is addressed in more detail in chapter three, in the section that deals with intent based-models of motherhood.

30. Of course, this is not to say that the role of a wife is limited to childbearing or motherhood in general.

31. Karen Marie Sly, "Baby-Sitting Considerations," 539, 547.

32. Sly's argument is a bit curious when she uses the term "prenatal baby-sitting." In her background material on surrogacy, she admits that in the standard surrogacy arrangement, "at least half of the fee [is] withheld until the child is delivered and the adoption had been formalized." Ibid., 543. There seems to be clear recognition that the fee pays for much more than gestational services, yet she seems intent on referring to the process as baby-sitting. If that is all that is involved, why is there any need to go through adoption proceedings, or the complex legal work in transferring parental rights?

33. Ibid., 547.

34. Ibid., 548.

35. Ibid., 562-63.

36. Andrews, "Control and Compensation," 550-551.

37. Thomas S. Bradley, "Prohibiting Payments to Surrogate Mothers: Love's Labor Lost and the Constitutional Right to Privacy," *John Marshall Law Review* 20 (1987): 734-35. Robert C. Black makes an even more explicit connection between the two when he states, "Statutes which make it a crime to *pay* a physician for delivering a baby or performing an abortion would unquestionably be held unconstitutional. Yet to say that a surrogate mother has the right to conceive and bear a child but not to be compensated *is to make essentially the same point* (emphasis added)." See "Legal Problems of Surrogate Motherhood," *New England Law Review* 16 (1981): 389.

38. This is essentially the argument made by Landes and Posner in their defense of a commercial adoption market. See Elisabeth M. Landes and Richard A. Posner, "The Economics of the Baby Shortage," *Journal of Legal Studies* 7 (June 1978): 323-48. The argument against making children objects of commerce in surrogacy also applies to commercial adoptions. The argument is addressed later in this chapter under the heading

"Commercial Surrogacy Involves Commodification of Children." The notion of a commercial adoption market is a topic to which I would like to return at a future time.

39. Andrews, "Control and Compensation", 551.

40. For example, see Note, "Developing a Concept of the Modern "Family": A Proposed Uniform Surrogate Parenthood Act," *Georgetown Law Journal* 73 (1985): 1291-1293; Lizabeth A. Bitner, "Wombs for Rent: A Call for Pennsylvania Legislation Legalizing and Regulating Surrogate Parenting Agreements," *Dickinson Law Review* 90 (Fall 1985): 253; Katz, "Surrogate Motherhood," 19-20; Laufer, "Can Surrogacy Co-Exist," 891-92; Bradley, "Prohibiting Payments to Surrogate Mothers," 742-43; Robert C. Black, "Legal Problems of Surrogate Motherhood," 381; Sly, "Baby-Sitting Considerations," 549-550.

41. In cases of gestational surrogacy, there is normally a biological link between the child and *both* social parents, since the "infertile" wife, not the surrogate, contributes the egg.

42. Katz makes this argument in contrasting surrogacy to black market adoptions. In surrogacy, "the child will have a proper home, in fact, the same one that he would have had if his parents had been able to conceive naturally or adopt independently." This is not to say, however, that the adopting parents in black market adoptions do not also desperately want a child, only that black market adoptions, being financially driven, do not offer the same guarantees of a healthy home as do contracting parents in surrogacy. See "Surrogate Motherhood," 25.

43. Joint Legislative Committee, *Commercial And Non-commercial Surrogate Parenting*, M36.

44. Andrews, "Control and Compensation: Laws Governing Extracorporeal Generative Materials," *Journal of Medicine and Philosophy* 14 (October 1989): 550.

45. Of course, the stranger's qualifications to be a parent may be equal or superior to the contracting, natural father. However, in black market adoptions, the only qualification given serious consideration is the ability to pay the necessary fees, and little weight is placed on the best interests of the child.

46. 434 U.S. 246 (1978).

47. 463 U.S. 248 (1983).

48. Ibid., 265.

49. 441 U.S. 380 (1978).

50. *Lehr v. Robertson*, 463 U.S , at 256.

51. 704 S.W. 2d 209 (Ky. 1986).

52. *In re Baby M*, 525 A. 2d 1128, 1164 (1987).

53. This may also be the case in gestational surrogacy, depending on how one defines motherhood. The following chapter will take up this question in more detail.

54. This real estate analogy is taken from Alexander Morgan Capron, "Surrogate Contracts: A Danger Zone," *Los Angeles Times*, 7 April 1987, B5.

55. Ibid.

56. Herbert T. Krimmel takes this a step further when he argues that the natural father is only claiming what is rightfully his, then there is no reason why he needs to pay the surrogate anything. Thus, to turn the argument of Judge Sorkow around, if the father cannot buy back what is already his, why does he need to purchase it in the first place? See Krimmel, "Surrogate Motherhood Arrangements," 109-10, n. 40.

57. H. M. Malm, "Commodification or Compensation: A Reply to Sara Ketchum," *Hypatia* 4 (1989): 132.

58. Bitner, "Wombs for Rent:," 253.

59. Black, "Legal Problems of Surrogate Motherhood," 381.

60. George Annas, "Death Without Dignity for Commercial Surrogacy: The Case of Baby M," *Hastings Center Report* 18 (April/May 1988): 22.

61. This objection is raised by Michigan State University philosopher Tom Tomlinson, cited in Leonard M. Fleck, "Surrogate Motherhood: Is It Morally Equivalent to Baby-Selling?," *Logos (USA)* 9 (1989): 144, n. 6.

62. The one exception encountered to date appears in Note, "Surrogate Parenthood, An Analysis of the Problems and a Solution: Representation for the Child," *William Mitchell Law Review* 12 (1985): 143-82.

63. This is taken from Sara Ann Ketchum, "Selling Babies and Selling Bodies," *Hypatia* 4 (Fall 1989): 119.

64. Of course, this same argument can be made against in vitro fertilization and other infertility treatments. The point being made here is simply that the arguments for commercial surrogacy are remarkably parallel to those made in favor of a free market approach to adoption.

65. Laufer, "Can Surrogacy Co-Exist?," 892, where he states, "The prohibition against baby selling is grounded in the assumption that the offer of compensation to an expectant mother while she is in an emotionally vulnerable state may invoke a coerced agreement. There is no such coercion in a surrogacy environment."

66. Andrews states, "reliance on the adoption analogy is misplaced [in attempting to ban payment to surrogates]. In traditional adoption, the child is going to a stranger. In surrogate motherhood, the child is going to his or her father. A stranger does not have a constitutional right to adopt someone else's child, and so the state can place all manner of restrictions in his way. A biological father does have a constitutional right to procreate his own biological child, and so restrictions on exercising that right must be justified by showing that they are necessary to avoid a substantial, imminent harm." Andrews, "Control and Compensation," 550.

67. The assertion that the right to procreate is empty if the fee is restricted is reminiscent of the *Webster* decision, in which the Supreme Court ruled that states could restrict abortion in public health facilities, that such a restriction was not inconsistent with the already established right to abortion. Critics of the decision objected to the decision, insisting that if public funding were removed, then access to abortion would be impossible for certain poor women, thus making the right to abortion empty for them. However, the Court responded by essentially holding that the right to abortion was a negative right, and the state had no obligation to fund abortions for anyone, only not to place obstacles in the way of a person who wanted to obtain one. The Court had ruled previously, in *Maher v. Roe* (432 U.S. 464, 1977), that the state was not obligated to provide funding for abortions through Medicare, even though the state had agreed to use such funds to pay for childbirth. In *Webster*, the Court justified a restriction on the use of public facilities for abortion on the same grounds that had been used in *Maher*, that "Missouri's refusal to allow public employees to perform abortions in public hospitals leaves a pregnant woman with the same choices as if the State had chosen not to operate

any public hospitals at all." (*Webster v. Reproductive Health Services*, 109 S. Ct., 1989, at 3052).

68. *DeShaney v. Winnebago County Dept. of Social Services*, 109 S. Ct. 998, 1989, at 1003.

69. Amicus Curiae brief of the ACLU of Southern California, presented to Orange County, California Superior Court in the Johnson v. Calvert case, cited in Joint Legislative Committee, *Commercial and Non-commercial Surrogate Parenting*, 94. They state, "There is simply no valid public policy reason to assume that the California Legislature, in making the sweeping ban on the sale or purchase of custody rights in all circumstances, intended that there be *any* exception at all. There is nothing in the language or the legislative notes of that penal statute to indicate any such intent."

70. Ibid.

71. Black, "Legal Problems of Surrogate Motherhood," 380.

72. See Coleman, "Surrogate Motherhood: Analysis of the Problems and Suggestions for a Solution," *Tennessee Law Review* 50 (1982): 71.

73. John A. Robertson, "Surrogate Mothers: Not So Novel After All," *Hastings Center Report* 13 (October 1983): 28-33, 28. This parallel clearly has limited application, and is only intended to apply to the legitimacy of the fee. If the framework for AID were adopted for surrogacy, it would likely cease to exist as a practice, since the presumption of AID is that the birth mother is the legal mother and her husband is the legal father. As noted earlier, current AID laws form a significant obstacle to surrogacy.

74. George J. Annas, "Baby M: Babies (and Justice) for Sale," *Hastings Center Report* 17 (June 1987): 13-15, 14.

75. See for example, *Planned Parenthood of Central Missouri v. Danforth* (requiring spousal consent prior to abortion), 428 U.S. 52 (1976) and *Doe v. Bolton* (requiring that abortions be performed only in accredited hospitals), 410 U.S. 179 (1973). However, in *Webster v. Reproductive Health Services, United States Law Review* 57 (22 July 1989): 5044-45, the Court ruled that states can prevent state facilities and resources from being used for abortions. In *Planned Parenthood v. Casey*, the Court has recently upheld the constitutionality of a Pennsylvania law that requires that a woman wait twenty-four hours before having an abortion, notify her husband if she is married, or notify her parents if she is a minor, and receive counseling about alternatives to abortion.

76. Mich. App., 307 N.W. 2d 438 (1981).

77. 431 U.S. 678 (1977). Keane made this analogy and the argument based on it in "Legal Problems of Surrogate Motherhood," *Southern Illinois Law Journal* (1980): 147, 153.

78. *Carey*, 431 U.S. at 687-88.

79. Fla., 293 So. 2d 59 (1974).

80. Joint Legislative Committee, *Commercial and Non-commercial Surrogate Parenting*, M32.

81. Ibid., M33.

82. Ibid., M33.

83. Here it is assumed that the surrogate contributes both the egg and the womb. There is considerable debate over whether or not a gestational surrogate has any parental rights to the child she carries. What makes someone a mother (genetics versus. gestation, for example) is the subject of the following chapter.

84. This response assumes that if a woman supplies the egg and gestates the child, as is the case in the majority of surrogacy agreements, she is the mother. This also assumes that the woman who gestates the child is also the mother. This will be argued in the following chapter.

85. 512 F. 2d 187 (1975).

86. 186 Kan. 311, 350 P. 2d 1 (Kan. 1960).

87. Wash. Rev. Code 9A.64.030 (1983), cited in Sly, "Baby-Sitting Consideration," 549, n. 46. Another exception that is mentioned in the law defines the type of consideration that may be paid, limiting it to medical and legal expenses involved with the birth and adoption of the child. It is unclear from the law whether that limit also applies between parents of a minor child, or whether it gives parents of the child the legal freedom to exchange more than simply those expenses for the parental rights to the child.

88. 8 Ill. App. 2d 344, 132 N.E. 2d 34 (1956).

89. Ibid., 132 N.E. 2d, at 35.

90. The issue of children being commodified as objects of barter will be taken up later in this chapter.

91. Ketchum, "Selling Babies ," 121.

92. Ibid., 122.

93. She states, "A market in women's bodies-whether sexual prostitution or reproductive prostitution-reveals a social ontology in which women are among the things in the world that can be appropriately commodified-bought and sold, and by extension, stolen." Ibid.

94. Malm, "Commodification or Compensation," 130. See also Heidi Malm, "Paid Surrogacy: Arguments and Responses," *Public Affairs Quarterly* 3 (April 1989): 59-60.

95. Malm, "Commodification or Compensation," 122.

96. Malm, "Paid Surrogacy," 60.

97. This section and the following one will not follow the format used thus far in this chapter. The evaluation of the arguments made will be woven throughout the general discussion of the argument.

98. See Christine Overall, *Ethics and Human Reproduction: A Feminist Analysis* (Winchester, Mass.: Allen and Unwin, 1987): 118, 124-26.

99. Janice G. Raymond, "Reproductive Gifts and Gift Giving: The Altruistic Woman," *Hastings Center Report* 20 (November/December 1990): 11.

100. Lori Andrews, "Surrogate Motherhood: The Challenge for Feminists," in *Surrogate Motherhood: Politics and Privacy,* ed. Larry Gostin (Bloomington: Indiana University Press, 1990): 171-176. See also her "Surrogate Motherhood: An Ethical Perspective," *Law, Medicine and Health Care* 16 nos. 1-2 (Spring 1988): 73-91.

101. Ruth Macklin, "Is There Anything Wrong With Surrogate Motherhood?: An Ethical Analysis," *Law, Medicine and Health Care* 16 nos. 1-2 (Spring 1988): 62-63.

102. See Sly, "Baby-Sitting Considerations:," 561-62.

103. Philip J. Parker, "Motivation of Surrogate Mothers: Initial Findings," *American Journal of Psychiatry* 140 (January 1983): 117-18.

104. Ibid., 1.

105. "Volunteer Surrogates Pour In," *Sunday Telegraph* (Sydney, Australia) 14 December 1980, cited in Gena Corea, *The Mother Machine: Reproductive Technologies from Artificial Insemination to Artificial Wombs,* (New York: Harper and Row): 229.

106. Robert H. Miller, "Surrogate Parenting: An Infant Industry Presents Society with Legal, Ethical Questions," *Ob/Gyn News* 18 (1983): 1, cited in Corea, *The Mother Machine,* 229.

107. Noel Keane and Dennis Breo, *The Surrogate Mother* (New York: Everest House, 1981), 236.

108. Corea, *The Mother Machine,* 245. At the time of this citation, in 1984, he had not yet brought any Asian women into the United States, but had already purchased advertising in different media outlets there and was beginning to negotiate the necessary details to have them brought to this country.

109. Ibid.

110. Ibid., 214-15.

111. *In the matter of Baby M,* 537 A. 2d at 1249 (1988).

112. This contract is the only aspect of surrogacy that is new, and thus to place it among the new reproductive technologies is somewhat misleading. This is not the case, however, when surrogacy involves in vitro fertilization and embryo transfer to a gestational surrogate. But the majority of surrogacy cases still involve the use of the surrogate's egg and womb.

113. *In the Matter of Baby M,* 537 A. 2d at 1249. As was discussed earlier, the court clearly pointed out that the profit motive dominated the Baby M transaction, since the broker, the Infertility Center of New York, failed to disclose some strongly negative psychological evaluations of Mary Beth Whitehead, since to do so would have undermined her suitability as a surrogate and jeopardized the entire arrangement. See Ibid., 1247.

114. This, of course, assumes a traditional definition of motherhood. This will be discussed further in chapter three. Suffice it to say here that most agree with the legal precedent that in cases in which the surrogate contributes both womb and egg, she is the mother. Most of the debate concerns the "motherhood" of the gestational surrogate.

115. George J. Annas, "Fairy Tales Surrogate Mothers Tell," in Gostin, *Surrogate Motherhood,* 49.

116. Ibid., 50.

117. Ketchum, "Selling Babies ," 118-19.

118. Michael Walzer, *Spheres of Justice* (New York: Basic Books, 1983), 100-102.

119. Arthur Okun, *Equality and Efficiency: The Big Tradeoff* (Washington, D.C., 1985), 6-10. Okun sees the entire Bill of Rights as enumerating a series of blocked exchanges. Cited in Walzer, *Spheres of Justice,* 100.

120. This is Okun's term, cited in Walzer, Spheres of Justice, 100.

121. Margaret J. Radin, "Market-Inalienability," *Harvard Law Review* 100 (June 1987): 1849-1937. Radin is against all surrogacy, though in a non-ideal world, is willing to prohibit only the commercial element. She is against surrogacy in general because it reinforces gender stereotypes, decreases the number of prospective parents for the already too high numbers of adoptable children, and reflects a too limited view of parent-child bonding, placing too much stress on the genetic element.

122. Ibid., 1904.

123. She does point out that when dissociated from some of the above things, such as work and politics, one does not cease to be a person. Further, some of those things can be incompletely commodified. However, these are integral to the person and cannot be

completely commodified, since she sees commodification existing along a continuum. Things like work and housing, which express a significant part of our identity, yet have a legitimate market value, are also incompletely commodified. Ibid., 1906, 1918-19.

124. Ibid., 1905-6.

125. This will be explored further in chapter three, when the subject of waiver of parental rights is taken up. The right to associate with one's offspring is clearly central to almost any concept of human flourishing, and thus cannot be the object of sale. Nor can it be waived irrevocably prior to the birth of the child.

126. Ibid., 1907.

127. Richard Titmuss, *The Gift Relationship: From Human Blood to Social Policy* (New York: Pantheon Press, 1971). Kenneth Arrow responded to Titmuss by denying that market conditions for blood actually reduce freedom of any choices. Arrow fails to see the same dilemma that is central to Titmuss' thesis. "Gifts and Exchanges," *Philosophy and Public Affairs* 4 (1972): 343-62. Peter Singer responded to Arrow in defense of Titmuss by arguing as a consequentialist that the laws of the marketplace actually do discourage altruism, particularly when one takes into account the social utility of altruistic behavior. Arrow has taken a too shallow view of freedom, isolating it from the end for which freedom is exercised and treating it too largely as an end in itself "Altruism and Commerce: A Defense of Titmuss against Arrow," *Philosophy and Public Affairs* 5 (1973): 312-20. Cited in Eugenie Gatens-Robinson, "Selling Spare Parts and Renting Useful Spaces," *Journal of Social Philosophy* 18 (Winter 1987): 28, 32-35.

128. Radin, "Market-Inalienability," 1926-27.

129. Ibid., 1927-28.

130. Ibid., 1916, 30.

131. Ibid., 1930. For the argument that even non-commercial surrogacy contributes to reinforcing gender stereotypes, see Raymond, "Reproductive Gifts," 7-11.

132. Cited in the decision by the New Jersey Supreme Court, *In the matter of Baby M*, 525 A. 2d, at 1128.

133. Ibid.

134. Annas, "Fairy Tales Surrogate Mothers Tell," 51.

135. Elizabeth Kane, *Birthmother* (New York: Harcourt Brace Jovanovich, 1988): 275. She has since changed her mind about surrogacy. See Annas, "Fairy Tales Surrogate Mothers Tell," 53, n. 32.

136. This misconception assumes some of the discussion in the following chapter on parental rights and the definition of motherhood. The debate over who is the mother revolves around the differences between the genetic and gestational surrogate. There is wide agreement that when the surrogate contributes both the egg and the womb, she is indeed the mother with full maternal rights. She is just not married to the father. Thus, she is much more than a reproductive carrier for the contracting couple.

3

PARENTAL RIGHTS AND THE DEFINITION OF MOTHERHOOD

INTRODUCTION

Some of the most vexing questions in surrogacy revolve around the issue of parental rights. With the ability to separate the genetic, gestational, and social components of motherhood successfully, new questions are being raised for which society has few legal, moral, or social precedents. Biology has always been presumed to determine parenthood, and, as a result, society has never been forced to examine the social and moral aspects of motherhood. Though society has always recognized the role of the social mother, one who is biologically unrelated to the child, in adoption and foster parenting, surrogacy presents cases in which these roles are separated by design instead of by the misfortune of someone who realizes she cannot keep the child she has borne. These tragic situations set up the distinction between biological and social motherhood. Now even the term biological mother must be clarified, since it encompasses both the genetic and gestational elements that can now be separated in surrogacy.[1] Legal precedent for gestational surrogacy will likely be established in the near future, since the California Supreme Court has ruled in the *Johnson v. Calvert* case.[2] This landmark decision will likely become the legal equivalent of the *Baby M* case for gestational surrogacy.

The issue of parental rights, along with the commercial element of surrogacy, is the most controversial element of any proposed position or legislation. In most surrogacy cases, there are at least two unrelated people making parental claims, and in gestational surrogacy, there are three people who have made biological contributions to the child. However, there could be as many as five people making custody claims upon any given child born of a surrogacy arrangement. In this extreme situation, the contracting couple could be genetically unrelated to the child, with the genetic materials supplied by anonymous sperm and egg donors. Through in vitro fertilization, the embryo could then be transferred to the uterus of another woman, who would gestate the child. It is difficult to see the reason why someone would actually undertake an arrangement like this one, especially since one of the principal reasons for surrogacy is to have a child genetically related at least to the husband of the contracting couple. But it does illustrate the importance of defining who the parents are, and their corresponding rights.

If commercial surrogacy is banned, that will dramatically decrease the number of available surrogates, greatly curtailing the practice. However, there will still be a need to resolve the issue of parental rights, since there will surely continue to be cases of altruistic surrogacy in which the surrogate will breach the informal agreement to transfer custody to the contracting couple. Simply because the arrangement is undertaken without a fee to the surrogate does not mean that there is no prospect of the surrogate's becoming attached to the child and refusing to give it up. Thus, any proposed legislation on surrogacy must address parental rights to anticipate situations in which custody conflicts arise. Further, in order to legitimate properly the child born of the arrangement, even if there is no custody dispute, parental rights must be clearly defined.

Some states will undoubtedly choose to regulate rather than ban commercial surrogacy. Though the majority of those that have enacted legislation have chosen to ban the commercial element of the practice, there is still great debate over the legality and morality of commercial surrogacy. It is not at all improbable that some states will elect to allow a fee to the surrogate and enact legislation to insure that there is no coercion or exploitation of the participating parties. In these states, the practice of surrogacy is likely to be significantly more widespread, and there may be proportionately more custody disputes, especially as the legal precedent allowing the surrogate to challenge successfully the enforceability of the contract becomes more widely known.[3]   In any contractual agreement, the relationships of the parties must be clearly defined. This is particularly so in surrogacy, since the relationships with the resulting child are so strong, and the possibility of irreconcilable conflict is greater.

There is general agreement that in cases in which the surrogate provides both the egg and the womb, she is both the natural and legal mother, thus possessing full maternal rights. This precedent was established by the *Baby M* court, and is disputed only by the advocates of intent-based parenthood, who generally favor viewing surrogacy within the parameters of contract law rather than family law.[4] According to the New Jersey Supreme Court, and those who follow its reasoning, to call her a surrogate is not only misleading, but incorrect.[5] The heart of the present debate concerns gestational surrogacy, in which two women make biological contributions. Thus, the majority of the discussion on maternal rights will focus on whether the genetic or gestational mother has priority in determining maternal rights, though there will be substantial interaction with the intent-based parenthood position.

The chapter will proceed as follows:

1. *The Definition of Motherhood.* Before any discussion of parental rights can proceed, who the parents are who possess those rights must be established. Claims to motherhood based on genetics, gestation, and intent will be examined. The conclusion drawn will be that gestation determines motherhood, and that the woman who gives birth to the child should be viewed as the legal mother, whether or not she contributes the egg.

2. *The Right to Associate with One's Children as a Fundamental Right.* This right will be established as a fundamental right. The legal precedent for this right will be explored, balancing the privacy claims of procreative liberty. The reality of this fundamental right argues against the concept of specific performance being applied to surrogacy contracts.

3. *No Enforcement of Pre-Birth Waivers of Parental Rights.* As a result of this fundamental right, it will be argued that the surrogacy arrangement should be viewed as unenforceable, and the contract voidable. Though the concept of specific performance has the appeal of simplicity, it is inappropriate when applied to surrogacy. In addition, there should be a recission period after the birth of the child in which the surrogate has the right to change her mind about surrendering custody of the child.

4. *Resolving Custody Disputes by a Dual Standard.* In the case of a breach of the agreement, how should custody be determined? Some suggest a presumption, usually in favor of the mother,[6] while others suggest adjudication on a case-by-case basis, entrusting to a court the responsibility of determining the best interests of the child.[7] This chapter will advocate a dual standard: the best interests of the child will determine custody, and if that is not determinative, then the strength of competing parental claims will be weighed, normally resulting in the surrogate being awarded custody.

5. *Conclusion: Adoption Law Preferred over Contract Law for Surrogacy.* The advantages of family law over contract law will be outlined and a summary of what surrogacy legislation under adoption law would look like will be presented. This will provide the basis for a more detailed legislative proposal in the following chapter.

DEFINITION OF MOTHERHOOD

Until the advent of in vitro fertilization, the definition of motherhood was not subject to debate. The mother was simply the woman who gave birth to the child. With the technological ability to separate the gestational and genetic components of motherhood, this maternal presumption now needs clarification. As Michigan Circuit Court Judge Marianne Battani expressed it in the 1986 *Smith v. Jones* surrogacy case, "We really have no definition of mother in our law books. Mother was believed to have been so basic that no definition was deemed necessary."[8]

This biological definition determined motherhood conclusively until recently. Though paternity was often unclear, there was no such problem with maternity, as long as the birth of the child was witnessed. Jewish law, for example, reflects this certainty of maternity in its insistence that a child born to a Jewish mother retains the Jewish heritage, irrespective of paternity.[9] A second presumption that has dominated the law concerning parental rights is the presumption of legitimacy. In order to guarantee proper child support and legitimation of a child, the father is presumed to be the husband of the woman who gives birth to the child. Though the presumption may be challenged, the law has been hesitant to recognize the rights of out of wedlock fathers, at the risk of illegitimating children. For example, California law holds this presumption, and it may be rebutted only by the husband or wife, under limited circumstances, one of which is that it must be successfully challenged within the first two years of the child's life.[10] Since paternal rights are not generally contested in surrogacy arrangements, in most cases the signature of the surrogate's husband on the contract is sufficient to rebut the presumption of paternity. Most would recognize the natural father as the legal father in surrogacy, thus seeing surrogacy as a valid exception to this presumption. The issue of the child's paternity in surrogacy is rarely debated; it is the definition of motherhood that is in question.

Genetics, gestation, and intent have all been suggested as criteria for establishing motherhood. Those who advocate either genetics or gestation are usually attempting to resolve the issue of motherhood within the context of gestational surrogacy. But those who advocate intent-based parenthood are arguing for a definition of parenthood that applies to all surrogacy cases, and whether the surrogate donates the egg or not is considered largely irrelevant. They are arguing that the psychological or social aspect of parenthood should be weighted more heavily than the biological aspects, and thus justify forcing the surrogate to uphold the terms of the agreement.

The Case for Genetics as the Determinant of Motherhood and a Critique

The case for the genetic link providing the basis for maternal rights centers around two landmark court cases dealing with gestational surrogacy. The decisions in these cases have affirmed the priority of genetics for determining motherhood, and are foundational in establishing the argument for genetics being the defining factor in motherhood.

In *Smith v. Jones*,[11] the first case of gestational surrogacy that went to court, a New York couple contributed the egg and sperm. In vitro fertilization was performed at a Cleveland hospital, and the fertilized egg was implanted in a Michigan woman. Though the contracting couple fully expected to have parental rights to the child the gestational surrogate was carrying, they were required to file for maternal rights under Michigan's Paternity Act. The law in Michigan was consistent with the presumption of paternity codified in law throughout the country. The law presumed that the surrogate was the legal mother since she was carrying the child, and that her husband was the legal father.

In this unprecedented decision, Judge Marianne Battani ruled that surrogacy constituted an exception to the presumptions of biology and paternity. Once blood tests were performed to verify the identity of the genetic mother, the surrogate was denied any parental rights. As Judge Battani expressed it, "The donor of the ovum, the biological mother, is to be deemed, in fact, the natural mother of this infant, as is the biological father to be deemed the natural father of this child."[12] The surrogate was considered, in effect, a human incubator, and the judge denied that she played any role other than providing the care and feeding for a child to whom she had no genetic connection, and thus no connection that would have gained her any rights as a mother. The judge recognized no contribution to the development of the child other than providing the gestational environment for its physical development. This decision set a precedent for enforcing the surrogate contract, since the gestational "mother" could not make any valid claim to parental rights.

Further judicial precedent was set in California in the *Johnson v. Calvert* case, thus strengthening the case for the priority of genetics in determining motherhood.[13] Here Anna Johnson was denied any maternal rights because she did not make any genetic contribution to the child she was carrying. Though Judge Richard N. Parslow did acknowledge that the contribution of the gestational environment to the child's psychological development is unclear, and the court heard a great deal of expert testimony concerning the gestational mother's role in the child's formation, he clearly sided with the genetic parents in giving them full parental rights. This is partially because the enormous influence of genetics on the identity of the child is virtually indisputable, as opposed to the influence of the gestational environment, which, according to Parslow, is still unclear.[14] He thus weighted an element that is clearly known more heavily than an element that is still the subject of much debate. Even if the gestational contributions of the surrogate were clearer, it is likely that he would still have decided in favor of genetics, given the long-standing recognition of the genetic aspect of parenthood.

His argument for genetics being the determinative element in motherhood (paternity was not at issue in either of these cases) focused on the impact of genetics in establishing a person's identity. He stated,

However, a surrogate carrying a child for a couple does not acquire parental rights. We've heard a lot about genetics in here. It's strange that right in the middle of the trial in all of the press in the country, we saw reports of new twin studies where they have once again seen what genetics mean in establishing who we are and what we are.

Who we are and what we are and identity problems particularly with young children and teenagers are extremely important. We know that there is a combination of genetic factors. We know more and more about traits now, how you walk, talk and everything else, all sorts of things that develop out of your genes, how long you're going to live, all things being equal, when your immune system is going to break down, what diseases you may be susceptible to. They have upped the intelligence ratio of genetics to 70 percent now.

Then there is the environment. Over the years experts flow back and forth between how much is genetics and how much is environment after you're born. *But genetics and what happens to you after you're born are the primary factors, as I understand it, of who we are, what we become* (emphasis added).[15]

Rather than choosing to recognize three legitimate parents, Parslow ruled in favor of genetics at the expense of gestation. Citing the testimony of psychologists at the trial, he rejected the notion that the child could have three legitimate parents who shared parental rights and custody. This was clearly not in the best interests of the child, since his flourishing was dependent on having a stable environment without the regimen of his primary caregivers being disrupted regularly by another "parent." The judge did not entertain the possibility that all three parents could have legitimate parental claims. If he had, he would have had to make a custody decision based strictly on the best interests of the child.

Parslow's decision was based on the strongest argument for considering genetics determinative in assigning maternal rights. The combination of genes is what gives each child his or her unique characteristics and traits, and those things form a substantial part of each child's identity. Genetics is determinative of many things in an individual's life, from facial features to tendencies to acquire certain diseases. Though clearly children in the womb can be damaged by the gestational environment by activities such as smoking and alcohol or drug use, the link between genetics and the identity and personality of the child is difficult to overstate. The priority of genetics is also suggested in cases in which the child bears a strong physical resemblance to one or both of the genetic contributors. Advocates of this position suggest that in cases like these, it is difficult to deny the very powerful influence of genetics, and even more difficult to deny parental rights to a child who looks like the ones who supplied the gametes. Thus, if the contracting couple supplies both egg and sperm, genetics is a powerful criterion for assigning parental rights to them.

In this situation, the surrogate mother is viewed as providing only the care and feeding of the child during the nine months of pregnancy. She contributes nothing to the physical features and traits of the child, assuming, of course, that she does not engage in behavior during the pregnancy that causes physical harm to the fetus. To take the idea of the human incubator a step further, if the embryo were implanted in another woman, the physical features would be the same. The child would look the same irrespective of who supplied the gestational environment. Because of this powerful connection between a child's genes and the important features that constitute his or her identity, it is argued that genetics should be the element that determines maternity.

This argument for genetics being the determining factor is further is supported by the strong desire of adopted children to reconnect with their natural parents. There is something significant about the genetic tie that frequently compels adopted children to go to great lengths simply to be reunited with their natural parents, even though they have no intention of living with them. In fact, this often happens once a person becomes an adult, when there is no possibility of the parent providing anything for the adoptee, as would be expected in the earlier years of the child's upbringing. There is simply the desire to unite with the one whose genes the person inherited. Of course, there are occasions when there are ulterior motives for seeking out a natural parent, for example, out of greed or anger. But often there is no desire other than to make a connection with the person to whom one is genetically related, because those genes have made a substantial contribution to the identity of the individual. This is not to minimize the contribution of the social parent in developing the character of the child. Rather, it is to show the powerful genetic contribution in contrast to that made by the woman who simply carries the embryo to term and brings the child into the world. This is further underscored by the growing number of children born from AID who are attempting to seek out a previously anonymous sperm donor.[16]

The genetic element is the reason some argue that it is better for the child to be raised by a parent with a genetic connection than by one who is not genetically related. Thus the best interests of the child may compel giving greater weight to genetics. Though clearly children have done well with adoptive and foster parents, supporters of the priority of genetics suggest that all other things being equal, it is better for a child to be raised by a parent with a genetic relationship. Of course, in most surrogacy cases, the surrogate provides the egg, and she is genetically related to the child. In these cases, the issue is not over parental rights, but custody.[17] In cases of gestational surrogacy, it is argued that it would be better for the child to be raised by two genetic contributors instead of one gestational contributor with no genetic link to the child, all other things being equal. As Sidney Callahan states,

The most serious ethical problems in using third-party donors in alternative reproduction concern the well-being of the potential child. A child who has donor(s) intruded into its parentage will be cut off from its genetic heritage and part of its kinship relations. Even if there is no danger of transmitting unknown genetic disease or causing physiological harm to the child, the psychological relationship of the child to its parents is endangered-with or without the practice of deception and secrecy about its origins.[18]

In the case of gestational surrogacy, if maternal rights reside in the surrogate, and if she wins custody of the child, then the child will be raised by a woman with whom he or she has no genetic connection. Of course, this can be done successfully, as in adoption. But that is an emergency solution for a problem situation. Surrogacy is neither of those things, though infertility is certainly unfortunate. But the preplanning that goes into surrogacy makes it very different from the rescue operation that adoption provides. It is argued that, all other things being equal, it would clearly be better for the child to be raised by two people who have the strong genetic connection than by a woman, and perhaps her husband (though Anna Johnson is single) who do not have such a connection. That is not to say that significant bonding and connectedness cannot happen apart from genetic relationship, only that in most cases, bonding is greatly intensified by genetics. One could also argue that two genetic contributors are to be favored over one gestational contributor for parental rights. Though this question properly belongs in the discussion of custody, not parental rights, proponents of this position suggest that, even if genetics and gestation are weighted equally, consideration should go to the contracting couple who have provided two parts genetics as opposed to one part gestation. Thus, gestational surrogates would have less of a claim to parental rights than would genetic surrogates.

A final argument in favor of genetics as the parental rights "trump card" is based on the concept that individuals own their own gametes.[19] Gametes are clearly transferable. The very notion of sperm and egg donation is premised on the idea that an individual owns his or her genetic material. It is a part of one's body just as is any other critical component. Whether it may be bought and sold is another issue, and it does not necessarily follow that since I own my gametes, I may therefore sell them. This is clearly not true with organs, though the same concept of ownership can be applied to them. The fact that a person does receive some compensation for sperm and egg donation, however, is consistent with the idea that he or she owns the sperm or eggs.[20]

When people anonymously donate sperm and eggs, they do so with the understanding that they are also relinquishing any parental claims on the child that will result from their donation. In other words, the genetic parents are the ones that initially hold parental rights, since they "own" the gametes. These rights can be surrendered upon donation of genetic materials.

In surrogacy, however, the contracting couple are not donating their gametes in the same way that anonymous donors do. They are clearly not relinquishing the parental rights that normally accompany genetic materials. They fully expect that they will be the legal and custodial parents of the child born out of the arrangement. Since they own their gametes, they thus have a claim on what becomes of their gametes when they are combined into a fertilized egg. This is similar to the way in which couples who undergo IVF own the embryos that are produced with their sperm and eggs. They control the disposition of the embryos that are not implanted.[21] If they own the embryos, then it follows that they also own the genetic materials necessary to produce them. It further follows that they have a priority claim on the child produced through the use of their genetic materials. This ownership may help explain the desire of infertile couples to have a child genetically related to them, and argues for the priority of genetics in determining motherhood.

There is little doubt about the influence of genetics in determining a person's identity and characteristics. Genetics determines a person's unique makeup, and sets him or her apart from any and all other individuals in the species. It surely is one of the strongest factors underlying the sense of bonding and connection felt between parent and child, and legitimately does motivate adopted children to go to substantial lengths to be reunited with their natural parents, often simply for the sake of being united.

However, in evaluating the argument that genetics should determine maternal rights, the question remains, "should it be the one overriding consideration that functions as the parental 'trump card'?" There are numerous cases in which genetics is not determinative by itself for parental rights. Take, for example, the case of anonymous sperm donors. In AID, the law reflects the notion that genetics is not determinative, since even if a sperm donor wished at a later point to press parental claims, the law would prevent him from doing so. It is true that the anonymous sperm donor voluntarily gives up any claim to parental rights upon donation, and if he were not anonymous, he likely could press for some sort of parental claim on the child. But the law recognizes that in cases of anonymous sperm donation,[22] the genetic connection counts for nothing, since, in order to legitimate the child, paternity is immediately vested in the husband of the birth mother.

To be consistent with how sperm donors are treated, egg donors are not automatically awarded maternal rights simply based upon genetics. With egg donors as well, the law recognizes that once the donation is made, any future claim for parental rights is forfeited. To treat sperm and egg donors consistently would be to deny both parental claims that are based on genetics alone.

The clear fallacy in the parallel between genetics determining paternity and genetics determining maternity is that, of course, genetics determines paternity, since there is little else to weigh in the consideration. Paternity is not divisible into separate biological components, as is the case with maternity. The better analogy for determining maternity is the one between anonymous sperm and egg donors, neither of whom are granted parental rights simply by virtue of genetics. This calls into question the use of genetics as the overriding consideration in determining motherhood. Thus, the genetic contribution should not be determinative by itself, in isolation from other factors.

Even in cases that do not involve anonymous donation of sperm or eggs, courts have been reluctant to award parental rights based exclusively on genetics. For example, in *Lehr v. Robertson*,[23] an unwed father who had never sought to establish a relationship with his child was denied veto power over the child's adoption by the mother's husband. The Court ruled, in essence, that genetics, by itself, did not give a man the right to block the adoption of the child he fathered. This is significant because the right to challenge an adoption that would result in the loss of all parental rights represents a basic exercise of those rights. The genetic connection, apart from a relationship with the child, does not give one the ability even to challenge successfully the loss of parental rights themselves. Justice Powell, for the Court, reasoned in this way:

Where an unwed father demonstrated a full commitment to the responsibilities of parenthood by coming forward to participate in the rearing of his child, his interest in personal contact with his child acquires substantial protection under the Due Process Clause. *But the mere existence of a biological link does not merit equivalent protection*. If the natural father fails to grasp opportunity to develop a relationship with his child, the Constitution will not automatically compel a State to listen to his opinion of where the child's best interests lie. Because he never established a substantial relationship with his child, the New York statutes at issue did not operate to deny him equal protection.[24]

The Court did not hold that the genetic link was not important, only that it was not determinative by itself. It appears that the combination of genetic contribution and a relationship with the child is the material of which parental rights are made. Genetics alone was not recognized as the deciding factor.[25]

In contrast to *Lehr*, in *Caban v. Muhammed*,[26] a genetic father with a well-established relationship with his children had parental rights recognized over and against the husband of the children's mother. The Court recognized an important element in this case, that Caban had maintained an ongoing relationship with the children. Thus, the state has an interest in allowing parental rights to continue to be exercised. Though the *Caban* situation is quite different from that in *Lehr*, the decision is consistent. Genetics is not considered the conclusive determinant of parental rights. Whether there is a relationship with the child or not, genetics alone does not determine parental rights, since maintaining the genetic tie often interferes with the important state interest of maintaining the legitimacy of children.[27]

In these cases, the Court affirmed that there are other interests at stake than simply genetic ties that determine parental rights. They are the state interests in the privacy and integrity of the marital family, the interests in the presumed father of the child to develop a relationship with the child born to his wife, and, most importantly, the interest in legitimating and providing for children born out of wedlock. The Court has affirmed the value of both genetics and the relationship elements of parenthood. However, there are other key interests that determine parental rights that may, at times, override even the interests of a person who has a genetic and relational connection to a child. Even though all of these cases deal with paternal, not maternal claims, they may be used to argue that genetics is not decisive for either, thus rendering highly questionable the insistence of advocates of genetic parenthood that with respect to surrogacy, maternity must be treated parallel with paternity.

The Case for Gestation as the Determinant of Motherhood and Its Justification

The view that gestation determines motherhood is actually the traditional view. In this view the woman who gives birth to the child is conclusively presumed to be the mother of the child, with full, uncontested maternal rights to the child. This is the position of the American College of Obstetricians and Gynecologists (ACOG), which affirms in its statement on surrogacy, "In the committee's view, the genetic link between the commissioning parent(s) and the resulting infant, while important, is less weighty than the link between surrogate mother and fetus, or infant that is created through gestation and birth. Thus, no distinction will be drawn between the usual pattern of surrogate parenting and surrogate gestational motherhood."[28] In addition, this is the position taken by the American Civil Liberties Union, in its policy statement on surrogacy. In defining motherhood in surrogacy arrangements, the ACLU states, "Whether the woman who gives birth to a child is a genetic parent is irrelevant to her parental rights."[29] Both of these positions reflect the view of the Warnock Report in England, that in gestational surrogacy, where the egg or embryo is donated, the "donation should be treated as absolute," and the donors have no inherent parental rights to the child. Thus the woman giving birth is regarded as the mother of the child.[30]

The notion that gestation should determine motherhood is based principally on the contribution the gestational mother makes during pregnancy and birth. She is anything but a human incubator, and makes a substantial contribution not only to the physical development of the child, but to its emotional and psychological development as well. As opposed to simply donating the egg, the gestational mother has built up what Ruth Macklin calls "sweat equity" in the child she is carrying.[31] The nine months invested in the child and the labor, literally, involved in giving birth, tilt the equation in favor of gestation. She clearly has made the greater investment in the child in terms of effort and time expended, and thus she should have a greater claim to motherhood. At the end of the process of birth, the woman who gives birth to the child will have contributed much more of herself than the egg donor in order to bring about the child's birth. For a woman who knows what pregnancy and childbirth involve, the contribution of the egg donor might even seem trivial compared to the rigors and the around the clock demands of pregnancy and birth.

George Annas suggests that gestation gives a woman a greater interest in the child she is carrying because of the biological investment being made.[32] Though this investment is difficult to define and more difficult to quantify, it does reflect the substantial difference in involvement between egg donation and the pregnancy and birth process.[33] It is simply not accurate to suggest that the woman who carries the child during gestation has no impact on the person into whom the child develops. Though the physical traits and many of the predispositions of the child have their source in the genes, there is a growing body of evidence that points to the gestational environment as a substantial contributor to the child's personality.[34]

Similarly, Katharine Bartlett of Duke University Law School argues that the nine-month investment of the gestational woman, in addition to the pain, risk, and sacrifice involved in carrying and giving birth to a child, greatly outweigh the contribution of the genetic donor.[35] Though she weighs the claims of the more common form of surrogate mother, whose own egg is involved, against the claims of the sperm donor–natural father, her argument fits well within the framework of this discussion. She responds to the argument that men and women should be treated equally in the reproductive arena. She rejects the notion that since men can sell their sperm, women should be able to sell their reproductive services, thereby setting up a contract-based view of surrogacy, awarding custody to the father instead of the mother under the terms of the contract. She replies to this notion by insisting that the woman's gestational contribution should be more heavily weighted than the man's genetic contribution, due to the burden involved in pregnancy and delivery. It should be noted that she immediately critiques this argument as reflecting an exchange view of parenthood that is no longer appropriate. However, her paradigm that places relationship, namely the mother's with the child, both in utero and in the process of giving birth, at the center of parenthood only strengthens the force of this argument, which she would likely accept when applied to the definition of motherhood.[36]

It is not only the investment of the gestational mother that gives her superior claim to motherhood; it is her contribution to the makeup of the child. To call her the human incubator, as did the Michigan Superior Court Judge Marianne Battani,[37] ignores many of the newly emerging facts of prenatal development. The woman who provides the gestational environment for the child makes an indispensable contribution, of course, to the child's physical growth and sustenance. But more importantly, she helps determine the emotional makeup, temperament, and disposition of the child, and in some cases, contributes to his or her physical form. In cases in which the gestational mother contributes to the child's physical form, the contribution is largely negative, since a pregnant woman taking tobacco, alcohol or drugs may damage the physical development of the child. To suggest that an embryo could be implanted in any woman and produce the same child as if it had been placed in another woman, runs counter to the facts of prenatal psychology. The gestational setting may not have a great influence on the physical features of the child, but it has a substantial impact on his or her personality. Thus, gestation is not a neutral element to the formation of the child.

Since the 1940s, with the pioneering work of psychiatrist Lester Sontag,[38] the field of prenatal psychology has been providing new information on the impact of the pregnant mother on her developing child. In some of his work, he studied the impact of stress during pregnancy on the behavior of children after birth. Many of the women involved had suffered significant trauma, such as the loss of a spouse or other family member. With such severe emotional stresses, the babies born later manifested psychosomatic problems and irritability, and in his view, set the stage for later problems in child and adult relationships.[39]

A further example of the connection between gestational environment and fetal development occurs in a longitudinal study of pregnant woman conducted by B.R.H. Van den Bergh of the Center for Developmental Psychology at the University of Leuven, Belgium. He concluded that not only is there continuity between fetal and neonatal behavior, but that the emotions of the mother can be linked to the child's temperament that is manifest after birth. He states, "maternal emotions during pregnancy are correlated with neonatal and infant behavior. These correlations indicate that children of high anxious pregnant women have gastro-intestinal problems, cry frequently and are perceived as having a difficult temperament."[40] Though he counsels caution in interpreting the results of his tests due to a lack of insight into what exactly causes this correlation, he suggests that a number of factors are likely involved, including maternal anxiety during pregnancy, negative perceptions of the pregnant mother toward the child, hormonal changes, and heredity.[41] Though the reasons for the correlation are not yet clear, the link itself is.

It is well known that smoking during pregnancy can have a deleterious physical effect on the child. But the impact of such behavior goes deeper than simply the physical effects. Dr. Michael Lieberman demonstrated that even the thought of smoking by the mother was enough to trigger emotional agitation and increased heartbeat on the part of the child.[42] These psychological effects of smoking may be even more damaging to the child, due to the chronic state of uncertainty into which they place him or her. Lieberman's study tied these emotions to a predisposition toward deep-seated anxiety in the child. Whether the anxiety is rooted in the mother's smoking is not the point, though that has been shown to be a significant factor. Rather, it is the anxiety itself, irrespective of the source, that has such an impact on the child.

Further studies show a link between attitudes of neglect toward the fetus by the mother and later emotional problems experienced by the child. For example, studies done on schizophrenic pregnant women indicate that there are often devastating scars left on the emotional makeup of the child.[43] Since these women suffer from schizophrenia, they are simply not capable of providing a nurturing, communicative environment for the child. This has a deep and lasting effect on the child. The child enters the world with more physical and emotional difficulties than is the case with emotionally healthy mothers.

These data were expanded by further studies that explored the attitudes of generally mentally healthy mothers toward their children. Though external stresses, particularly intense, long-term ones that are incapable of resolution, contributed to both physical infirmity and emotional instability in the child,[44] many child development researchers hold that the mother's attitude toward the child in utero is critical. For example, a German psychologist at the University of Constantine in Frankfurt, Monika Lukesch, noted a significant difference in both the emotional and physical health of children who were born to accepting mothers, or those mothers who were looking forward to their pregnancies, as opposed to rejecting mothers, or those who were not.[45] All of the two thousand subjects in her test were from similar socio-economic backgrounds, were of similar intelligence levels, and received similar levels of prenatal care. The only significant difference was their attitude toward the children they were carrying. She concluded that the mother's attitude toward the child was the most important determinant of the overall health of the newborn.

A similar study reached the same conclusion. Dr. Gerhard Rottmann of the University of Salzburg studied 141 women, placing them into one of four categories depending on their attitudes toward their developing children.[46] There were Ideal Mothers, who wanted the child both consciously and unconsciously, as was evident by the testing performed on each woman. These women gave birth to the healthiest children, both emotionally and physically. At the other end of the continuum there were the women with the strongest negative feeling toward their child, whom he called the Catastrophic Mothers. These had the most trouble during pregnancy and as a result gave birth to the greatest number of premature and low birth weight children, who manifested tendencies toward emotional disturbances. In between these two, there were the Ambivalent Mothers, who were outwardly happy about the pregnancy but were actually uncertain about wanting their children, the Cool Mothers, who had a deep-seated desire for children but were not, at the time of the pregnancy, ready for children due to complicating factors such as career concerns and financial insecurities. In both of these last two groups, the fetus picked up the mixed signals from the mother, and, significantly, the last group gave birth to an unusually high number of lethargic and apathetic children.

Other tests demonstrate the capacity of the fetus to recognize the mother's speech,[47] and even to recognize types of music.[48] This points to the ability of the fetus to learn in utero, and has been the impetus for an entire discipline, prenatal education, aimed at conditioning the fetus to learn by responding to specific stimuli.[49] The debate in the literature is not over the ability of the fetus to learn, but whether experiences in utero influence specific behavior or incline the child more generally toward certain dispositions.[50] One specific example of the ability of the fetus to learn is in response to auditory stimuli in utero. Brent Logan, of the Prenatal and Infant Education Institute, studied the effect of "imprinting" variations in the sound of the mother's heartbeat, and concluded that prenatal sensory enrichment through exposure to various sounds in utero can influence the fetus's neurological development and aptitude significantly.[51] As a result, prenatal instruction is becoming an applied science of its own. The issue is not whether the fetus can learn in utero, but how to maximize the gestational period to give the fetus increased neurological aptitude.

These studies that have opened the field of prenatal psychology and instruction show the impact of the gestational mother on the personality development of the child. Psychiatrist Dr. Thomas Verny has concluded that the unborn child's personality does indeed begin to form in utero, and that the woman who carries the child plays a formative role in either assisting or hindering that development. He states,

The single most gratifying aspect of our new knowledge [about prenatal psychology] is what it reveals about the pregnant woman and her role in shaping and guiding her unborn child's personality. [these studies] show one of the ways personality characteristics and traits begin forming in utero. Our likes and dislikes, fears and phobias--in other words, all the distinct behaviors that make us uniquely ourselves--are, in part, also the product of conditioned learning. My point is that since we have finally identified some of the early experiences which shape future traits and characteristics, a woman can now begin actively influencing her child's life well before birth.[52]

To be sure, the areas in which prenatal psychology are most helpful are preventive, that is, the mother can do certain things and avoid others that will prevent negative outcomes for her child.

Thus, minimizing the impact of the gestational environment and calling the woman who bears the child simply a carrier do not harmonize with the facts. Because of the immense contribution of the gestational mother, to the child's physical and emotional development, gestation should weigh very heavily in the determination of motherhood and attendant maternal rights.

Similar in importance to the investment and contribution of the gestational mother is the bonding that occurs between her and the child she is carrying. Though significant bonding can take place between any two individuals, the combination of biological investment and the resultant bonding weighs heavily in favor of gestation as the determinant of motherhood.[53] That is, the combination of biology and relationship that is inherent in gestation argues for motherhood being vested in the woman who bears the child. In most pregnancies, this bond is a central part of the pregnant woman's self-concept, and though children do not normally entirely define a woman's life, they are surely integral to what defines her as a person. In most instances, the loss of this bond causes a great deal of grief when a pregnancy is lost. This is even the case in adoption, in which the birth mother realizes that giving up the child is in both the child's and the mother's best interests. One reason many states have a period in which a birth mother can regain custody of her child prior to an adoption becoming final is that they recognize the strength of this bond. Similarly, most states do not hold a birth mother to a pre-birth consent to adoption, since she cannot know the strength of the bond she will feel with her child prior to birth, and thus cannot give genuinely informed consent. In cases in which a surrogate changes her mind and wants to keep the child, it is reasonable to see this bond as similarly important and self-defining. Though one should be careful about affirming a "biology is destiny"[54] concept of self for women, that is not to say that pregnancy, childbirth, and motherhood are not highly determinative of a woman's sense of self.

This sense of bonding is what makes pregnancy essentially a relationship, not only physiologically, but emotionally. Gestation creates motherhood because of the intense, intimate relationship that is created as a woman carries a developing child. Egg donation and a $10,000 fee paid to the surrogate do not compare with the bonding that has been established during pregnancy.

As opposed to paternity, in gestational motherhood the biological connection and the relationship are essentially one and the same. The Supreme Court in *Lehr*, and reaffirmed in *Caban*, implied that biology (i.e., gestation) may be sufficient to bring maternal rights, but not paternal rights. The Court held that the biological connection in paternity gave the natural father the unique opportunity to develop a relationship that no other man can have. But should he fail to do so, biology alone does not guarantee parental rights.[55] Implied by the Court's decision is that for paternity, as opposed to maternity, biology and relationship do not necessarily go together. The gestational link in motherhood carries the relationship with it. Thus, for mothers, in a way unlike that of fathers, the biological tie creates a relationship.[56] This is borne out by the assumption in many states' adoption laws that mothers are always sufficiently related to their children to give them the right to veto an adoption motion. The converse assumption is clearly not the case for fathers.[57] Rothman summarizes the argument for gestation in this way: "Any pregnant woman is the mother of the child she bears. Her gestational relationship establishes her motherhood. We will not accept the idea that we can look at a woman, heavy with child, and say the child is not hers. The fetus is part of the woman's body, regardless of the source of the egg and sperm. Biological motherhood is not a service, not a commodity, but a relationship."[58]

The picture painted by Rothman is a compelling one, that a woman eight to nine months pregnant, having established a physical relationship and emotional bond to the child she is carrying, is surely the woman with the greater maternal rights claim to the child. She, not the egg donor, is the one who has already established a bond with the child, though it is true that the egg donor, as well as the sperm donor, anticipate a very strong bond with the child when they presumably will gain custody. However, their bond is only anticipated and potential, and thus is qualitatively different from the bond currently experienced by the gestational mother. Though I disagree with the notion that the fetus is part of the woman's body,[59] it certainly comes much closer to the situation in surrogacy than does the concept of genetics being determinative for motherhood. Even if one does not accept the idea that the fetus is part of the woman's body, because of the bonding of pregnancy, it is certainly more the gestational mother's than the egg donor's.

Katharine Bartlett of Duke University Law School makes a similar argument by insisting that the relationship emphasis of adoption law makes a better set of parameters for surrogacy than does contract law. The responsibilities as well as the rights and the privileges of parenting flow out of relationship, not contract. With the relationship that is inherent in the gestational role, making motherhood dependent on genetics and enforcing the contract against the gestational mother ignores the powerful combination of biology and current relationship that makes the claim of the gestational mother so strong. Reassigning motherhood by dissociating gestation and relationship is thus contrary to the phenomenon of bonding that characterizes pregnancy. Bartlett states, "[surrogacy] presupposes that the biological mother-child bond is easily severed, that pregnancy and childbirth is a process which does not necessarily entail enduring human emotion and permanent connectedness, that women can have children and give them up if the price is right, and that women who make such agreements and change their minds are acting improperly, even pathologically."[60]

The ideal for any woman being recruited as a surrogate is the ability to effect this dissociation. For example, a book that advertises itself as a leading consumer's guide to new reproductive technologies underscores the importance of this dissociation. It states, "The surrogate must begin to erect an emotional barrier, so that she experiences the child not as hers but as the child of the couple."[61] It is common for surrogate practitioners to seek out women who have both a strong desire for children and at the same time, the ability to abandon such a desire. Women who can both attach deeply to children and who can also detach from them just as substantially, are clearly the best candidates. Surrogate practitioners appear to have a deep ambivalence about the bonding that occurs in utero. In fact, there is a growing body of literature produced by the surrogacy industry that gives instructions to potential surrogates on how to dissociate during the course of their pregnancy.[62]

It is undeniable that this dissociation does occur in some surrogacy cases. Lawyers who arrange surrogacy contracts frequently testify that in many successful surrogacy arrangements, no bond is established between surrogate and child, even when there is a genetic connection. The child is turned over to the contracting parents and there is no dispute concerning custody. It may be true that mother-child bonding is not an entirely universal experience, and that, parallel to adoption, surrogates do sometimes successfully relinquish custody. However, it does not follow that a surrogacy contract should be enforced and the child turned over to the genetic parents when the gestational mother has indeed established a significant bond with the child. In those cases in which the surrogate desires to keep the child and thus breaches the terms of the agreement, denying motherhood to the woman who carries the child runs contrary to the powerful combination of a biological and relational connection. If the surrogate desires to relinquish the child to the couple who initiated the surrogacy arrangement, then she is free to do so, parallel to adoption. But if she chooses to maintain the bond created in utero, then, by virtue of the already established bond, she, not the genetic contributor, should have maternal rights. If she elects to give up the child, it must be with the assumption that it is hers, as the mother, to give or to keep.

This significant bond between mother and child established during pregnancy is one reason why a gestational surrogate often grieves over the loss of her child, similar to the way in which a birth mother in adoption grieves over giving up her child. The grieving process is further similar to the way in which parents mourn the loss of a child who is stillborn or who dies as a result of a late-term miscarriage.[63] This suggests that the sense of loss is not dependent on genetics, but rather on the relationship formed in utero, thus giving the gestational mother something very significant not experienced by the genetic contributor. The unique relationship formed between the gestational mother and the fetus she is carrying argues strongly for the priority of gestation over genetics in the determination of motherhood and the attendant maternal rights.

The Case for Prenatal Intent to Parent as the Determinant of Motherhood and a Critique

Attempting to take into account the possibilities made available by new reproductive technologies, advocates of a third view of motherhood link parental rights with the pre-conception intent to become parents and raise the child produced by non traditional reproductive methods. Three slightly different approaches to intent-based parenthood will be considered in this section. First,

Andrea Stumpf, writing in the *Yale Law Journal*, has suggested a matrix for determining motherhood that is focused on the entire reproductive process, rather than simply birth.[64] Second, Marjorie Maguire Schultz of the University of California, Berkeley, Law School argues for an intent-based determination of motherhood in order to provide for a gender-neutral basis for parenthood.[65] Finally, English philosopher Edgar Page, from the University of Hull, suggests that the couple who initiated the surrogacy contract should be vested with parental rights, and the surrogate viewed as an in utero egg donor who rents her gestational capacities to give birth to a child that legitimately belongs to the contracting couple.[66]

Stumpf begins with the observation that surrogacy does not fit into any already established scheme in the law, and because of this, in many cases, the law has been stretched to accommodate something that it did not originally intend to address. As a result, the cases that have come to the courts are, in her view, the object of an arduous process that does not necessarily serve the child's best interests, nor adequately protect the parties to the arrangement.[67]

She proposes a new way of viewing the legal status of reproductive technologies in general, focusing on the entire process of reproduction rather than on one specific element, that is, birth. Her matrix includes four phases of the process, the first two of which are central for her view of new reproductive technologies, the last two of which have been the traditional focus of the law.[68]

The first phase is the "Child Initiating Stage," in which the contracting couple initiate the process of reproduction with their intent to conceive a child. She cites the way in which the courts have traditionally ignored what she calls the psychological or mental aspect of procreation, and insists that it is the one that should govern the vesting of parental rights in non traditional reproductive methods. The second stage is the "Preparation Stage," in which the surrogate, the lawyer, and the inseminating physician join the contracting couple in the process. This stage includes the drawing up of the contract and culminates in the successful implantation of a fertilized egg in the surrogate, whether by AID or IVF. The third stage is the "Gestation Stage," which ranges from the time of implantation to its climax at the birth of the child. The issues raised here are principally those of the surrogate's right to privacy, and Stumpf insists that the surrogate be afforded the same privacy rights as pregnant women in traditional families. The final stage is the "Child-Rearing Stage," in which the presumption in Stumpf's system would be for parental rights to be vested in the contracting parents. Should the surrogate seek to rebut this presumption, she would be seeking to regain, not retain, maternal rights. Thus, the surrogate has very few protected rights except during the pregnancy.

In Stumpf's system, stage one is the critical one, and her views here determine the parental rights outcome at stage four. In contrast to both contract and criminal law, which both acknowledge the component of intent in actions and events, family law has traditionally not given much weight to this mental aspect.[69] The courts have historically relied on biology primarily because it is easier to ascertain, it is permanent, and the relational links that emerge out of biology have already been formed by the time most family law cases get to court.[70] But in doing so, courts have ignored the psychological facet of the parent-child relationship.

Stumpf argues that this psychological facet of reproduction should be the controlling one in determining parental rights. She states,

The psychological dimension of procreation preceded and transcends the biology of procreation. Motherhood can be a product of both mental and physical conception; reductionist modes of legal reasoning have ignored this fullness. Prior to physical conception of a child, the beginnings of a normal parent-child relationship can come from mental conception, the desire to create a child. When the child's existence begins in the minds of the desiring parents, biological conception of the child declines in importance relative to psychological conception with respect to the full life of the child. The mental concept of the child is the controlling factor of its creation, and the originators of that concept merit full credit as conceivers. The mental component must be recognized as independently valuable; it creates expectations in society for adequate performance on the part of the initiators as parents of the child. The rights and obligations of initiating parents should reflect their position of relative importance. Use of the surrogate method, manifesting procreative intent, should invoke the legal presumption that the child belongs to the intenders. Understanding the infertile wife's role as mother makes clear that surrogate arrangements render the biological link obsolete as the legal determinant of "mother."[71]

Stumpf points out that the mental component of procreation is an aspect of the entire process, thus her insistence that it be regarded as inherently valuable. Yet she moves quickly from suggesting that it should be *a* component of the process to its being *the controlling* aspect of the process, with no argument in between to justify that leap. In the final analysis, the psychological dimension places the contracting couple into a position of absolute, not relative, importance in determining parental rights to the child. While attempting to balance the components of procreation, she ends up minimizing the biological in favor of the psychological. Intent alone gives the legal presumption of motherhood, apart from any biological contribution or relational connection.

One need not admit that "biology is destiny" in order to hold that biology does play an important part in procreation.[72] But when the surrogate's psychological intent to parent develops during the pregnancy, that should be recognized too. Thus the combination of psychology and biology that Stumpf wants to balance is indeed balanced when the surrogate desires to keep the child. Just because the mental intent to become a parent develops after conception, or even after birth, does not make it less significant than the intent of the contracting woman.

There are other scenarios in which the intent to parent does not chronologically precede biological conception. For example, in cases of unplanned pregnancies, frequently women change their minds about abortion as the intent to parent develops with the woman's connection to the fetus. Even women who initially set aside the intent to parent in order to give up a child for adoption, reserve the right to change their mind, even after birth, allowing for the intent to parent to resurface. There is no reason why the pre-conception intent to parent should be weighted more heavily than an intent that develops during pregnancy and birth. In cases in which the intent does develop in the surrogate, she combines all the elements of motherhood that Stumpf is attempting to balance. Thus there is no reason why the surrogate should not be considered the mother instead of the contracting woman.

Two important assumptions undergird Stumpf's position. First, she is assuming that the psychological aspect of conception is a more important one than the biological one. Her statement that the mental aspect transcends the biology of procreation appears to be based primarily on the chronological relationship between the intent to conceive and the procreative action that follows it. To be sure, the mental intent to conceive does create expectations on the part of the intending parents. But the fact that intent, even with the expectations that such an intent brings, precedes biology in creating a child does not dictate that intent necessarily supersedes biology. Nor does it follow that intent to parent should be the overriding consideration in determining parental rights. Stumpf assumes a position that is at the heart of the surrogacy debate, and then builds a new legal matrix around that assumption. However, her position begs the question of why the mental aspect of procreation should have priority over the biological one.

A second assumption that she makes is that surrogacy should be promoted and that the currently inadequate legal scheme should be changed to accommodate it. She states, "Without exception, legal treatment [of surrogacy] has been fundamentally inadequate. The realities of surrogate arrangements are being obscured, and the ends of these arrangements are being obstructed. . . . These well-established presumptions [of biology and legitimacy, that govern AID] disregard the fundamental aspects of surrogate arrangements and legally define the status of the parties in a way that misallocates rights and obligations."[73]

However, the law that governs AID is not the only legal framework from which to view surrogacy. She omits any consideration of adoption law, which is a much closer analogue than AID law, and many believe that existing adoption law is both appropriate and fitting for surrogacy. Of course, applying adoption law to surrogacy will produce a different outcome, since the arrangements will involve more risk to the contracting couple. Current law only misallocates rights and obligations if one assumes that surrogacy should be encouraged, or at least accommodated. But that assumption about surrogacy in general is at the heart of the debate. The difficult issue needing resolution is not the adequacy of the legal system to handle surrogacy, though clearly the system did not anticipate it.   That is not to say that current law cannot comfortably accommodate it. But if one assumes that surrogacy needs to be promoted, then any legal matrix that does not do so can be described as inadequate. Her legal framework is built on the unsubstantiated assumption that surrogacy is, at worst, morally neutral, and at best, something that should be actively promoted. Her concept of mental conception is built around protecting the rights of the contracting couple at the expense of the rights of the surrogate. In Stumpf's scheme, the surrogate only has recognized and well-protected rights in the gestational stage. Though attempting to balance the rights of the parties, her bias toward surrogacy forces her to favor the rights of the contracting couple and minimize the rights of the surrogate.

For example, she admits that "both biology and psychology are critical to procreation."[74] Yet just prior to that she insists that the infertile wife should be seen as a maternal figure too. But in her attempt to balance the two women in the arrangement, she clearly favors the intending woman. She states, "Understanding the infertile wife's role as mother makes clear that surrogate arrangements render the biological link obsolete as the legal determinant of mother."[75] Her role as the initiator of the surrogacy alone is what gives her full maternal rights. If biology is critical to procreation, then why does it apparently play no role in determining who has legal maternal rights to the child born of the procreative arrangement? If it is so crucial to making procreation happen, then there is no reason why it should not be a significant determinant of parental rights. Though Stumpf acknowledges the biologically obvious, it is treated as only a token contribution, having nothing to do with maternal rights.

She further admits that "motherhood can be a product of both mental and physical conception; reductionist modes of legal reasoning have ignored this fullness."[76] While being rightly critical of reductionism in legal reasoning, it appears that she is employing a similar reductionist mode of reasoning in giving priority to the psychological aspects of procreation. By ignoring the biological connection, she ignores the fullness of motherhood that she attempts to capture.

In discussing the constitutional aspects of surrogacy, Stumpf defends the right to conceive using collaborative methods as a corollary of the right to privacy. In comparing surrogacy to other right to privacy cases involving abortion, she adds the complicating factor of a third person whose rights must be added into the equation. In abortion, the rights of the mother and the child must be balanced. But in surrogacy, the rights of the child and two mothers must be balanced. She states, "Because even infertile mothers can exert their right of psychological conception, they too have a procreative right that courts should preserve."[77] Yet in drawing the connection between her stage one (the child-initiating stage) and stage four (the child-rearing stage), the infertile woman's right to conceive mentally becomes a pre-emptive right to raise the child. Thus, her procreative right is not *a* right that courts should preserve; it is *the* exclusive determinant of maternal rights, protected at the expense of the woman who is the central focus of stages two and three. Whether there is even a constitutionally protected right of psychological conception is not the point. What began as an attempt to balance the rights of all parties quickly becomes an argument in favor of the exclusive right of the intending woman to the child based only on her intent to conceive. Even the title of her stage four "The Child-Raising Stage-- Balancing Rights in Favor of Psychology" reflects this bias, which in the final analysis, is no balance at all.

In stage four, Stumpf proposes a "presumption of appropriation for the initiating parents."[78] That is, the child should be transferred to the intending parents' custody immediately at birth. She acknowledges the conflict with the traditional presumptions of biology and legitimacy, but weights the mental conception of the child more heavily than the physical conception, even insisting that the initiating couple had a relationship with the child prior to its conception, and thus prior to the surrogate's involvement in the process. She states, "The fact that the initiating parents mentally conceived of the child and afforded it existence prior to the surrogate mother's involvement must be acknowledged."[79] She further claims that their connection with the child should be favored over the gestational mother's. In her response to Harvard Professor Carol Gilligan's critique of surrogacy, in which Gilligan favors the attachment of the gestational mother over contract considerations,[80] Stumpf insists that "the surrogacy contract also brings into being an attachment of the initiating parents to the child. Attachment does not arise from physical experience or possession, and denying the initiating parents the child would infringe upon a care-based relationship. In Gilligan's own words, it is a dilemma of connection, not of contest."[81]

In the first place, it is not clear in which way a mentally conceived child exists at all in any objective sense. The child is not afforded existence in any tangible way until the fertilized egg is implanted in the uterus as an embryo. The relationship between the contracting couple and the yet to be conceived child exists only in their minds, and in no way can it be compared to the connection between the child and the gestational mother. There can be little doubt that at birth, the stronger connection is between the child and the mother who gives birth.[82] As far as the child is concerned, she is the only mother that he or she has had any relationship with. The intending mother/child connection exists only in her mind, and in that sense, it is a one-way relationship. It is difficult to see how there can be a relationship that could not possibly be acknowledged by one of the parties in the relationship. So there are questions about the objective existence of a child that is only in the minds of the contracting couple. Further, that can hardly be the basis for limiting the undisputed connection between the child and the gestational mother.

Intent without biology contributes little to the creation of the objective entity known as a child. For example, infertile couples who may have had the mental intent to conceive for years have made little tangible progress toward realizing their dreams of having a child, if they have not made the biological connection between egg and sperm. Furthermore, biology can and does work in the absence of the intent to conceive. The myriad of unplanned and unwanted pregnancies, especially among teenagers, bears eloquent witness to biology working against the mental intent to conceive. Of course, in surrogacy, the intent to conceive begins the entire process. But if artificial insemination or in vitro fertilization is not successful with the surrogate, the mental intent to conceive counts for very little in the actual realization of the couple's goal.

A position similar to Stumpf's is argued by Professor Marjorie Maguire Schultz.[83] She suggests that intent-based notions of parenthood make the surrogacy contract valid and enforceable, and she criticizes the *Baby M* decision for failing to recognize what to her is the determinative aspect of parenthood. Her desire is to have a system of parental rights that does justice to the idea of gender neutrality, as opposed to the traditional version of parenthood with its male bias.

Because reproductive technology now allows for specificity of reproductive purpose by separating all the component parts of procreation, it increases the available options for both the biologically and socially infertile.[84] This latter category includes those who desire to raise children but who are either unable or unwilling to change aspects of their intimate lives in order to do so. For example, gay couples or single adults who desire to be parents now may do so, without the usual sexual relations necessary to conceive. However, these people are not infertile in the accepted medical sense of the term. In addition, those who wish to separate procreation from child rearing now may do so, and of course, options for the biologically infertile are also greatly expanded.

This expansion of options is a very significant part of the argument Schultz makes for intention-based parenthood. Her thesis is that "Legal rules governing procreative arrangements and parental status should recognize the importance and legitimacy of individual efforts to project intentions into the future. Where such intentions are deliberate, explicit and bargained for, where they are the catalyst for reliance and expectations, as is the case in technologically-assisted reproductive arrangements, they should be honored."[85] Thus, intent to parent, as clearly expressed in surrogacy, should be the overriding determinant of parental rights. Modern reproductive technology has given intention potentially a much more significant place in decisions about becoming a parent. With the technology now available to separate out intentions from the other aspects of procreation, and given the importance of intentions in determining the moral meaning of an action, Schultz argues that "intentions that are voluntarily chosen, deliberate, express and bargained-for, ought presumptively to determine legal parenthood."[86] She then sets out what an intent based surrogacy policy would look like, and finally, views the *Baby M* case through this framework.

Though she extensively lays out the implications of an intent-based surrogacy policy and gives detailed analysis of the *Baby M* case, very little in her work actually defends the priority of intentions in determining parenthood. Though she interacts carefully with other significant aspects of surrogacy that conflict with her conclusions (for example, commercial aspects of surrogacy, revocation of the contract by the surrogate, and the use of the technologies by traditional versus non-traditional families), the priority of intention as opposed to genetics and gestation is more assumed than argued for in her framework. The argument in her work concerns the implications of intent-based surrogacy, not the place of intention itself. The closest she comes to arguing for intention superseding genetics and gestation occurs in the analysis of the New Jersey Supreme Court's reversal in the *Baby M* case. She insists that the court entirely overlooked the crucial role of reproductive intention in its decision. Calling this oversight "profoundly wrong-headed,"[87] she states, "To ignore the significance of deliberation, purpose and expectation--the capacity to envision and shape through intentional choice--is to disregard one of the most distinctive traits that makes us human. It is to disregard crucial differences in moral meaning and responsibility."[88]

Certainly intention is a critical component of moral action, and the ability to shape one's future through conscious choices is an important part of what makes an individual a person. But to move from there to insisting that intention be the major and overriding factor in determining parental rights ignores critical biological facts. It ignores the fact that in procreation intention alone creates virtually nothing, and that procreation can take place apart from reproductive intent. Intention only begins a process that cannot be completed without the biological components. To take intention as the sole factor in determining parental rights is to ignore the more important role of both genetics and gestation.

Schultz asserts that the pre-conception intent of the contracting couple takes precedence over the emerging intent of the surrogate, in cases in which the surrogate desires to keep the child.[89] But what makes the surrogate's claim a powerful one is the combination of intent and a biological connection.[90] The reason the surrogate's developing intent to parent must be considered strongly is that she has a fundamental right to associate with the child she bears.[91] This is not to say that she has exclusive parental rights, only exclusive maternal rights. She does not have the right to sole custody. That must be shared with the natural father. But neither does his or his wife's pre-conception intent to parent give either of them exclusive parental rights. Take the case of a birth mother who intended to give up her baby for adoption to a couple who arranged prior to the child's birth (through their intent to parent) to adopt the child. The changed intent to parent of the birth mother is enough to give her sole maternal rights. Very few would envision a scenario in adoption in which the pre-conception intent would be once and for all determinative of parental rights. Yet for the parallel in surrogacy, this is precisely what Schultz proposes. If intent is important, it must be important for more than the contracting couple alone.

At the heart of Schultz's proposal is her assumption that the law should accommodate the new reproductive technologies. It appears that she assumes that the law must encourage new reproductive technologies, and that attempts to suppress them are suspect, if not "wrong-headed" (Schultz's term). Though she does favor some regulation of surrogacy to protect the parties involved, there is little doubt about her advocacy of surrogacy. She states, "The critical, overarching question for legal policy is not *whether* but *how* to accommodate the new developments."[92] Of course, this may mean simply that the law may not ignore new developments, pretending that they do not exist at all. But in her critique of the *Baby M* decision, she seems to assert that the law should be reformulated to encourage new reproductive technologies in general. She states that the New Jersey Supreme Court "assessed the surrogacy arrangement under which Mary Beth Whitehead agreed to bear a child for William and Elizabeth Stern through a pre-modern lens of conventional procreational and family patterns. In so doing, it failed to create a legal framework responsive to the growing role of personal intention in reproductive and parenting decisions."[93]

However, this begs the question of "why change the lens simply because of new reproductive technologies?" The need to do so is assumed throughout the work. One could argue that present adoption law is well suited to accommodate surrogacy arrangements. Of course, if one disagrees with the conclusions reached by applying adoption law to surrogacy, then it is easy to see the law as being inadequate. But there is no reason why the law must be changed simply to accommodate new technologies in any field, apart from moral arguments about the merits of any such technology. This is even more the case when these technologies involve intimate parts of life and fundamental rights. In her critique of the *Baby M* decision, she insists that the New Jersey Supreme Court's approach will not provide an adequate basis for surrogacy. She states, "the Court's approach will fail to provide a framework in which the multiple issues of reproductive technology can be successfully resolved."[94] For Schultz, successful resolution means resolution in favor of encouraging surrogacy and awarding custody and parental rights to the contracting couple. However, the law can successfully resolve issues around surrogacy by simply applying adoption law to the cases in dispute. There is clearly a value judgment inherent in her use of the term successfully that implies that the only successful resolution is one that protects the contracting couple at the expense of the surrogate. That value judgment is assumed throughout the work, not argued.

She does deal with the issue of who the mother is in surrogacy, briefly evaluating the claims of both genetics and gestation, and acknowledging the difficulty in making this maternal rights decision. She states, "I would argue that there is no persuasive basis for a categorical preference for either a gestational or a genetic contributor to receive exclusive recognition as mother."[95] However, her solution to this difficulty is to eliminate both genetics and gestation from any consideration in the determination of maternal rights, arguing that "personal intention seems a desirable basis for selecting between two biological claimants who are arguably equally situated."[96] To say that intention should be considered is one thing; to insist that it is the decisive consideration is quite another, particularly since intention, by itself, accomplishes very little in actually conceiving a child. It is difficult to see how an aspect that makes so little real difference can be given overriding importance in determining parental rights. Further, if intention is to figure prominently into the equation for parental rights, then the changing intention of the surrogate must be considered as well, since, should her intent develop as the fetus develops within her, she now combines the intent to parent with a biological and relational connection to the child.

A more novel approach has been proposed by British philosopher Edgar Page, who justifies surrogacy as in utero egg donation and rental of gestational capacities of the surrogate.[97] Assuming that children are not transferable, since they are not commodities, he rules out what he calls "total surrogacy," in which a couple, through sexual intercourse, conceives a child and transfers parental rights to another. (At this point, he also rules out genetic surrogacy, in which the surrogate supplies both the egg and the uterus.) There is no difference between that scenario and adoption, and under British law, private placement adoptions are illegal. However, under AID and egg donation laws, gametes are transferable and donatable. In most situations of gamete donation, the donation is made and any rights to the resulting child are relinquished. But in gestational surrogacy, the contracting couple "donates" the gametes, but with no corresponding intent to give up parental rights. Thus he justifies gestational surrogacy under AID, egg donation, and IVF laws.

He sets up the following scenario to justify genetic surrogacy, showing that it is no different from gestational surrogacy. Certainly it would be acceptable, though unusual, for the egg donor to be a fourth party (the contracting couple and the surrogate being the first three). Perhaps the infertile wife cannot produce eggs, and for some unknown reason, the couple desires that the egg come from someone other than the surrogate, perhaps to avoid potential custody disputes. It would be acceptable in his system for the contracting husband's sperm to fertilize the egg from a donor and implant it in the surrogate, who in turn, gestates the child. Under this system, it would appear that there would be no reason why the surrogate could not be both the third and fourth parties combined into one. In fact, in the majority of surrogacy cases, this is precisely what occurs. In this case, it would be acceptable to have the egg removed and donated, fertilized, and then re-implanted in her uterus, where she provides the gestational environment for the child. Page calls this "an absurd position" in which, under the Warnock Committee recommendations, genetic surrogacy is banned, but if the surrogate had her egg removed from her body, donated it, and, following fertilization, had it implanted in her uterus, it would be legitimate.[98] To deal with this situation, he proposes in utero egg donation, in which all genetic surrogates actually become simply gestational surrogates, having donated the egg in utero to the contracting couple. Thus surrogacy, in Page's view, works toward an approximation of normal parenthood under AID and egg donation laws rather than as an unnatural substitute for it.[99]

The difficulty with this position is that it, too, begs the question of what makes a person a mother. He assumes that genetics takes priority over gestation, and contrary to the Warnock report, that the mother is the genetic contributor, not the woman who gives birth to the child. But this is only an assumption, and nowhere is there an argument for this priority. For example, Page states, "Let us now return to the question as to who should be recognized as the mother of the child, the genetic mother or the gestator,[100] when a woman is pregnant by embryo transfer, the embryo not being genetically related to her. The question is basically the same question as: which of the two women have the rights and duties of the mother? The woman who gestates the child could not have these rights as the child's genetic parent; she is not the genetic parent. Therefore, on my view it [motherhood] will be a matter of whether the rights and duties have been transferred to her."[101] Thus, parenthood resides solely in genetics. A gestational surrogate could not be a genetic parent because she did not contribute gametes. But that begs the question of why the genetic "parent" should be the mother if she does not bear the child. His system depends on that unsubstantiated assumption. One can argue that there is no difference between genetic and gestational surrogacy, and come to the opposite conclusion, that maternal rights belong to the woman who bears the child, irrespective of genetic contribution.

This assumption is important in his initial differentiation between genetic and gestational surrogacy, prior to his scenario of in utero egg donation. He states, "the difference is that in gestatory surrogacy the child belongs to the commissioning parents from the outset as they do not at any stage relinquish their rights and duties in respect to it (by donating their gametes)."[102] Yet this entirely ignores the physical and psychological contribution of the woman who gestates the child, assuming without argument that genetics determines parenthood.

In conclusion to the discussion of the determinant of motherhood, given the fact that genetics alone is not treated as determinative in many cases, and that intent is not an adequate substitute, the woman who bears the child, irrespective of the genetic contributor, should be designated the child's mother. She provides a powerful combination of biological and even psychological contribution to the child's physical and emotional development, and the closest bonding and connection to the child she is carrying. Once the mother is determined to be the woman who gives birth to the child, other fundamental rights come into focus after birth, should the surrogate breach the agreement and decide to keep the child.

THE RIGHT TO ASSOCIATE WITH CHILDREN AS A FUNDAMENTAL RIGHT

The right to privacy has been invoked to support the rights of the contracting couple to procreate by utilizing collaborative methods of reproduction. This right is recognized under the general umbrella of the right to privacy in decisions concerning one's family matters, which includes the rights of parents, apart from unwarranted state intervention, to make the critical decisions about how they will raise their children. To this point in the surrogacy debate, the privacy right has been invoked to undergird the rights of the contracting couple to undertake a surrogacy arrangement. As it was argued earlier, though privacy cannot be claimed to support commercial surrogacy, it is legitimate to use it to support altruistic surrogacy.

However, there are rights to privacy involved in surrogacy other than the right to procreate. The right of parents to associate with their children, apart from neglect or unfitness, has long been recognized as a fundamental constitutional right. Once the two legal parents have been identified in any surrogacy arrangement (the natural father and the woman who gives birth to the child), then they both may exercise their rights to initiate and develop a relationship with the child, rear the child, and make decisions concerning the child's upbringing. To insist that the surrogate has a fundamental right to associate with the child she bears does not necessarily mean that she has the right to exclusive custody. In custody disputes, it may be in the child's best interest to reside with the natural father and his wife, as was determined in the *Baby M* case. There, the New Jersey Supreme Court ruled that Mary Beth Whitehead was the legal mother, having contributed both egg and womb, but that the child would be better off in the primary custody of the Sterns'. Whitehead then received extensive visitation rights. Both the custody and visitation award are consistent with the parties' fundamental right to parent.

However, the right of one parent to associate with a child cannot be enforced at the expense of the right of the other to do the same.[103] Neither can the right to use third party reproductive collaborators (who end up with fundamental parental rights) be exercised at the expense of the surrogate's fundamental parental right to associate with her child. Though there is a fundamental procreative right involved in surrogacy, it should not be enforced by denying other fundamental rights to the surrogate. Enforcing the agreement denies one parent the right to be involved in her child's life. However, failure to enforce the contract does not infringe on the contracting couple's right to use surrogacy to procreate. It simply does not allow them to sever a mother's tie to her child. They may still use surrogacy to produce a child, but the use of a surrogate does not guarantee them exclusive custody over the child born out of the arrangement. This is essentially the reasoning followed in the *Baby M* decision of the New Jersey Supreme Court. There, the court recognized the right of a surrogate to the companionship of her child as a "recognized fundamental interest protected by the constitution."[104] This did not conflict with the natural father's rights to procreation, since the court held that his right to procreate is "very simply the right to have natural children whether through sexual intercourse or artificial insemination."[105] As Capron and Radin commented on this case, "William Stern had a right to father *Baby M* but not to insist that she be turned over to him to raise or that the Whiteheads be forced to fulfill their promise to relinquish their parental rights to the Sterns."[106]

Viewing surrogacy in light of the right to privacy can lead to confusion concerning the fundamental rights of the participants, which often leaves the surrogate without rights once the child is born.[107] For example, John and Susan Phillips, writing in the *Kentucky Law Journal*, argue for the right for all parties to enter a surrogacy arrangement as an extension of the fundamental right to privacy in procreative decisions. But when it comes to enforcing the contract, as they suggest the law should do, they confuse procreative liberty and the right to associate with one's children, thereby entirely neglecting the surrogate's similar rights. They state, "If a surrogate mother chooses to bear a child through artificial insemination she has a fundamental right to so decide. The right is no less fundamental because she later terminates her parental rights in favor of the natural father. Similarly, the natural father's decision to beget a child is a protected choice. A man's right to father children and enjoy the association of his offspring is a constitutionally protected freedom. There is no rational justification for diluting this paternal prerogative solely because the children will be fathered through artificial insemination."[108]

Just because an infertile couple has the procreative liberty to enter an altruistic surrogacy arrangement, it does not follow that they should automatically obtain exclusive parental rights to the child. Procreative liberty only refers to the right to conceive and bear a child. In most cases, parental rights do follow from procreative liberty, and the Phillipses have recognized that the natural father has the right to associate with the child he has fathered. But so does the surrogate. The Phillips acknowledge her freedom to enter the arrangement, but deny her corresponding right to associate with her child. Just because the child is fathered through artificial insemination does not mean that the surrogate has irrevocably surrendered the fundamental right to associate with her child, and it does not create a paternal prerogative for parental rights. Both have the right to enter the arrangement, though not for the commercial benefit of the surrogate. Both have the right to associate with the child of which they are the legal parents, though they can voluntarily waive that right. However, they cannot waive that right for a fee, either in surrogacy or in adoption.[109] The man's right to procreate by utilizing surrogacy cannot override the surrogate's parental rights. Procreative liberty and parental rights, though they go together in most procreative settings, are separate in surrogacy. Procreative freedom for the intending couple only provides parental rights when the surrogate voluntarily relinquishes her parental rights, not when she wants to keep her child. After the child is born, the issue is not procreative liberty, but the right to associate with one's children.

This fundamental right of parents to associate with their children was first articulated in *Pierce v. Society of Sisters*.[110] There the Court struck down an Oregon statute that required all children of school age to be enrolled in public schools. It was held that this constituted an unreasonable interference with the liberty of parents to direct the upbringing of their children. Implicit in this decision is the more fundamental right of parents to be involved with their children's lives, which cannot be cut off without clear evidence that it is in the child's best interests that such action be taken.

Two other cases that affirm this right involve laws concerning termination of parental rights. In *Stanley v. Illinois*,[111] the Court affirmed that "the rights to conceive and to raise one's children have been deemed essential, basic civil rights of man and far more precious than property rights. It is cardinal with us that the custody, care and nurture of the child reside first in the parents, whose primary function and freedom include preparation for obligations the state can neither supply nor hinder."[112] Of course, the nuclear family was assumed in this case, and the Court did not anticipate surrogacy when it made this decision. But that does not minimize the rights of parents, even if they do not live together, as was the case with the Stanleys, to exercise their unique opportunity for a relationship with their children.

This right was more clearly affirmed in *Santowsky v. Kramer*.[113] Here the issue was the constitutionality of a New York statute that held that only a "fair preponderance of evidence" was required to prove parental neglect and thus terminate parental rights over the objections of the parents. The Court ruled that the due process clause required more than that quantum of evidence, based on the importance of the parent-child relationship and the possibility of error on the investigators' part that might result in irrevocably terminating that relationship. About the importance of the parent-child tie, the Court stated, "This Court's historical recognition that freedom of personal choice in matters of family life is a fundamental liberty interest protected by the Fourteenth Amendment. The fundamental liberty interest of natural parents in the care, custody and management of their child does not evaporate simply because they have not been model parents or have lost temporary custody to the State. Even when blood relationships are strained, parents retain a vital interest in preventing the irretrievable destruction of their family life."[114]

In view of this fundamental right, due process must be scrupulously observed when considering a parent's unfitness to exercise this right. Though parents can voluntarily relinquish their parental rights, they cannot be forced to do so in the absence of clear evidence of neglect or gross incompetence as a parent, and in those cases, their right to due process must be respected. It would appear that, if the mother is indeed the woman who bears the child, her maternal rights cannot be terminated by enforcing the surrogacy arrangement, assuming that she has not abandoned the child,[115] and is a fit parent. Demanding specific performance of the agreement thus violates this fundamental constitutional right, and would constitute unwarranted government intrusion into the rights of the surrogate. Failing to enforce the agreement might be an intrusion into the contracting couple's procreative liberty, but enforcing the agreement would be a far more severe intrusion on the surrogate's right to parent her child. This is because procreative liberty is essentially a negative right, and by refusing to enforce the agreement, the state does not prevent a couple from using collaborators to conceive a child. Rather, it prevents the couple from receiving sole custody of the child, at the expense of the surrogate. There is nothing in any of the Court's decisions on procreative liberty that implies that the state must take positive steps to insure the successful completion of any procreative endeavor. The state should not take steps to prevent the use of third parties, but once the child is conceived and born, the state should not remove the child from the care and custody of either of the two legal parents without sufficient cause and without observing due process. The state should not terminate the rights of the mother to protect the contractual interests of the contracting couple. Nor should the state terminate the surrogate's parental rights even on the grounds of the child's best interests, though custody and visitation decisions may be made on this basis.

Not only do parents have a right to associate with their children, but the children have the reciprocal fundamental right to a relationship with their parents. A 1983 California Appeals Court decision recognized the reverse side of a parent's rights in *Michelle Marie W. v. Ronald W.*[116] There the court held that a minor child who is refused the opportunity to establish the paternity of his or her father is deprived of a fundamental interest. The court stated that such a refusal "deprives one of the classes whose interest is at stake, the children, of a fundamental right. The right of a child to establish a relationship with a parent is the most fundamental right a child possesses and can be equated in importance with personal liberty and the most basic of constitutional rights."[117]

NO ENFORCEMENT OF PRE-BIRTH WAIVERS OF PARENTAL RIGHTS

Because of the fundamental right of a mother to associate and develop a relationship with her child, any surrogacy arrangement that involves a pre birth or pre-conception agreement to relinquish parental rights and custody should be void and unenforceable. This critical part of the surrogacy contract cannot be upheld without violating the surrogate's constitutional rights of privacy. Applying contract law to surrogacy and insisting that "a deal's a deal" fails to protect the surrogate's fundamental rights, and upholds the contracting couple's rights at her expense.

Specific performance of the agreement does have its attraction.[118] It would be short and simple, offering a clear solution to some of the difficult conflicts in surrogacy that sometimes must be worked out over extended time periods in the courts.[119] In addition, when competent adults make a deal, they are normally expected to abide by its terms, since promise keeping is considered a very important value in society. In addition, enforcing the contract will serve as a warning to potential surrogates and would discourage those not capable of surrendering the child and parental rights, thereby increasing the effectiveness of the screening process and facilitating a smoother completion of the arrangement.

However, even under contract law doctrine, assuming a contract framework for surrogacy, the arrangement cannot be enforceable. Courts traditionally have been reluctant to order specific performance for personal service contracts.[120] They are difficult to supervise adequately by the courts, and forcing individuals into performing personal services could be interpreted as involuntary servitude, in violation of peonage laws and the Thirteenth Amendment. Courts have traditionally been hesitant to force individuals into undesired personal associations. Given the intensely personal and private nature of surrogacy, it is unlikely that courts would enforce such a services agreement. The normal solution is for courts to award damages, not to force someone to perform a service against his or her will. In situations of altruistic surrogacy, in which no fee is paid to the surrogate, this presents further complications for applying contract doctrine. Normally, when there is no consideration paid, the promise made is unenforceable.[121]

In surrogacy, few of these personal service contract considerations actually apply.[122] Once the child has been born, enforcing the agreement would work to sever the relationship between the participants rather than forcing them to continue a relationship. Further, performance under the contract is simple to monitor. Custody must be surrendered and a waiver of parental rights must be signed. Both can be easily witnessed. In the lower court decision in the *Baby M* case, Judge Sorkow concluded that surrogacy was an arrangement for reproductive services only, but he awarded the child to the contracting couple on the basis of specific performance.[123] The one aspect of contract law that does appear to apply is that promises made without payment of consideration are unenforceable. Even if medical expenses are paid, that would not likely be seen as consideration, since without the agreement the mother would not have incurred those expenses. Thus the surrogate could not be said to have received a benefit from such reimbursement, since it was all paid in relation to the pregnancy. This is one aspect of contract law that does apply to surrogacy. As presented in the framework of this analysis, which would allow only non-commercial arrangements, such altruistic surrogacy would still be unenforceable under contract law.

Even if commercial surrogacy were allowed, the contract should still be unenforceable. Though consideration is paid to the surrogate, which creates the expectation of performance, she has a fundamental right to associate with her child since she is the legal mother of the child. The contract cannot be enforced if it involves compromising her essential rights as a parent. She cannot be forced to turn over custody or sign away her parental rights, even if the natural father is one of the parties to the agreement. His involvement raises conflicts in the next part of the process, the determination of custody. It does not suggest that he and his wife should have a superior parental rights claim as a result of the contract. A court can decide on primary custody for the father without suggesting that the surrogate is not the mother.

Since the surrogate is the legal mother of the child, the only way in which her parental rights can be terminated is by voluntary adoption. One can view surrogacy as a pre-conception agreement to adoption, but as is the case in many states' adoption laws, a pre-birth consent to adoption is not considered enforceable. One of the reasons for this is that a mother cannot give truly informed consent to adoption prior to birth of the child. She cannot really know what it is going to be like for her to give up this particular child, even if she has had one or more children prior to this pregnancy. For example, Phyllis Silverman, a social worker who testified in the *Baby M* case, reported that contemplating giving up a child in the abstract was a far different matter from actually surrendering a living child to another person after the child is born.[124] When comparing the pre-adoption attitudes of mothers with the actual experience, the overwhelming majority of them admitted that giving up their child "felt worse than they ever imagined."[125] The choice to relinquish parental rights must be made with full awareness of the pain and difficulty involved, and this cannot occur until after the mother has had a chance to experience what a relationship with this child is like after birth.

A second reason why pre-birth waivers are not enforceable is that the pain involved and damage incurred by a woman when forced to relinquish her child against her will can be substantial. Since the right to associate with one's child is so fundamental, and the pain involved with giving up one's child involuntarily is often great, it is best not to enforce the contract. Studies show that women who give up children for adoption, because they believe it is in the child's best interests, nonetheless suffer significantly.[126] In surrogacy, when the mother is not unfit, the pain can be similar, if not greater. Silverman concluded in her testimony in the *Baby M* case that enforcing surrogacy contracts will result in "depression, loss of self-worth, destruction of self-identity, difficulty in forming or continuing close personal relationships, and a grieving process that will continue every day for the rest of the mother's life. The impact on these women will be enormous and it will be permanent."[127] There is no reason to presume that the experience of surrogates will be significantly different simply because they entered the pregnancy expecting to give up their child.

Under the adoption laws of many states, a consent to adoption is not considered valid until a period of time after the child's birth has elapsed. Such a recision period in surrogacy would enable the surrogate to make a fully informed decision to surrender her child for adoption to the contracting couple, and would minimize the pain involved in so doing. The child should remain in the surrogate's custody until the end of the recision period. At that time, should she still wish to give up the child for adoption, she may do so. Until the time that the adoption is finalized by the courts, she may change her mind, as is the case with many states' adoption laws. At that time, the consent to relinquish parental rights is irrevocable. However, if she chooses to retain her maternal rights, then the question of custody arrangements with the father needs to be considered.

RESOLVING CUSTODY DISPUTES ACCORDING TO A DUAL STANDARD

In the *Baby M* case, the litigation necessary to resolve competing custody claims continued for more than two years. Even after the child was established in the Sterns' home, they ran the risk of losing the child, or at least sharing custody (which finally did occur) and thereby disrupting the stable environment that the child critically needed for her early formative years of development. Similarly, in the *Johnson v. Calvert* case, the child was more than two years old when the California Supreme Court's decided the case. Given that these types of interruptions in the child's environment are normally not in the child's best interests, it would seem, at first glance, that some measures need to be taken to insure that these kinds of drawn-out and costly court battles over custody are minimized when the surrogate wants to keep the child.

Yet the alternative to these scenarios is to invoke some sort of presumption for either parent, based on which parent has a stronger parental claim to the child. Some have suggested that the natural father should automatically be awarded custody, with the surrogate having some visitation rights.[128] Under this arrangement, the child is immediately turned over to the contracting couple at birth, not allowing the additional bonding that takes place when breast feeding is initiated to occur, and the couple does not have to fear that the surrogate will change her mind after custody is initially surrendered.   The basis for this presumption in favor of custody to the father is that the father is the one who initiated the agreement for the purpose of obtaining a child, whereas the surrogate entered the agreement for the purpose of providing a child for someone else.   However, this arrangement makes non-enforcement of the contract somewhat illusory, and actually enforces it indirectly.[129] There is little difference between the surrogate's being forced to give up her child, except for visitation, under this presumption, and simply enforcing the contract.   In the former, though she does not technically lose parental rights, practically, she loses most of the opportunity to form a significant relationship with her child. She loses this opportunity without any proof of unfitness or any proof that such an arrangement would be in the child's best interests.   In addition, if AID laws are not changed, a presumption in favor of the biological father runs the risk of illegitimating the child, since it is unlikely that either one of the natural parents would consent to a stepparent adoption by the other couple.[130]   Normally the presumption of paternity is rebuttable if the husband of the child's mother refuses to take responsibility for the child, or if blood tests conclusively establish that someone else is the child's father.   But the normal assumption, which is conclusive after a set period of time, as in the *Michael H.* case, is that the child's father is the husband of the child's mother.

On the other hand, surrogacy could function under a presumption in favor of the surrogate mother.   Though this has been criticized as a return to the tender years presumption that has a gender bias built in that is harmful to women,[131] others have argued for it based on the model of the mother as the primary caretaker of the child from birth and thus the one with the greater investment and bonding with the child.   This is further based on the fact that the least detrimental alternative to the child is almost always to avoid disruption in primary relationships between the child and the person who is the primary caretaker.[132]   Though this presumption is not gender based by definition, since the primary caretaker could just as easily be the father or another relative, in surrogacy, the primary caretaker model will invariably suggest custody for the mother, since normally she is the primary caregiver for the child in the period immediately following birth.   Though not technically the tender years presumption, practically, the result is the same in surrogacy.   To adopt this presumption would involve neglect of the natural father's desire to have a child (which was the reason surrogacy was initiated by him and his wife), and makes the custodial destiny of the child dependent on biology alone, leaving the father and mother unequally situated with respect to custody.

A further alternative is to use the best interests of the child standard as the guideline for custody placement. This would place all surrogacy conflicts concerning parental rights in the courts, and would result in delays and perhaps even traumatic disruptions in the child's environment, neither of which could be considered in the child's best interests. The best interests standard itself has been criticized in recent years for forcing judges to make value judgments on what is best for a child which may not, in fact, be in the child's best interests, given our pluralistic culture; for forcing judges to predict the future concerning which parent would provide a better home setting; for (in surrogacy) having little or no information about the contracting couple's past parenting experience to weigh what kind of parents they would be; and for discriminating against those with a lower socio-economic place or against those with lifestyles that the judges do not understand or approve of.[133] However, deficiencies in the way the standard is applied do not necessarily mean that surrogacy custody disputes should not end up with a court deciding them. It simply means that judges should be more sensitive to issues of fairness and to their limits, given the limited amount of information available to them.

In surrogacy cases, it is not difficult to imagine situations in which the best interests standard would not produce a clear preference for one parent over another. The alternative would then be shared custody, with the child alternating between the family units. In most cases, this would not be in the child's best interests. Even though this is commonly done in divorce custody settlements, in most of those cases, the children are older and the regular change in living situations is not nearly as disruptive, since they are more equipped to deal with the changes. That is clearly not the case for a newborn or an infant. It is critical that there be stability in the small child's home environment, and the kind of custody arrangement that would be most fair to both parents would be most harmful to the child. Since society has rightly and consistently preferred the interests of children over the rights of adults, even their fundamental rights, it is not unreasonable to keep what is best for the child at the forefront of custody considerations even if it involves less than full exercise of one of the parent's rights.

A combination of the above alternatives moves the parties toward fairness while respecting the best interests of the child.[134] Such a dual standard scheme for determining custody would first apply the best interests standard in order to determine custody. This would decide cases in which there is a clear indication of one parent's superiority over the other as the primary caretaker. For example, it might favor a married father over a single mother, or a family with a stable income over one in which the parents are unemployed (though the court should not discriminate strictly on the basis of the amount of income of a household), or a family with a stable marriage over a family with a history of marital problems. Application of the standard at this first stage of the custody determination would have to indicate clearly the greater fitness of one parent over the other. This step would either rule out one of the parents based on gross unfitness, or eliminate one parent as being clearly less capable of providing a stable home for the child. In most surrogacy cases, if screening of the surrogate is properly done prior to conception, then the custody determination would likely need to move on to a second step.[135]

The second step would involve comparing the strength of competing parental claims, and in all likelihood, granting primary custody to the surrogate, on the basis of the combination of her biological contribution, of gestation and bonding formed in utero. In essence the same factors that give the surrogate maternal rights also give her primary custody, all other things being equal. Though the inherent bias toward the mother based on biology may appear to be a step backward from society's movement toward gender equality, this takes into account the reality that men and women are not situated equally in their relationship to a newborn, especially if the man and woman are not married and not living in the same household. In effect, to deny these biological differences is to penalize women with their greater involvement in pregnancy and childbirth. As Wolf states, "Considering gestation and birthing allows one to consider more fully which parent is already beginning a relationship, is more involved with, and has more immediate responsibility for the newborn. To rule those factors off the course would penalize the parent with the greater involvement and assume that women should be considered just like men in their relationship to a newborn."[136]

Thus the initial custody decisions would be made by applying the best interests standard, and should that not be conclusive, a presumption for the primary caretaker, most likely the surrogate, should be invoked. Visitation rights for the non-custodial should be established on a consideration of the child's interests, since it is often detrimental for the child to alternate between two parents who do not get along. The rights of adults to associate with their children, though fundamental, nevertheless are subordinate to the best interests of the children.

CONCLUSION: ADOPTION LAW PREFERRED OVER CONTRACT LAW FOR SURROGACY

Given the nature of the fundamental rights involved, it seems best to apply family law rather than contract law to surrogacy, both in general and when custody disputes arise. Historically, contract law has not been widely applied to family settings, partly because of the courts' long-standing reluctance to become involved in domestic disputes.[137] Though courts intervene more frequently to safeguard children's best interests, this historical laissez-faire attitude of the courts is still the norm today.

Since a surrogacy contract can easily be considered a prenatal adoption agreement, it seems best to apply adoption statutes to it. Simply because surrogacy is a new and novel reproductive arrangement, it does not follow that the law must be changed to accommodate it. If on moral grounds one decides that commercial surrogacy governed by the contract should not be encouraged or allowed, then there is no obligation for the law to stretch in order to give the endorsement of the state to it.[138]

In general terms, adoption law as applied to surrogacy would embrace the moral conclusion made so far concerning commercial, contractual surrogacy. These adoption principles should guide the formulation of specific legislation to deal with surrogacy. A legislative proposal will follow in the next chapter. The key principles include the following:

1. In keeping with the moral analysis of the commercial aspects of surrogacy, there should be no payment directly to the surrogate, beyond reasonable and documented medical expenses, and reimbursement for lost wages due to the pregnancy.

2. Any agreement to relinquish parental rights prior to birth should be considered void and unenforceable.

3. The surrogate should have the right to change her mind and keep the child during a recision period after birth. No consent to adoption should be considered valid until this period has passed. The recision period for surrogacy should be the same as the recision period allowed by any particular state's adoption laws.

4. If the surrogate decides to keep the child, primary custody should be decided by application of a dual standard: the best interests of the child standard to take into account any clear differences between the parties' ability to provide a stable home for the child, and if there is not a clear difference, then the parental claim standard, to weigh the strength of competing parental claims. In most cases, this will result in a presumption for the surrogate.

5. Once primary custody has been decided, visitation rights should be decided by applying the best interests standard. This is the one aspect of surrogacy law that differs from adoption, because in a custody dispute in surrogacy, one parent is not relinquishing parental rights, only primary custody. Assignment of visitation rights reflects custody law in a divorce proceeding.

Though this proposal does not fully protect all the rights of all the parties, it does offer maximum protection of the rights of the adult participants in the arrangement, consistent with the overriding concern, the best interests of the child. If, in the process of ensuring that children are not commodified and that mothers are not forced against their will to relinquish parental rights, surrogacy agreements become more risky and uncertain, then so be it. The law has no duty to accommodate a new technology in general, nor this reproductive arrangement in particular, simply because it opens up new possibilities. After moral analysis, society, through state legislatures, may decide that these possibilities are not in the public interest, and thus that surrogacy contracts should not be enforced, because they are against public policy.

NOTES

1. See for instance, Laurence D. Houlgate, "Whose Child? In re Baby M and the Biological Preference Principle," *Logos (USA)* 9 (1988): 161-77. Houlgate wrote in the aftermath of the *Baby M* case, prior to any gestational surrogacy cases gaining national attention. When he describes his biological preference principle, he does not distinguish between genetic biological preference and gestational biological preference. He states, "Let me extract from this [the *Baby M* case] the following principle: in a contest for custody between a biological parent and one who has no biological relationship to the child, the state should prefer the biological parent. That is, when deciding who shall be granted the status of legal parent, the state should always prefer the biological parent to all other contestants. I shall call this the 'biological preference principle'" (Ibid., 162).

He favors the surrogacy contract as a way of defeating this presumption, since his principle is only a presumption and not an absolute. It is clear, in view of more recent gestational surrogacy cases, that he needs to clarify his biological preference principle to identify which biological mother has the priority in determining maternal rights.

See also Ruth Macklin, "Artificial Means of Reproduction and Our Understanding of the Family," *Hastings Center Report* 21 (January-February 1991): 6.

2. Philip Hager, "State High Court to Rule in O.C. Surrogacy Case," *Los Angeles Times*, 24 January 1992, A1, 12. In May 1993, the State Supreme Court ruled in favor of the Calverts, upholding the decisions of the lower and appeals courts.

3. Of course, if surrogates are not successful in pressing lawsuits, then the number of challenges brought by surrogates will likely be fewer. The frequency of lawsuits depends significantly upon the frequency of success in winning them. However, with the increased publicity surrounding surrogacy and a few Court decisions in favor of surrogates, the likelihood of further Court challenges increases.

4. See for example, Andrea Stumpf, "Redefining Mother: A Legal Matrix for the New Reproductive Technologies," *Yale Law Review* 96 (1986): 197-208; Marjorie Maguire Schultz, "Reproductive Technology and Intent-Based Parenthood: An Opportunity for Gender Neutrality," *Wisconsin Law Review* 1990, no. 2 (1990): 297-398. These two articles will be discussed later in this chapter.

5. However, the discussion in this chapter will proceed using the accepted nomenclature for surrogacy.

6. See for example, Martha Field, *Surrogate Motherhood: The Legal and Human Issues* (Cambridge, Mass.: Harvard University Press, 1988), 126-43. For a critique of her maternal presumption, see Frances H. Miller, "Surrogate Fatherhood (Review of *Surrogate Motherhood* by Martha A. Field)," *Boston University Law Review* 70 no. 1 (January 1990): 169-83.

7. See Susan M. Wolf, "Enforcing Surrogate Motherhood Agreements: The Trouble with Specific Performance," *New York Law School Human Rights Annual* 4 no. 2 (Spring

1987): 403-8. She is uncomfortable with the prolonged nature of custody battles, but is more uneasy with the unfairness involved in a custody presumption.

8. This case will be discussed below under the genetic determinant for motherhood. The quote appears in "Surrogate Has Baby Conceived in Laboratory," *New York Times* 17 April 1986, A26, cited in Stumpf, "Redefining Mother," 187, no. 1.

9. Stumpf, "Redefining Mother," 187, n. 2.

10. Calif. Evid. Code, Sec. 621, cited in *Michael H. v. Gerald D.* (491 U.S. 110, 117-18, 1988). The relevant portion of the law states, "The issue of a wife cohabiting with her husband, who is not impotent, is conclusively presumed to be a child of the marriage." The presumption may be rebutted by blood tests performed within the first two years of the child's life.

11. *Smith v. Jones*, no. 85-53201402 (Mich. Cir. Ct., Wayne County), 14 March 1986. Cited in Donald DeMarco, *Biotechnology and the Assault on Parenthood* (San Francisco: Ignatius Press, 1991): 174-76. For comment on this case see, Nancy Blodgett, "Who is Mother: Genetic Donor, Not Surrogate," *American Bar Association Journal*, 1 June 1986, 18.

12. From the *Smith v. Jones* case, cited in Macklin, "Artificial Means of Reproduction," 9.

13. See the background discussion of this case in chapter four.

14. Parslow stated it this way in the decision, "The gestational environment is still not clear. We've heard some experts testify in this case both ways on that. It's difficult. Obviously, you can't interview a child. We know that there are various chemical things that go on and we know that there may be some factors there combined with the genetic factors that make you susceptible to some things and have strength and immunity from others, but *there is still much disagreement as to the influence of the gestational environment* See Calif. Super. Ct. AD 57638, October 22, 1990, cited in Joint Legislative Committee on Surrogate Parenting, *Commercial and Non-commercial Surrogate Parenting* (Sacramento: Joint Publications Office, November 1990): 108.

15. Ibid., 107-8.

16. Macklin, "Artificial Means of Reproduction," 9.

17. Advocates of intent-based parenthood would argue that the contracting couple, irrespective of genetic contribution, should be the legal parents due to the psychological aspects of parenthood. This will be discussed further below.

18. Sidney Callahan, "The Ethical Challenge of the New Reproductive Technology," in *Medical Ethics: A Guide for Health Care Professionals*, ed. John F. Monagle and David C. Thomasma. Frederick, Md.: Aspen Publishers, 1987.

19. See Macklin, "Artificial Means of Reproduction ," 9. The concept of gametes, and the parental rights that accompany them, being transferable is taken from Edgar Page, "Donation, Surrogacy and Adoption," *Journal of Applied Philosophy* 2 (October 1985): 165. His position justifying the contracting couple as legal parents is an intriguing one, and will be addressed later in this chapter.

20. One of the differences between organs and sperm/eggs (and also blood) is that the latter are renewable and organs are not. Though eggs are technically not renewable, a woman has many more eggs during her lifetime than she will actually use. This clearly sets eggs apart from non-renewable bodily organs.

There is a significant difference between the compensation received for egg donation and that for sperm donation. The reason for this disparity is that the process of donating eggs is much more involved than the relatively simple process of donating sperm. However, this difference in no way detracts from the notion that a person owns his or her genetic material.

21. However, there are some limits on what the genetic contributors can do with the embryos. They cannot be sold, but they can be donated to another infertile couple. They can be stored, and the law concerning destruction of unused embryos varies from state to state. In general, however, the couple does make the decision as to whether the embryos are donated to another couple or stored for their future use. Though there are limits, this does not undermine their essential ownership of the unimplanted embryos.

22. It should be noted that the overwhelming majority of sperm donations are made anonymously.

23. 463 U.S. 248 (1982).

24. Ibid., 248-49.

25. The precedent for this case was set five years earlier in Quilloin v. Walcott (434 U.S. 246 (1978)). The Court ruled that an unwed father, who had made no attempt to have a relationship with the child and was not seeking custody or visitation at the time of the adoption proceedings, cannot block a stepparent adoption of the child. The state was not required to weigh the parental claims of unwed fathers similarly to divorced fathers, which was the equal protection claim made by the natural father. The state was assuming that divorced fathers at one time had a significant relationship with the child, and that the divorce did not constitute abandonment of that relationship. As Justice Marshall stated in the unanimous majority opinion, "the State was not foreclosed from recognizing this difference in the extent of commitment to the welfare of the child" (Ibid., 256).

26. 441 U.S. 380 (1979). A more recent, and more complicated, case (*Michael H. v. Gerald D.*, 491 U.S. 110, 1988) makes a similar point but with more pointed language denying the value of genetics alone in determining parental rights. Michael was seeking to be declared the legal father of his natural daughter, Victoria, with the attendant parental rights, asserted over the husband of Victoria's mother, Carole. Michael was arguing, in essence, that he had a constitutionally protected liberty interest in his genetic link and continuing relationship with Victoria.

Michael's argument was that genetics plus relationship gives one a protected liberty interest that should be constitutionally protected. Justice Scalia's majority opinion clearly stated that genetics alone does not automatically warrant an award of parental rights. In fact, it is not even genetics plus relationship that gives a person irrefutable parental rights, if to affirm those rights would involve inquiries about a child's paternity that would be "destructive of family integrity and privacy." Thus in this case, the genetic tie of Michael to Victoria was not determinative. The issue was whether Michael's genetic tie plus his relationship to Victoria merits granting him parental rights, even though his relationship consisted of a total of eleven months. As Justice Scalia stated in the majority opinion, "This is not the stuff of which fundamental rights qualifying as liberty interests are made" (Ibid., 125, 127).

27. In his dissent, Justice Stewart chided the majority for its refusal to acknowledge this foundational element of family law. He stated, "The State's interest in promoting the welfare of illegitimate children is of far greater importance than the opinion of the Court

would suggest. It [the statute in question] provides a means by which an illegitimate child can become legitimate-a fact that the Court's opinion today barely acknowledges" (Ibid., 395).

Interestingly, the dissents by both Justices Stewart and Stevens suggest that there is what Susan Wolf calls a "biological asymmetry" between the unwed father and mother. That is, the maternal presumption inherent in the New York statute in question is appropriate, and according to Stewart, to hold differently would "defy common sense"; he calls consent of the mother for adoption "indispensable" (Ibid., 395). Wolf points out that this asymmetry suggests that the only type of surrogacy that should be allowed is gestational surrogacy. Where there is no genetic contribution, there is no corresponding difference in the parental claims of natural father and mother as there is in genetic surrogacy, thus avoiding the problems inherent in the *Calvert* case. This suggestion, however, assumes that genetics takes priority over gestation in determining maternal rights. To be sure, Wolf's point in the article is not to define motherhood, but to outline issues that surface when the surrogate breaches the agreement. But her assumption about the place of genetics is clear, with the implication that there would be no legitimate parental rights dispute in cases of gestational surrogacy. See Wolf, "Enforcing Surrogate Motherhood Agreements," 407-8, nn. 79, 81.

28. American College of Obstetricians and Gynecologists, Committee on Ethics, *Statement on Surrogate Motherhood* (Washington, D.C.: ACOG, 1990), 2. Also cited in Larry Gostin, ed. *Surrogate Motherhood: Politics and Privacy* (Bloomington: Indiana University Press, 1990): 300-303.

29. American Civil Liberties Union, *Policy on Surrogate Parenting* (New York: ACLU,1987): 1. Also cited in Gostin, *Surrogate Motherhood,* 293-99. Though the ACLU statement does vest full parental rights in the gestational mother, interestingly, on the surface, it does not do so at the expense of the genetic mother. The statement is quite clear that she also has a parental rights claim. However, should the surrogate breach the agreement, her parental rights cannot be involuntarily terminated, so it is difficult to see the real benefit accruing to the genetic contributor if the surrogate decides to keep the child.

30. United Kingdom, Department of Health and Social Security. *Report of the Committee of Inquiry into Human Fertilization and Embryology*, 1984. Cited in Page, "Donation, Adoption and Surrogacy," 162.

31. Macklin, "Artificial Means of Reproduction," 9.

32. George J. Annas, "Redefining Parenthood and Protecting Embryos: Why We Need New Laws," *Hastings Center Report* 14 (October 1984): 51. See also George J. Annas and Sherman Elias, "Non-coital Reproduction," *Journal of the American Medical Association* 255 (3 January 1986): 67; "In Vitro Fertilization and Embryo Transfer: Medicolegal Aspects of a New Technique to Create a Family," *Family Law Quarterly* 17 (1983): 216-217.

33. Houlgate, "Whose Child?," 167. Regarding Annas's, "Redefining Parenthood," article, Houlgate suggests that Annas has in mind more of the relational, or nurture element in pregnancy that gives a woman a greater claim to the child. This may be a part of his reasoning, but it is not apparent from the part of the article he cites. It appears that he has Macklin's "sweat equity" concept in mind in his argument.

34. This will be explored in more detail later in this chapter.

35. KatharineBartlett, "Re-expressing Parenthood," *Yale Law Journal* 98 (1988): 329-30.

36. Her paradigm for parenthood will be discussed below.

37. See the above discussion of *Smith v. Jones*, the first case in which a Court decided maternal claims in gestational surrogacy.

38. See for example, L. W. Sontag, "Parental Determinants of Postnatal Behavior," in *Fetal Growth and Development*, ed. Harry A. Weisman and George R. Kerr (New York: McGraw Hill, 1970).

39. L.W. Sontag, "Somatopsychics of Personality and Body Function," *Vita Humana* 6 (1963): 11-24.

40. B.R.H. Van den Bergh, "The Influence of Maternal Emotions During Pregnancy on Fetal and Neonatal Behavior," *Pre- and Peri-Natal Psychology* 5 (Winter 1990): 127.

41. Ibid., 128.

42. Cited in Sontag, "Parental Determinants," 265.

43. See for example, the work of Melvin Zax and associates in Melvin Zax et al., "Birth Outcomes in the Offspring of Mentally Disordered Women," *American Journal of Orthopsychiatry* (April 1977): 218-30, and Zax et al., "Perinatal Characteristics in the Offspring of Schizophrenic Women," *Journal of Nervous and Mental Disorders* 157 (1973): 191-99.

44. See for example the work of Dr. Dennis Stott, "Follow-up Study from Birth of the Effects of Prenatal Stresses," *Developmental Medicine and Child Neurology* 15 (1973): 770-87. On the specific role of fathers in creating or reducing stress in the mother, see Stott, "Children in the Womb: The Effects of Stress," *New Society* (19 May 1977): 329-31.

45. Monika Lukesch, "Psychologie Faktoren der Schwangerschaft," (Ph.D. dissertation, University of Salzburg, 1975), cited in Thomas Verny, M.D. and John Kelly, *The Secret Life of the Unborn Child* (New York: Dell Publishing, 1981): 47, 219.

46. Gerhard Rottmann, "Untersuchungen uber Einstellung zur Schwangerschaft und zur fotalen Entwicklung," in *Geist und Psyche*, ed. Hans Graber (Munich: Kindler Verlag, 1974), cited in Verny and Kelly, *The Secret Life of the Unborn Child*, 48.

47. Verny and Kelly, *The Secret Life of the Unborn Child*, 21.

48. Ibid., 21-22. See also A.H. Rosenfeld, "Music: The Beautiful Disturber," *Psychology Today* 12 (1985): 51.

49. Peter Hepper, Research Fellow at the School of Psychology at the Queen's University of Belfast has recently stated that, "there can be little doubt that the foetus can learn in the womb." See his "Foetal Learning: Implications for Psychiatry," *British Journal of Psychiatry* 155 (1989): 289-93, in which he cites the following studies as evidence of fetal learning: A. J. DeCaspar and W. P. Fifer, "Of human bonding: newborns prefer their mothers' voices," *Science* 208 (1980): 1174-76; A. J. DeCaspar and A. D Sigafoos, "The Intrauterine Heartbeat: A Potent Reinforcer for Neonates," *Infant Behavior and Development* 6 (1983): 19-25; A. J. DeCaspar and P. A. Prescott, "Human Newborns' Perception of Male Voices: Preference, Discrimination and Reinforcing Value," *Developmental Psychobiology* 17 (1984): 481-91; A. J. DeCaspar and M. J. Spence, "Prenatal Maternal Speech Influences Newborns' Perception of Speech Sound," *Infant Behavior and Development* 9 (1986): 133-50; L. Salk, "Mothers' Heartbeat as an

Imprinting Stimulus," *Transactions of the New York Academy of Science* 24 (1963): 753-63.

50. Hepper states, "Whether such experiences [in the womb] exert specific effects on behavior or act more generally to predispose the individual's behavior in certain ways is yet to be determined, but one thing is certain-the prenatal period cannot be overlooked." Hepper, "Foetal Learning," 292.

51. Brent Logan, "Teaching the Unborn: Precept and Practice," *Pre- and Peri-Natal Psychology* 2 no. 1 (Fall 1987): 22. The way in which this prenatal imprinting is helpful is described by Logan as follows, "Since auditory stimulation has proven the key to early neurological health yet the vast majority of brain cells become nonfunctional shortly before birth--while children who have received prenatal sensory enrichment are exhibiting what can be held as the reverse of this reductive process--an exclusive connection between the demonstrated prime imprinting mechanism and postnatal achievement is drawn, from which advantage can be taken during the main chance for neuronal retention and organization."

52. Verny and Kelly, *The Secret Life of the Unborn Child*, 16, 20, 22.

53. See Note, "Rumplestiltskin Revisited: The Inalienable Rights of Surrogate Mothers," *Harvard Law Review* 99 June 1986: 1952. See also the discussion of market inalienability applied to surrogacy in chapter two.

54. To be sure, biology includes genetics, but the emphasis on biology as it determines a woman's self-concept concerns the aspect of her biology that is uniquely female, that is, her ability to gestate and give birth to a child.

55. See *Lehr v. Robertson*, 463 U.S. 248 (1982).

56. Janet L. Dolgin, "Status and Contract in Surrogate Motherhood: An Illumination of the Surrogacy Debate," *Daily Journal Report* 90 no. 12 (28 December 1990): 2-18, 7.

57. Ibid.

58. Barbara Katz Rothman, "Surrogacy Contracts: A Misconception," *Daily Journal Report* 90 no. 12 (28 December 1990): 17-21, 20.

59. It seems that Rothman wants to have it both ways in her argument. She rightly wants to affirm the value of the developing relationship in gestation, yet also suggests that the fetus is only a part of the woman's body. It is difficult to see how someone could have the kind of intimate relationship she envisions in pregnancy with something that is not even seen as a separate entity. Given the bonding inherent in gestation, in my judgment, the argument that the fetus is part of the woman's body is not necessary, and detracts from her central point that the essence of motherhood is the relationship.

60. Bartlett, "Re-Expressing Parenthood," 333-34. Ironically, the New Jersey Superior Court, in upholding the Baby M contract, pointed out that Mary Beth Whitehead was acting irrationally and inappropriately by the extreme measures she took in order to keep Baby M, clearly reflecting the strength of the bond established in utero. The faulty logic in the lower court's decision was recognized by Chief Justice Wilentz in the New Jersey Supreme Court's decision. The Court rightly questioned how Whitehead could be faulted for exercising maternal protection of her child, which in any context except surrogacy, would be viewed as admirable, and perhaps even heroic. See *In re Baby M*, 525 A. 2d, 1167-1168, *In the matter of Baby M*, 537 A. 2d 1227 (1988).

61. Lori Andrews, *New Conceptions* (New York: Ballantine, 1985): 221.

62. Bartlett, "Re-Expressing Parenthood," 334, n. 180.

63. Houlgate, "Whose Child?," 167.

64. Stumpf, "Redefining Mother," 187-208.

65. Schultz, "Reproductive Technology," 297-398.

66. Page, "Donation, Adoption and Surrogacy," 161-72.

67. Stumpf, "Redefining Mother," 188.

68. Ibid., 193.

69. Ibid., 195.

70. Ibid., 195, n. 30.

71. Ibid., 195-97.

72. Stumpf recognizes the tendency of Western law and history to "squeeze the woman's role of mother into a biological pigeonhole. Despite a professed search for unbiased justice, Western law has followed the myopia of Western society by focusing on the biological discrepancy between, rather than the psychological similarity of, maternity and paternity." Ibid. 197-98, n. 42.

73. Ibid., 188, 190.

74. Ibid., 197, n. 40.

75. Ibid., 197.

76. Ibid., 194.

77. Ibid., 200-201.

78. Ibid., 205.

79. Ibid.

80. See Carol Gilligan, "The 1984 James McCormick Mitchell Lecture: Feminist Discourse, Moral Values and the Law-A Conversation," *Buffalo Law Review* 34 (1985): 11-64.

81. Stumpf, "Redefining Mother," 205, n. 69.

82. Of course, this is not to deny that there are times in which this mother-child connection does not come to fruition, particularly in cases in which mothers reject their children at birth, or in cases in which the bond develops only after birth. But normally, when comparing the connection between the woman who has only mentally conceived a child and the woman who has carried it, there is little doubt that the stronger connection is the latter.

83. Schultz, "Reproductive Technology," 297-398.

84. This is Schultz's term. Ibid., 314-16.

85. Ibid., 302-3.

86. Ibid., 323.

87. Ibid., 377.

88. Ibid., 398-99.

89. Ibid., 178.

90. Certainly one must take into account whether the surrogate's intention is so late in developing as to make it suspect, and other factors must be taken into account to adequately assess the claim of a connection. For instance, in *Johnson v. Calvert*, Anna Johnson's claim to a bond with the child was widely considered questionable due to earlier strong statements which she had made about the baby belonging to the Calverts.

91. The clear constitutional precedent for this will be outlined later in this chapter.

92. Schultz, "Reproductive Technology," 301.

93. Ibid., 373.

94. Ibid., 377.

95. Ibid., 332.

96. Ibid.

97. Page, "Donation, Adoption and Surrogacy," 162-72.

98. Ibid., 167-68.

99. Ibid., 171.

100. The assumption is inherent in the description of the two women, which Page already calls the genetic contributor the mother.

101. Ibid., 164.

102. Ibid., 167.

103. It should be noted that occasionally this is done in divorce custody settlements, when governed by the child's best interests. If those interests mandate a similar resolution of surrogacy custody disputes, then the interests of the child take priority over the interests of the adults in question. Normally in custody disputes this fundamental right is maintained, and both parents receive access to their child or children.

104. *In the matter of Baby M*, 537 A. 2d, at 1255.

105. Ibid., 1253.

106. Alexander Morgan Capron and Margaret J. Radin, "Choosing Family Law over Contract Law as a Paradigm for Surrogate Motherhood," *Law, Medicine and Health Care* 16 nos. 1-2 1988: 43, n. 38.

107. See for example, in Andrea Stumpf's reproductive matrix discussed earlier in this chapter, that the surrogate only has substantial rights during the stages of conception and gestation. Once the child is born, she loses all parental rights.

108. John W. Phillips and Susan D. Phillips, "In Defense of Surrogate Parenting: A Critical Analysis of the Recent Kentucky Experience," *Kentucky Law Journal* 69 (1980-81): 877-931, 922-923.

109. The following section takes up the subject of enforcing prebirth waivers of parental rights by the surrogate. The surrogate's waiver of parental rights does not become irrevocable until a recision period has passed, consistent with the particular state's adoption laws. Until that point, she can only conditionally waive her rights to the child she is carrying. Thus, it is not accurate to say that she can contract a waiver of parental rights, since the concept of a contract implies that its terms cannot be revoked if one of the parties changes his or her mind about those terms. In other words, a revocable contract is not really a contract in the accepted use of the term.

110. 268 U.S. 510 (1925).

111. 405 U.S. 645 (1972).

112. Ibid., 651.

113. 455 U.S. 745 (1981).

114. Ibid., 753.

115. Though her pre-conception intent to relinquish parental rights could be seen as the equivalent to abandonment, surely her change of heart is sufficient to rebut that original intent.

116. 139 Cal. App. 3d 24, 188 Cal. Rptr. 413 (1983).

117. 139 Cal. App. 3d at 29, 188 Cal. Rptr. at 416.

118. Wolf, "Enforcing Surrogate Motherhood Agreements," 378-80.

124   *Parental Rights and the Definition of Motherhood*

119. These conflicts include not only those of competing parental rights claims but also the conflict between the commercial and the personal when questions of children and the woman's body as property are considered. Ibid., 381-89.

120. Margaret Townsend, ""Surrogate Mother Agreements: Contemporary Legal Aspects of a Biblical Notion," *University of Richmond Law Review* 16 (1982): 470.

121. Capron and Radin, "Choosing Family Law," 40.

122. Wolf, "Enforcing Surrogate Mother Agreements," 391-92.

123. *In re Baby M*, 217 N.J. Super., 372, 398, 525 A. 2d, 1157, 1170-71 (1987).

124. Phyllis R. Silverman, "Report of Phyllis R. Silverman for use in the Baby M litigation," October 23, 1986, 4. Cited in Field, *Surrogate Motherhood*, 73, n. 89.

125. Cited in Field, *Surrogate Motherhood*, 200, n. 87.

126. See for example, Robin Winkler and Margaret van Keppel, *Relinquishing Mothers in Adoption* (Melbourne, Australia: Institute of Family Studies, 1984) and Suzanne Arms, *To Love and Let Go* (New York: Alfred Knopf, 1986).

127. Silverman, "Report of Phyllis R. Silverman," 5. Cited in Field, *Surrogate Motherhood*, 73-74.

128. See for example, Elizabeth Rose Stanton, "The Rights of the Biological Father: From Adoption and Custody to Surrogate Motherhood," *Vermont Law Review* 12 (1987): 120. Her view is a pure contract position, in which this presumption for the natural father extends to assigning legal parenthood to him and his wife. Thus, the presumption for the natural father is made at the expense of the surrogate. This goes a bit further than simply a guideline for determining custody, but still reflects the bias toward the father.

129. Joan Mahoney, "An Essay on Surrogacy and Feminist Thought," in Gostin, *Surrogate Motherhood:* 183-97,191.

130. Barbara Cohen, "Surrogate Mothers: Whose Baby Is It,?" *American Journal of Law and Medicine* 10 (Fall 1984): 241-85, 271, n. 210.

131. The tender years doctrine states that the mother should have primary custody of young children because of their need for a mother during the "tender years" of their development. On the gender bias built into this doctrine, see Miller, "Surrogate Fatherhood," 169-170. See also Wolf, "Enforcing Surrogate Mother Agreements," 407.

132. Martha A. Field, *Surrogate Motherhood*, 126-130.

133. Rene R, Gilliam, "When a Surrogate Mother Breaks A Promise: The Inappropriateness of the Traditional Best Interests of the Child Standard," *Memphis State University Law Review* 18 (Spring 1988): 530.

134. Wolf, "Enforcing Surrogate Motherhood Agreements," 406.

135. This would be the case especially if commercial surrogacy is banned and there is no significant potential for recruiting poor women to serve as surrogates solely for the money.

136. Wolf, "Enforcing Surrogate Motherhood Agreements," 408.

137. June Carbone, "The Limits of Contract in Family Law: An Analysis of Surrogate Motherhood," *Logos (USA)* 9 (1988): 147.

138. I am assuming that there normally is and should be a connection between law and morality. Though this is not universally accepted, the law has historically sought validation from recognized moral principles. The debate over the relationship between law and morality will be addressed briefly in chapter four.

4

MORAL ANALYSIS OF CURRENT SURROGACY LAW

INTRODUCTION

Beginning in the early 1980s and particularly in the aftermath of the *Baby M* case, many states began to develop legislation to address the complexities of the surrogate motherhood arrangement. They worked from a confusing judicial precedent that began in 1981, which includes seven key cases to be discussed below. The states that have enacted legislation and the courts that have ruled on surrogacy contracts have worked from different approaches to the substantive issues involved in surrogacy. Different positions have been taken on the key issues addressed thus far: commercialization of surrogacy, the definition of mother, clarification of parental rights, and the enforceability of the contract. Internationally, nations in Europe and provinces in Australia and Canada have adopted positions that have also included different approaches to the central issues. The purpose of this chapter is to evaluate both the judicial precedent and the laws that have been enacted by state legislatures according to the moral framework of surrogacy developed to this point. The chapter will also provide a survey of the legal landscape in surrogacy as of July 1993, both nationally and internationally, with a summary of the degree to which these statutes and commission recommendations conform to the moral framework of this work.

This analysis of surrogacy's broader legal background in this chapter includes the following:

I. Analysis of the key court cases that have set an ambiguous judicial precedent.

II. Survey of state laws on surrogacy that have been enacted as of July 1993.

III. Survey of international law, from Europe, Canada and Australia.

IV. Analysis of attempts to place surrogacy within the framework of existing adoption and AID laws.

Until this point in this work, the assumption has been made that what is moral in surrogacy should also be legal. That is, the moral conclusions reached in chapters two and three should be the basis for a surrogacy statute. Specifically, any surrogacy law should reflect the position that child selling is immoral, and forcing a mother to give up her child against her desire in order to enforce a surrogacy contract is also immoral.

The degree to which morality should be translated into law has been the subject of great debate. One of the clearest voices insisting on the separation of law and morality is found in John Stuart Mill's *On Liberty,* which suggests that the primary basis for determining whether an action should be the subject of law is whether there is evidence of clear harm done either to other individuals or to society at large by allowing the action. He stated in his central thesis that, "The only purpose for which power can be rightfully exercised over any member of civilized community against his will is to prevent harm to others."[1] He added that prevention to harm to oneself is not a sufficient basis on which to enact a moral position into law.[2] Mill thus seeks to maximize individual freedom within the bounds of prevention of harm.

The debate over the relationship between law and morality intensified in England in the late 1950s with the publication of the Wolfenden Report, which recommends that homosexual sexual relations no longer be considered punishable by law. The Report suggests that there must be "a realm of morality and immorality which is not the law's business."[3]   By contrast, Lord Patrick Devlin argues that, "the suppression of vice is as much the law's business as the suppression of subversive activities."[4] He argues that every society has the right to do what is necessary to preserve its own existence and to insist on moral conformity by the coercive power of law to insure society's survival.[5] He further insists that society has the right to follow its own moral consensus in determining which actions are serious enough to warrant criminal sanctions.[6]

The debate was advanced in 1958 in the exchange of papers between Oxford Professor H. L. A. Hart and Harvard Law Professor Lon Fuller.[7] While Hart does not deny that legal systems are strongly influenced by morality and that there are places in the law where law and morality intersect, he does deny an inherent connection between law and morality. That is, simply because a law contradicts standards of morality, it does not follow that the law in question is not a valid law. On the other hand, just because something is morally desirable, it does not follow that such a moral rule is a valid law.[8] The validity of a law is dependent on its having been legislated into law by a bona fide legislative body, not on its relation to any moral norm.

Fuller suggests that the distinction between law and morality is not a particularly helpful one and instead proposes the distinction between order and good order. All law produces order in society, yet there is a clear difference between order produced by the law and a good order in which the individual citizens recognize that the law that provides such an order is necessary, right, and just.[9] He insists that a legal system cannot be built on law alone. Rather, the authority of the law depends on the moral attitudes that undergird it, giving it the competence to order society that it claims to have. This is what Fuller calls a "morality external to law."[10] Any valid law must be accepted not only as a law but as a good and just law. Further, a legal system must have an "internal morality," that is, basic norms that clearly point to the source of the laws and a basic procedure by which the laws are made.[11]

While accepting the notion that not all morality can or should be legislated,[12] the present moral analysis of surrogacy law will proceed from the position that effective law requires a moral undergirding such that the laws that are passed can be accepted as valid laws that are in accord with generally accepted standards of morality. That is, the positivist separation of law and morality is rejected as an inadequate foundation for law.

Though the positivists fear that law would be used to enforce an oppressive, specifically religious moral vision, there is nothing inherent in positivism's separation of law and morality that protects society from the threat of totalitarianism. Positivists regard this as an extreme charge, but without any necessary connection to morality that enables laws to be received as good laws, there is the possibility that the law could be used for totalitarian ends. As an example, Fuller cites the tradition of legal positivism in Germany for a century prior to the rise of Hitler and concludes that the positivist attitudes in the German legal profession were actually beneficial to the Nazis.[13] He states, "German legal positivism not only banned from legal science any consideration of the moral ends of law, but it was also indifferent to what I have called the inner morality of law itself. The German lawyer was therefore peculiarly prepared to accept as "law" anything that called itself by that name, was printed at government expense and seemed to come "von oben herab." In light of these considerations, I cannot see either absurdity or perversity in the suggestion that the attitudes prevailing in the German legal profession were helpful to the Nazis."[14]

Though Professor Hart admits that morality can be used to critique laws, moral considerations cannot be used to render laws on the books null and void. Fuller cites the case of the German informer laws that existed under Hitler that formed quite a dilemma for the German legal system as it was being reestablished after World War II. Informer laws provided capital punishment for individuals who spoke out against the German government under Hitler. They became a convenient method to dispose of enemies, and even spouses, during the period in which they were in force. Here law was used for a most perverse end, and as a result of moral considerations, post-war German courts declared that these laws were not valid laws. Yet Professor Hart insists that people's statements against the government were genuinely unlawful, and he would correct this gravely unjust law by a retroactive statute. The difference is that Hart still sees the prior law as a valid law, and Fuller, with the postwar Germans who were trying to salvage their legal system, would see the informer law as inherently invalid due to moral considerations. As Fuller states it, "The fundamental postulate of positivism--that law must be strictly severed from morality--seems to deny the possibility of any bridge between the obligation to obey and other moral obligations."[15]

A second tension with legal positivism is its inability to resolve adequately the "hard cases" that inevitable arise. As Professor Ronald Dworkin suggests, the hard cases are invariably solved by appeal to principle; that is, judges in these cases decide them with respect to their own political morality.[16] There is more involved in resolving hard cases, ones that the law does not directly address, than simply resolving interpretive difficulties, as Professor Hart suggests.[17] Rather, one must appeal to principles that have moral considerations at the core.

For law to be effective in the long run apart from excessive coercion, laws must be seen as good and just laws, which are necessary and right. Morality thus provides a framework in which the making of laws takes place, and provides the basis on which laws are accepted, not only as laws per se, but as good laws to which individuals can give their voluntary obedience.

Just because one recognizes that there needs to be a moral foundation for law, it does not follow that all morality must be enacted into law. For a legal system to be effective, the laws must be seen as consistent with widely held standards of morality. That does not mean that everything dictated by these standards must be the object of legislation. For instance, the law regularly distinguishes between reasonable precautions and works of supererogation. It is not legally required for someone to jump into the river to save a drowning person, even though moral demands might dictate otherwise. However, the law would require a precautionary railing on the bridge to prevent people from accidentally falling in.

Similarly, private activity between consenting adults is generally considered an area the law must leave alone, falling under right to privacy. Yet society has made dueling illegal, even though it fits under this heading of privacy. In most states, prostitution is also illegal, and it too is in the area of privacy. Though the law does not generally dictate in areas of private morality, that is not an absolute. In most cases, the law should be kept to a minimum in these areas.

When it comes to commercial surrogacy, it would appear that it, too, belongs in the area protected by the right to privacy. Indeed, many advocates of surrogacy appeal to the notion of procreative liberty that is inherent in the right to privacy to support the practice. Why should commercial surrogacy be prohibited by law when private behavior such as adultery is not? The reason is that there are constitutional as well as moral issues involved in surrogacy. The key moral issues in surrogacy are at the heart of the constitutional provisions that are violated by commercial, contract-enforced surrogacy. It was concluded in chapter two that surrogacy constituted the purchase and sale of children, in violation not only of basic moral principles that protect the dignity of human beings, but also in violation of the Thirteenth Amendment, which is based in large part on such moral principles. Similarly, it was concluded in chapter three that the right of a mother to associate with her child is such a fundamental right (clearly implicit in the right to privacy) that it generally cannot be stripped from her against her will. Thus, surrogacy contracts that are enforced when the surrogate desires to keep the child violate not only moral but constitutional principles. The intersection of morality and the law in the Constitution suggests that the moral considerations in surrogacy should be translated into a law that prohibits commercial, contract-enforced surrogacy. This intersection between morality and the law in the Constitution is what makes surrogacy different from adultery, and is the reason adultery is legally permitted and surrogacy should be prohibited. It is hoped that this helps explain why such an extended discussion of child selling in chapter two and the right of a mother to associate with her child (of course, the definition of mother is critical to this latter point) is included in this work. Surrogacy law should reflect the moral conclusions not solely because they are moral considerations, but because there are constitutional considerations at stake too, that are undergirded by the moral conclusions drawn in this work.

JUDICIAL PRECEDENT

The following cases are the major surrogacy cases in the United States. Though not an exhaustive discussion of every surrogacy case that has gone to court to be resolved, this discussion includes the major precedent-setting cases that have given direction to legislators in formulating state laws. Though the cases included do not address each of the key issues in surrogacy, and though different approaches have been taken by different courts, taken as a whole the judicial precedent gives an indication of how the courts have attempted to resolve many of the key issues in surrogacy. Each case will be presented, including the relevant facts and the heart the decision of the judge or judges, followed by an analysis of the key issues discussed to this point in the work (commercialization, definition of motherhood, parental rights and enforceability of the contract). The cases are arranged chronologically.

Doe v. Kelley (1981)[18]

John and Jane Doe, pseudonyms for the actual couple, had been married since 1965, and had two children, ages eleven and seven. The court was not able to determine whether those children were born from their marriage or adopted, since the Does were non-responsive when asked this question during the proceedings. Jane Doe had undergone a tubal ligation, rendering her unable to have children, and they hired Mary Roe (again a pseudonym), John Doe's secretary, for $5,000 plus medical expenses and continued medical insurance, sick leave, and pregnancy disability insurance from Doe, to bear his child as a surrogate. In effect, he would continue to pay her during the time she missed from work due to the pregnancy. The reason for the surrogacy arrangement was to provide the Does a child that would be biologically related to John Doe, suggesting that their two children were adopted. The arrangement was brokered by attorney Noel Keane, and he represented the couple in the proceedings.

The couple had filed suit against the Michigan Attorney General, seeking to have the Michigan law that prohibited exchange of money for adoption and "related proceedings" declared unconstitutional. The lower court ruled against them, and the decision was affirmed on appeal.

The couple argued that the law infringed on their right to privacy as established by *Carey v. Population Services*[19] and *Griswold v. Connecticut*.[20] They appealed specifically to these two cases to show that the due process clause protects liberty of personal choice in family matters.

The Appeals Court recognized a right to procreative liberty as a fundamental interest protected by the constitutional right to privacy, but denied that this could be extended to paid surrogacy contracts. Judge Kelly stated,

While the decision to bear or beget a child has thus been found to be a fundamental interest protected by the right to privacy, we do not view this right as a valid prohibition to state interference in the plaintiffs' contractual arrangement. The statute in question does not directly prohibit John Doe and Mary Roe from having the child as planned. It acts instead to preclude plaintiffs from paying consideration in conjunction with their use of the state's adoption procedures. In effect, the plaintiffs' contractual agreement disclosed a desire to use the adoption code to change the legal status of the child. We do not perceive this goal as within the realm of fundamental interests protected by the right to privacy from reasonable governmental regulation.[21]

The decision thus did not prohibit all surrogacy arrangements, only those that involve a fee to the surrogate mother beyond reasonable medical expenses. The court saw the fee arrangement as clearly inconsistent with state adoption law and refused to honor the plaintiffs' implied request that contract law be applied here. The judge rightly maintained a distinction between the right of the couple to utilize the services of a third party in procreation, and the right to pay her a fee. Though Judge Kelly did not specifically identify surrogacy as baby selling in the decision, his appeal to adoption law throughout as the framework for his decision makes it clear that he is treating surrogacy in the same way that the law treats black market adoption, as essentially the sale of children. Since there was no desire of the surrogate to keep the child, issues of parental rights, the definition of motherhood, and enforceability of the contract did not arise and were not addressed.

Syrkowski v. Appleyard (1983)[22]

In a non-adversarial proceeding, George Syrkowski initiated an action under the Michigan Paternity Act to have himself declared the legal father of a child born to Corinne Appleyard as a result of a surrogacy arrangement. She did not desire to keep the child, and her husband submitted a statement of non-consent, indicating that he did not consent to his wife's artificial insemination, thereby revoking any claim to parental rights. The parties agreed that Syrkowski was the natural father, that he and his wife should be awarded full custody, that his name should be entered on the birth certificate as the legal father and that the child should bear his surname.

The Michigan attorney general argued at the hearing that the circuit court did not have authority to extend the Paternity Act to surrogate motherhood contracts. Under the Michigan law, when a woman, with her husband's consent, bears a child as a result of artificial insemination, her husband is presumed to be the child's father, though this can be challenged. Even though Appleyard responded with his statement of non-consent, the trial court refused to grant paternity to Syrkowski.

On appeal, the decision of the lower court was affirmed. The appeals court determined that Syrkowski's petition for paternity was beyond the intent of the Paternity Act. With a strong appeal to the original intent of the statute when written,[23] the court insisted that the Paternity Act was designed to provide financial support for children born out of wedlock (and in most states, to keep those children from the stigma of illegitimacy), and that the surrogacy arrangement did not fall under the scope of the act, and thus the challenge to the presumption of the law was not accepted.

The court appealed to *Doe v. Kelley* in raising the question of whether surrogacy arrangements were against public policy. It did not make any decision on the legitimacy of surrogacy contracts per se, but was hesitant to give approval to the arrangement apart from further study of the effects on all the parties involved: "We view the surrogate mother arrangement with caution as we approach an unexplored area in the law which, without a doubt, can have a profound effect on the lives of our people. The courts should not be called upon to enlarge the scope of the Paternity Act to encompass circumstances never contemplated thereby.   Studied legislation is needed before surrogate arrangements are recognized as proposed under the facts submitted herein."[24]

In this case, even though the enforceability of the contract was not at issue, the issues of parental rights were addressed by the court. The decision here shows the obstacle that artificial insemination laws place in the way of surrogacy. Although the presumption of paternity is rebuttable, the court refused to allow a surrogate's husband to revoke parental rights, even when it was beyond reasonable doubt that he was not the natural father. Thus, it would appear at this point that there would be little recourse to contracting parents in Michigan through the courts, since the court appealed to the legislature to provide direction for future court action.

Since there was no dispute between the parties concerning custody of the child, and since the Appleyards did not desire to exercise their parental rights under Michigan's Paternity Act, the presumption of paternity should have been conclusively rebuttable here. In cases of altruistic surrogacy, when the natural father and his wife wish to adopt the child and are not opposed by the surrogate or her husband, the surrogate should be able to waive her parental rights so that the child can be adopted by the natural father and his wife. However, the reason it was so important to obtain an order of filiation that had Syrkowski's name on the birth certificate and that awarded him full custody of the child is so that state laws prohibiting payment for adoption could be circumvented. In most surrogacy cases, the natural father's wife must still adopt the child, and thus the fee paid to Mrs. Appleyard was still for her waiver of parental rights, thereby violating state law. That is why the proposed order of filiation was written to include full custody being awarded to Syrkowski, thus enabling them to avoid the obstacles of adoption law altogether. Had this case not involved such an attempt to avoid the adoption laws, the Court should have allowed the transfer of parental rights to occur, but prohibited the payment of the fee to the surrogate. Though it is not clear the degree to which the existence of the fee played an important part in the judge's decision, the court nevertheless refused the waiver of parental rights on the grounds that the Paternity Act could not in general be extended to surrogacy. In refusing the order, as a matter of public policy, the court placed a significant obstacle in the way of surrogacy.

In this case, the waiver of parental rights by Appleyard should have been recognized. The child was assured of both legitimacy and support by the Syrkowskis. Though the court did not comment on the definition of motherhood per se, it is clear from the decision that the surrogate was considered the legal mother (and her husband the legal father). However, she should have had the right to waive her parental rights, though not for a fee. The fee was not specifically addressed, though it seems that the court was hesitant to give any encouragement to commercial surrogacy without further public policy analysis. In this case, the fee should have been returned and the transfer of parental rights allowed, thus treating this as a case of altruistic surrogacy. If the surrogate refused to return the fee, then it is difficult to see how the court could have allowed a waiver of parental rights without it being the sale of a child.

In re Baby Girl (1983)[25]

In this Kentucky case, the issue was the same as in *Syrkowski*, only the claim was initiated by the surrogate who wished to relinquish parental rights. The decision and the reasoning were practically identical to that in *Syrkowski*.

This action came to court as the result of a petition of the surrogate and her husband, who wished to terminate their parental rights under the Kentucky Termination Act.[26] At the time of the petition, the child had been turned over to the contracting father, who had left the state to return to his home, since he was not a resident of the state of Kentucky. The couple petitioned the court to terminate parental rights, transfer custody of the child to the biological father, hold him to be the natural father, and issue a birth certificate for the child that named him as the legal father.

The court denied the motion for the couple's order of termination, with a rigid adherence to the presumption of paternity. The decision was based on two principal arguments. First, the presumption of paternity is so strong that a statement of artificial insemination is not adequate to rebut it. The court ruled that, "A long line of cases holds that a child born in wedlock is presumed to be the legitimate child of the husband and wife. Evidence that the child's mother is married and that there was opportunity for procreation within the period of gestation raises a conclusive presumption that the child is the husband's legitimate child. The mere affidavit as to artificial insemination without other positive proof of non-access is not sufficient for this court to assume and adjudge the donor to be the natural and biological father of the child."[27] It would appear that had the contracting father provided additional evidence of his biological connection to the child, the court may have decided differently. "The presumption is so great that it cannot be overcome except by evidence of strong character and so convincing as to remove question of reasonable doubt."[28] What would have constituted convincing evidence is not clear from the decision, but this line of reasoning does not place an insurmountable obstacle in the way of surrogacy arrangements.

However, the second argument of the court makes it more difficult for surrogates and contracting couples in the absence of clear legislation. Here the court's reasoning was very similar to the Michigan court in *Syrkowski*. The judge ruled that surrogacy arrangements were beyond the scope that was intended by the Kentucky Termination Act. He stated, "At the outset, it appeared to this court that the parties and their counsel were seeking legal determinations far beyond the scope permitted by the Termination Act as enacted by the Kentucky legislature. The Termination Act is not a paternity act and it contains no provision under which a court may adjudge paternity of a child as sought in this action."[29] Thus even if clear proof of paternity could be established, there was no way the law could be applied in this case, since it dealt with surrogacy, not ordinary adoption, in which the child was placed privately by individuals, not by the appropriate state agency. The judge stated that "The termination statute was enacted by the legislature for the purpose of providing a procedure by which a birth parent may terminate his or her parental rights and place custody of the child with a licensed child-placing agency for adoption. By such procedure the birth parents were removed from the adoption proceedings and this contributed greatly to the security and stability of the placement. In this case there has been placement of the child by petitioners and acceptance of the child without any written permission or authority from the Cabinet of Human Resources."[30] The only significant difference here was that the child was privately placed, as opposed to being placed by a public agency. Even though in surrogacy the contracting couple adopts the child,[31] the court denied this parallel and ruled that the adoption laws essentially do not apply to surrogacy arrangements.

Clearly the reason for prohibiting private placement is to ensure the child's best interests, and avoid a black market adoption situation. As in *Syrkowski*, it would seem that the waiver of parental rights should have been allowed, particularly if the natural father were to undergo a blood test to provide conclusive proof of paternity. However, the fee should not be allowed, and as in *Syrkowski*, should the surrogate refuse to return the fee, the presumption of paternity with which the Court worked should be applied. It appears that the court was attempting to prohibit private placement adoption for a fee by invoking the presumption of paternity and not allowing consent to artificial insemination to rebut the presumption.

People v. Keane (1985)[32]

Though not a surrogacy case per se, this case has important implications for the practice, particularly the termination of parental rights necessary for a surrogacy arrangement to be completed.

Attorney Noel Keane was charged with illegally placing a child for adoption and giving money for such placement. The latter charge was dismissed in the lower court, and the dismissal was affirmed by the court of appeals. The former charge is the focal point of the Appeals Court decision.

In this case, a Trisha Shearer, a fifteen year old girl with an unwanted pregnancy, and her mother, Judy Wood, contacted Keane about placing the yet unborn child for adoption. Marvin and Sandra Barsky, a California couple, agreed to adopt the child and paid all of Shearer's medical expenses as well as the cost of her stay at a home for unwed mothers. On the day that Shearer and the child were discharged, the child was transferred to the custody of the Barskys, although Shearer was having serious regrets about the adoption and was emotionally very upset. Keane intervened and physically took the baby from the attending nurse and handed the child to the Barskys, who promptly flew home to California. Keane eventually engineered the return of the child to the custody of Shearer, but was charged with violation of the Michigan Adoption Code, which states, "A child shall not be placed in a home for the purpose of adoption until an order terminating parental rights has been entered."[33]

The part of the decision that relates to surrogacy is that private brokers are not lawful administrators of an adoption. The decision stated that "under the code, direct consent adoptions are prohibited. Private parties, including lawyers, can no longer act as middlemen between the biological mother and the adoptive parents. Only licensed private agencies, the Department of Social Services and the probate courts can arrange and approve adoptions."[34] Since adoption of the child born to a surrogate by at least the wife of the contracting couple is essential to complete a surrogacy contract, this places a serious obstacle in the way of fulfilling the contracts. This decision is the precursor to the later law established in Michigan that criminalizes surrogacy brokering. In addition, a child cannot be placed in an adoptive home until a court order for the termination of parental rights has been entered. This is done in accordance with adoption law, which gives the birth mother an opportunity to change her mind subsequent to an original statement of consent to relinquish parental rights. This again places a serious obstacle to the pre-conception consent to waive parental rights called for by most surrogacy contracts.

This case does not directly address the fee to the surrogate, though it is at the heart of the prohibition of private placement adoptions. The court rightly prohibited the use of brokers to arrange adoption contracts. Further, in refusing to allow Keane to privately arrange custody prior to the adoption order being finalized, the court rightly recognized the right of the birth mother to change her mind before the waiver of parental rights becomes irrevocable. It is assumed that the mother is the woman who gave birth to the child, and the enforceability of the contract was not at issue.

Surrogate Parenting Associates, Inc. v. Commonwealth of Kentucky (1986)[35]

This case constitutes the first comprehensive surrogacy case, in which the court ruled on more than one aspect of the practice. Prior to this, the courts had ruled on only specific elements of the surrogacy arrangement in question. Here, however, the legitimacy of surrogacy in general is addressed.

In this case, heard finally by the Kentucky Supreme Court, the attorney general had brought a suit seeking to revoke the corporate charter of Surrogate Parenting Associates, Inc. (SPA). The suit claimed that the operation of SPA violated three Kentucky laws: (1) KRS 199.590(2), which prohibits the exchange of money or other consideration in relation to an adoption; (2) KRS 199.601(2), which prohibits voluntary termination of parental rights prior to five days after the birth of the child; (3) KRS 199.500(5), which states that consent to adoption will not be valid if given prior to five days before birth of the child.[36] The lower court ruled in favor of the corporation. It was reversed by the court of appeals, and the appeals court was reversed by the Kentucky Supreme Court, which held for SPA. The Supreme Court held that surrogacy did not constitute baby selling, and thus did not violate KRS 199.590(2). The judges stated in their decision that "The fundamental question is whether SPA's involvement in the surrogate parenting procedure should be construed as participation in the buying and selling of babies as prohibited by KRS 199.590(2). We conclude that it does not, that there are fundamental differences between the surrogate parenting procedure in which SPA participates and the buying and selling of children as prohibited by KRS 199.500(2) which place this surrogate parenting procedure beyond the purview of present legislation."[37]

The judges interpreted the law as intending to keep the public from the coercive and exploitive forces of a black market in babies. They reasoned that there was a fundamental difference between surrogacy and adoption, in that in the former, the decision to give up one's child is made prior to conception, presumably as a result of a rational, well thought out decision, not under the pressure of an unwanted pregnancy. Surrogacy, in which the infertile wife is alleviated actually is a parallel to artificial insemination to alleviate a husband's infertility. The judges stated that "The process [of surrogacy] is not biologically different from the reverse situation where the husband is infertile and the wife conceives by artificial insemination. No one suggests that where the husband is infertile and conception is induced by artificial insemination of the wife that the participants involved have violated the statutes now in place."[38]

The second key argument of the justices involved the amendment of KRS 199.590, the statute in question, to include in vitro fertilization as a legitimate form of assisted reproduction. The attorney general argued that the amendment's silence on surrogacy strongly implied the legislature's disapproval of the practice, an implication that the court rejected.[39]   Instead, they extended the permission granted to in vitro fertilization to include surrogacy, as a form of medically assisted conception. The court ruled that "The in vitro fertilization procedure sanctioned by the statute and the surrogate parenting procedure are both similar in that both enable a childless couple to have a baby biologically related to one of them when they could not do so otherwise. The fact that the statute now expressly sanctions one way of doing this does not rule out other ways by implication. In an area so fundamental as medically assisting a childless couple to have a child, such a prohibition should not be implied."[40]

The judges affirmed the circuit court opinion that the legal relationship between natural father and child takes surrogacy out of the realm of adoption and beyond the reach of adoption law. Thus, the only legal question in the event of a dispute is one of custody, resolved by the best interests of the child standard. Regarding the waiver of parental rights, the court held that the surrogacy contract (as would be all custody contracts in Kentucky) was voidable, but not illegal and void. That is, the surrogate has the right to change her mind in accordance with existing adoption law.[41] Should she change her mind, the parties would be in the same position as any mother, father, and child who were not under the surrogacy contract.

In one of the dissenting opinions, Judge Vance denied the contention of the majority that surrogacy did not constitute baby selling. He seemed to take the intent of the statute in question (KRS 199.590(2)) further than simply protecting the public from the excesses of the baby black market. Rather, the simple fact that children are being exchanged for money violates the law, irrespective of the circumstances surrounding the exchange, whether it is undertaken under duress or not.[42]

In a second dissent, Judge Wintersheimer pressed the necessity of the adoption framework when dealing with the surrogacy fee. He insisted that it is assumed that adoption is an essential part of the arrangement. He stated, "Once the obvious certainty of the infertile wife's presence is recognized, it cannot be logically denied that the certainty of adoption must logically follow. The purpose of the language of the contract is merely to avoid KRS 199.590(2). It is an obvious subterfuge."[43] He further argues that surrogacy threatens the stability of the family, opens the possibility of exploitation of women, and gives a second party (the adopting couple) the right to control one's fundamental right to reproductive privacy.

This is the first of the court decisions that gave validity to surrogacy contracts, though not entirely without limits. The fee was found legal, but the surrogate has the right to change her mind and keep the child, within Kentucky's adoption law framework.

Clearly the dissenting opinions are more in keeping with the moral analysis of surrogacy undertaken in this work. Judge Vance rightly recognized that the exchange of money for parental rights constitutes an unlawful, morally objectionable form of baby selling, regardless of the circumstances surrounding the exchange. He recognized that with a portion of the fee being held in escrow until parental rights are transferred, it is difficult to see how that does not constitute baby selling.   The majority's insistence that surrogacy is fundamentally different from black market adoptions is overstated, as was shown in chapter two. The majority appealed to procreative liberty, specifically the *Carey* decision, to give a basis for allowing surrogacy. Yet they failed to distinguish between the right to arrange surrogacy and the right to sell the child that results from that arrangement. Further, they insisted that when the natural father is involved in the transaction, as in surrogacy, applying the term adoption is not appropriate. Yet they did not recognize that the natural father's paternity does not give him sole rights to the child; at best, he has the equivalent of joint tenancy in property. The fee functions as the purchase price for the other party's interest in the property, making it difficult to escape the charge of baby selling. Finally, the majority insisted that when the Kentucky statute in question was amended to include in vitro fertilization, that extended to surrogacy as well. Yet as Judge Wintersheimer pointed out in his dissent, the legislature had other opportunities to adopt legislation that would allow paid surrogacy and did not.[44] He concluded that the legislature did indeed reject surrogacy as a violation of public policy.

However, in cases of a contractual dispute, the Kentucky decision does reflect the moral analysis of this work.   Though motherhood is not technically defined, it was not necessary here since the woman who gave birth also contributed the egg. The decision rightly allows a surrogate time to change her mind before her waiver of parental rights becomes final, and considers that the contracts are not inherently void, but voidable if contested by the surrogate. Should that happen, parental rights are vested in the natural father and the surrogate. The issue of custody determination is not addressed, though it may be reasonably assumed that the court would decide it on the best interests of the child standard.

In the Matter of Baby M (1988)[45]

In this widely publicized case, William Stern had a special interest in fathering a child to whom he was genetically related, since he was the only living member of his blood line, most of his relatives having been killed during the Holocaust. His wife, Elizabeth, had a mild case of multiple sclerosis and she believed that the health risk of pregnancy was significant, though she was technically not infertile.

The Infertility Center of New York matched the Sterns with Mary Beth Whitehead, a woman of moderate means with two children already. She agreed to artificial insemination and to surrender custody of the child upon birth for a $10,000 fee and payment of all associated medical expenses. If she miscarried prior to the fifth month, she would receive no fee, but if miscarriage came after the fifth month, or if the child was stillborn, she would receive $1,000. After the child was born, Whitehead deeply regretted her decision to surrender custody. At her request, the Sterns allowed her to take the child for a week, after which time she fled the area with the child. The child was later recovered in Florida by force and returned to the Sterns. Whitehead then sued for custody of the child.

In a decision handed down in March 1987, the lower court ruled that the surrogacy contract was valid.[46] Judge Harvey Sorkow ruled that Whitehead was not coerced into signing the contract and therefore it should be enforced. Using the analogy between sperm donation and a woman renting her womb, he ruled that the equal protection clause entitled a woman to sell her reproductive capacities. The court further reasoned that since the legislature did not have surrogacy contracts in mind when it enacted the adoption laws in question, they were irrelevant. Thus, the laws governing termination of parental rights and transfer of consideration for adoption did not apply to surrogacy. The Court concluded that Whitehead breached a valid contract when she refused to surrender the child and give up custody.

Even though the contract was upheld, a custody hearing was held since the best interests of the child were the primary concern. At the hearing, the Whiteheads were strongly criticized, based on their refusal to obey the court order and their subsequent flight from the state. Ironically, Whitehead's fitness as a mother was questioned on the basis of her refusal to give up her child and the lengths to which she went to insure that she could keep the child. The judge awarded custody to the Sterns since they would be able to provide a more stable home for the child. This was later criticized by the New Jersey Supreme Court for giving too much weight to socio-economic standing at the expense of relational qualities that constitute parenthood.[47]

On appeal, the decision was reversed, though the custody outcome remained the same. In February 1988, Judge Robert Wilentz, writing for a unanimous court, ruled that surrogacy contracts violated state laws that prohibit the transfer of money for adoptions. The court used a family law model instead of the contract law scheme followed by the lower court, to decide the case. The court determined that surrogacy is, in effect, baby selling and there are some things, including human life, that cannot be bought and sold. They cited as evidence the fee structure of the contract, in particular the fact that significantly less money was to be paid to Whitehead if the baby was miscarried or stillborn. In their judgment, clearly the Sterns were paying for a child and full parental rights. Judge Wilentz stated, "One of surrogacy's basic purposes, to achieve adoption of a child through private placement 'is very much disfavored.' Its use of money for this purpose--and we have no doubt whatsoever that the money is being paid to obtain an adoption and not, as the Sterns argue, for the personal services of Mary Beth Whitehead--is illegal and perhaps criminal."[48]

The court also cited New Jersey laws that supported the fundamental rights of genetic parents to participate in raising their children. Since Whitehead was not an unfit mother and had not abandoned her child, there was no good reason to deny her right of association. In addition, the contract violated laws that stipulated a time period for a birth mother to change her mind prior to giving up her child irrevocably for adoption. Further, the contract violated established New Jersey public policy on custody that gave the natural parents the right to determine who would raise the child. Precedent dictated that that decision cannot be made prior to the child's birth. Judge Wilentz stated, "In addition to the inducement of money, there is the coercion of contract: the natural mother's irrevocable agreement, prior to birth, even prior to conception, to surrender the child to the adoptive couple. Such an agreement is totally unenforceable in private placement adoptions. The surrogacy contract violates the policy of this state that the rights of natural parents are equal concerning their child, the father's right no greater than the mother's. The whole purpose of the surrogacy contract was to give the father the exclusive right to the child by destroying the rights of the mother."[49]

The adoption of the child by Elizabeth Stern (facilitated by Judge Sorkow immediately after the lower court ruling) was voided and the Whiteheads were to receive visitation rights to be decided by a lower court. They did not receive custody since the court held that the best interests of the child would be served by the Sterns receiving custody. Even though Whitehead announced a pregnancy by another man shortly thereafter and separated from her husband (later marrying the other man), visitation rights were not terminated.

The court was critical of the Infertility Center of New York for inadequately screening Whitehead and for allowing money to be the primary motivating factor in the arrangement:

Mrs. Whitehead was examined and psychologically evaluated. The Sterns never asked to see it and were content with the assumption that the Infertility Center had made an evaluation and had concluded that there was no danger that the surrogate mother would change her mind. It is apparent that the profit motive got the better of the Infertility Center. Although the evaluation was made, it was not put to any use and understandably so, for the psychologist warned that Mrs. Whitehead demonstrated certain traits that might make surrender of the child difficult and that there should be further inquiry into this issue in connection with her surrogacy. To inquire further, however, might have jeopardized the Infertility Center's fee. The record indicates that neither Mrs. Whitehead nor the Sterns were told of this fact, a fact that might have ended their surrogacy arrangement.[50]

This was one of the few surrogacy cases to this point in which the surrogate changed her mind about surrendering custody of the child, and it illustrates the variety of complications that could occur. For example, if William Stern dies, even though Elizabeth Stern is the social mother of the child and has established the stronger bond with her, custody could revert back to Whitehead. At the least, she could make a strong case, being the natural mother, though the court would be guided by the best interests standard. Similarly, should the Sterns divorce, Whitehead would again have grounds to mount a custody challenge, since the social mother has no legal parental rights. Then the situation would parallel the recent Orange County, California, case in which the contracting couple divorced and three people sued for custody of the child.[51] In addition, there could be issues of child support in the future. Suppose that as *Baby M* grows up, she desires to live with Whitehead. Would Stern be liable for child support? A good case could be made that he would. Similarly, should Whitehead become financially able, perhaps through book or film royalties, would she become liable for child support? Again, a good case could be made that she would.

This case continues the precedent set in Michigan that discourages surrogacy, without prohibiting it outright. The fee is considered the unlawful sale of a child. The contract is not enforceable, since it violates the surrogate's fundamental right to associate with the child she has borne. Should the surrogate contest the contract, she is considered the legal mother with full maternal rights. Yet it contrasts with the ruling handed down in Kentucky in the *Surrogate Parenting Associates* case and with the *Johnson v. Calvert* case in California.

Johnson v. Calvert (1990)[52]

This was the first case of gestational surrogacy to be contested and receive wide public attention. Mark and Cris Calvert hired Anna Johnson during the fall and winter of 1989-90 to be a gestational surrogate for their child, carrying an embryo that had been created by in vitro fertilization, using the egg and sperm of the Calverts (Cris Calvert was able to produce an egg, but not carry a pregnancy). She was to be paid $10,000 plus associated medical expenses for giving birth and surrendering custody of the child to the Calverts. On January 15, 1990, the three parties signed an agreement stipulating that Anna Johnson would relinquish the child at birth and make no claims to parental rights. On January 19, 1990, a fertilized embryo of the Calverts' (accomplished by IVF) was implanted in Johnson's uterus. The child was born on September 19, 1990.

Toward the beginning of the seventh month of pregnancy, Johnson began to have second thoughts about giving up the child she was bearing. One month prior to birth, she sued for custody of the child. When the child was born, temporary custody was awarded to the Calverts, with daily visitation allowed to

Johnson. These were later reduced to twice weekly until the final custody hearing.

Orange County, California Superior Court Judge Richard N. Parslow ruled that the surrogacy contract was valid and not inherently exploitive. He drew a clear distinction between this case and *Baby M* when he stated at the beginning of the decision, "This is, as we have talked about, an in vitro fertilization embryo transfer case. It's not an adoption relinquishment case, it's not a baby selling case, it's not a Baby M type case where we had natural parents on two sides of a situation competing. It's none of those things."[53] Since Johnson had no genetic stake in the child, no parental rights were recognized for her. He compared Johnson's role to a foster parent who does not at any time during performance of that function assume any parental rights. He stated, "I further find that Anna's relationship is analogous to that of a foster parent providing care, protection and nurture during the period of time that the natural mother, Crispina Calvert, was unable to care for the child. However, a surrogate carrying a genetic child for a couple does not acquire parental rights."[54]

Parslow ruled that genetics took precedence over gestation, and that the best interests of the child would be served by custody with the Calverts, in any case. Even if Johnson did have a genetic relationship with the child, the Calverts would likely have been given custody under the best interests standard. There was testimony that undermined Johnson's fitness as a mother. Her roommate testified to the neglect of her current child, and the fact that she was a single mother with minimal financial resources and difficulty holding a job. These factors clearly contributed to the custody decision. In addition, the sincerity of her bond to the child was questioned, since it was never mentioned until the seventh month, and then in contradiction to numerous earlier statements to the Calverts that she was carrying *their* child.

Judge Parslow essentially applied contract law to the dispute, since, in his view, this was not an adoption case, nor was it two competing natural parents vying for custody. He stated, "I'm finding that in my view surrogacy contracts in the in vitro fertilization cases are not void nor against public policy. I believe that provision (regarding relinquishment of the child) is enforceable by either specific performance, arguably even by habeas corpus, if necessary."[55]

Since there were no parental rights to be claimed by the surrogate, Judge Parslow reasoned that the fee did not constitute baby selling, since by definition it was not paid for the relinquishment of parental rights. Rather it was paid for gestational services rendered. He stated, "I see no problem with someone getting paid for your pain and suffering. And so if it's agreeable that they be paid for that service, they are not selling a baby, they are selling, again, the pain and suffering, the discomfort, that which goes with carrying a child to term."[56]

Judge Parslow encouraged the legislature to make appropriate surrogacy laws to prevent these kinds of public custody battles. His recommendations deal only with gestational surrogacy and include the following:[57] (1) Intensive psychological evaluation of the parties should be conducted by an agency that is not in the business of brokering surrogacy arrangements; (2) The wife of the contracting couple, that is, the genetic mother should be medically unable to carry a child to term; (3) There should be a clear understanding prior to implantation of the fertilized embryo that the child will be transferred to the custody of the genetic parents immediately after birth and, that the surrogate has no parental rights; (4) Motherhood should be redefined since separation of the genetic and gestational aspects is now possible; and (5) The surrogate should have previously carried at least one child to term. However, until the legislature enacts any of these recommendations into law, the decision has clearly opened the door to at least gestational surrogacy in a way that the *Baby M* case did not. It is not clear if Judge Parslow's ruling would have been different had Johnson been both the genetic and gestational mother of the child. Though the final custody outcome was the same in this case and the *Baby M* case, in that the contracting couple received custody of the child, the approach taken was quite different. The California court emphasized contract law as opposed to the adoption law framework followed in New Jersey. In doing so, the California court redefined motherhood. The mother in this case is clearly the woman who made the genetic contribution to the child. The reason that adoption law did not apply here, according to the decision, is that there were no parental rights to be waived. Judge Parslow took the genetic contribution to be the only one that mattered in determining parental rights, and in doing so, ignored the substantial contribution of the woman who gestates the child.

As was shown in chapter three, the gestational mother contributes not only nine months of "sweat equity" in the child but also makes a significant contribution to the temperament of the child. In view of the analysis of this work, Judge Parslow assigned motherhood to the wrong person. The contract should not have been enforceable, since enforcing it involved violating a fundamental right to associate with the child she bore. Neither should the fee have been allowed, since it indeed did pay, in part, for the transfer of parental rights. However, it is not difficult to see how Parslow's ruling is consistent with his definition of motherhood. If Anna Johnson is not the mother, then the fee cannot be paid for transfer of parental rights and can be for services only. Further, if she is not the mother, then there is no fundamental right that is violated if the contract is enforced. Rather, in his view, the fundamental rights of the parents, that is, the Calverts, to associate with their child are violated by not enforcing the contract. This may explain the extreme measures, even by habeas corpus, that Parslow recommended to insure that the terms of the contract are followed. The approach taken by Parslow demonstrates the centrality of properly defining motherhood, since the other key issues in surrogacy are dependent on one's view concerning who is the mother. His ruling was affirmed by the appeals court and the California Supreme Court.

Moschetta v. Moschetta (1991)[58]

The most recent surrogacy case to make headlines, also in Orange County, California, has exposed further complications that can arise in surrogacy arrangements. In June 1990, Elvira Jordan bore a child, Marissa, from her egg and the sperm of Robert Moschetta. In November, he separated from his wife Cynthia and took the child. In filing for legal separation, Cynthia filed for custody, even though the child had no genetic link to her. She claimed that significant bonding with the child had taken place and that her contribution as the social mother should weigh equally with her estranged husband's genetic contribution. Jordan also filed for custody, claiming that she did not enter into the surrogate contract to bear a child for a couple that was not going to stay together to provide a stable home for the child. She further alleged that the Moschettas put on a facade of marital stability during the pregnancy, since they knew that Jordan was unlikely to surrender the child unless she was convinced that their marriage was stable. She claimed a parental right based on her genetic and gestational contributions to the child. So three "parents" all claimed a right to custody.

On January 15, 1991, Superior Court Judge John Woolley awarded temporary custody to Robert Moschetta, the natural father, visitation rights to his estranged wife, and neither custody nor visitation rights for the surrogate/natural mother. However, on appeal, in April 1991, Jordan was granted parental rights and the Superior Court Judge Nancy Wieben Stock ruled that she was entitled to shared custody with the natural father.[59] In effect, she was to play the role of day care provider, since she was to enjoy her custody of the child during the time when the father was away at work. He would have the child in the evenings and on weekends, and she would have the child for forty hours weekly during the day.[60] There is no appeal pending.

The issues addressed in this case concern parental rights and enforceability of the agreement, not the fee paid to the surrogate. The judge correctly recognized the parental rights of Elvira Jordan and allowed her to share custody of the child. What makes this case difficult is the role of the social mother and the clear bonding that had taken place between her and the child. But since it is often not in the child's best interests to have custody divided between two parents who do not get along, and who are even hostile as is the case here, it is not surprising that the judge did not award any rights or visitation to Cynthia Moschetta. While wanting to recognize the important role of the social mother, there had been no adoption proceedings undertaken in order to get parental rights transferred. With the recognition of Jordan as the mother and with the child's best interest mandating not splitting custody between three parents, Cynthia Moschetta was left with no legal stake in the child. Though it does seem unfair to her, it is justifiable given the definition of motherhood presented in chapter three.

CONCLUSION

Though not without exceptions, the judicial precedent set by the above cases is one of caution about encouraging the practice of commercial surrogacy. Though no case has addressed all the key issues involved in surrogacy, the majority of the cases taken together give a fairly consistent view of the practice. Except for *Surrogate Parenting Associates, Inc. v. Kentucky* and *Johnson v. Calvert* in California, the courts have rightly ruled that the surrogacy contract is void and unenforceable, applying adoption law rather than contract law to surrogacy. When addressed, the courts have further agreed that commercial surrogacy does indeed constitute baby selling and should be prohibited. Though it has not been an issue except in the *Johnson v. Calvert* case, the normal presumption concerning motherhood has been followed, that the mother is the woman who gives birth to the child. The assumption behind the presumption has been accurate in most cases, that the woman who gives birth is also the genetic contributor to the child. When there is no biological connection to the child, the Courts have not been inclined to recognize any rights for the infertile wife of the natural father, thereby denying any parental rights to the anticipated social parent. The normal presumption of paternity has not been followed in most cases, since it can be rebutted by a blood test.

Thus, in cases of genetic surrogacy, the thrust of the judicial precedent is consistent with the moral analysis of this work, that prohibits a fee to the surrogate, defines the mother as the woman who gives birth to the child, and considers the contract unenforceable. The Kentucky Supreme Court, in *Surrogate Parenting Associates, Inc. v. Kentucky* took an entirely different approach, following contract law as opposed to adoption law. The Orange County, California Superior Court, in *Johnson v. Calvert* defined motherhood based on the genetic contribution, not gestation. A different view of the enforceability of the contract and the legitimacy of the fee followed from that definition. But the majority of cases that have come to the Courts have been resolved in a way compatible with the moral analysis of this work.

SURVEY OF STATE LAWS

To date, as of July 1993, fifteen states have enacted legislation to deal with surrogacy. So far the law has generally followed the judicial precedent set in Michigan and New Jersey, for the most part, looking on surrogacy contracts with disfavor. Most states consider them unenforceable, and some make it illegal for the surrogate or a third party broker to receive a fee beyond expenses.

So far, attempts to formulate a national policy through Congress have failed.[61] In 1987, Rep. Luken of Ohio introduced a bill that resembles Great Britain's Surrogacy Arrangements Act.[62] It would have prohibited commercial surrogacy and advertising for surrogacy arrangements. The bill did not come before the entire House, failing to make it out of subcommittee. A similar bill was introduced in 1989 by Reps. Boxer of California and Hyde of Michigan, which imposes criminal sanctions on the brokers, but no penalty to the contracting couple. It too has yet to come before the entire Congress.

This section on state law will include a survey of the fifteen states that have passed legislation on surrogacy, followed by comment on the degree to which each state law conforms to the moral framework presented in this work. Each law will be surveyed to see how it addresses the central moral issues in surrogacy: commercialization of surrogacy, definition of mother, clarification of parental rights, and enforceability of the contract.

Arizona[63]

Though the law does not prescribe penalties, commercial surrogate contracts are considered illegal. The law states, "No person may enter into, induce, arrange, procure or otherwise assist in the formation of a surrogate parentage contract."[64] The surrogate is considered the legal mother of the child, and her husband is presumed to be the legal father, though that presumption is rebuttable. The law does not distinguish between genetic and gestational surrogacy, outlawing both.

Here the commercial elements of surrogacy found objectionable in chapter two are prohibited. The law rightly ascribes motherhood to the surrogate and gives her parental rights, and since the contract is illegal, it is also unenforceable. The law appears to go further than simply outlawing commercial surrogacy to prohibit altruistic surrogacy, a questionable extension given the discussion of procreative liberty in chapter one.

Arkansas[65]

The law here does not make any definitive statements on the key moral issues of the enforceability of surrogacy contracts or the legality of commercial surrogacy. It addresses the important issue of parental rights, but leaves the status of surrogacy contracts ambiguous.

The law focuses on the presumption of parentage of a child born by artificial insemination, consistent with AID laws. Any child born to a woman by artificial insemination is to be legally regarded as the natural child of the woman and the woman's husband, if he consents to the artificial insemination in writing. There is an exception in the case of a surrogate mother, in which case the child will be legally that of the natural father and his wife (called the woman intending to be the mother). Thus, an exception is made to the normal presumption of paternity in artificial insemination cases. This would seem to open the door to enforce surrogacy contracts, but nowhere in the law is it clearly stated that such is the case. The birth certificate, however, reflects the normal presumption, not the exception. That is, on the birth registration, the mother is the one who gave birth, but this may be changed upon an appropriate court order, presumably so ordered in the case of surrogacy.

The language of the law does not make it clear whether specific performance of the contract can be enforced. To date the law has not been interpreted by any Arkansas court to help specify exactly what the law encompasses. According to the bill's sponsor, Rep. Henry Wilkins, its purpose was to prevent a situation in which a deformed child would not be claimed by either the contracting couple or the surrogate.[66] It is not a comprehensive statement on surrogacy, as are many other state laws, and it leaves a great deal of room for further interpretation by the courts. However, a study commission was appointed by the legislature in 1989 to make a more thorough study and present recommendations. So it seems that the legislature realized that this recently enacted law should not be the last word on the subject.

The general thrust of this law conflicts with the moral framework for surrogacy presented in this work. By allowing an exception to the normal presumption of parentage, it defines the mother as the intending parent, not the woman who carries the child. The law makes no distinction between genetic and gestational surrogacy, so that even a surrogate who supplies the egg will not be considered the legal mother of the child. This conflicts with the majority of court cases cited earlier and with the definition of motherhood in chapter three. Though the law does not specify that the contract will be enforced, it may be assumed that a court order to change the birth certificate of the child born to the surrogate will be sufficient to prevent the surrogate from making a successful claim for custody of her child. Thus, for all practical purposes, the contract is enforceable, violating the fundamental right of the surrogate to associate with and raise her child. The law is a good example of the extent to which other issues in surrogacy depend on the definition of motherhood, which may be the reason that the law is focused on that issue.

Florida[67]

Under the Florida law, surrogacy is called a pre-planned adoption agreement, into which parties may legally enter, though it is not a binding agreement. The term surrogacy is not used and the surrogate herself is called a "volunteer mother." The contracting couple are called the "intending parents."

There are numerous conditions attached to a pre-planned adoption agreement, making surrogacy consistent with Florida adoption law: (1) Only reasonable medical living expenses of the surrogate can be paid. A fee to either her or the broker (beyond legal expenses in connection with the adoption) is prohibited. (2) The surrogate's consent to relinquish parental rights, though agreed upon prior to conception, may be rescinded at any time up to seven days following the birth of the child. Thus the agreement may not contain any provision that requires the surrogate to relinquish parental rights irrevocably. Even the payment of reasonable expenses cannot be conditioned upon surrender of parental rights, nor can payment be dependent upon the health of the child. (3) The surrogate will assume responsibility for the child in the event that the contracting couple terminate the agreement prior to transfer of custody of the child. (4) The surrogate will adhere to reasonable medical care during the pregnancy, submitting to normal medical evaluation to monitor the pregnancy.

The law further requires that any termination of parental rights be done in accordance with existing adoption law, thereby forbidding any fee and requiring the consent of the volunteer mother be executed only after birth of the child. Penalties for violation of the law in surrogacy agreements overlap with sanctions for violating adoption laws; violation is a third degree felony with penalties of up to $5,000 fine and five years imprisonment.

This law reflects many of the features of the legislative proposal presented in the forthcoming conclusion. It is consistent with most of the moral analysis in chapters two and three. It only allows non-commercial surrogacy, though it does allow for brokers to act as middlemen in arranging the contracts, a feature not included in the proposal in chapter six. It respects the fundamental rights of the surrogate to keep the child if she so desires and rightly contains a recision period in which she can change her mind prior to irrevocably giving up parental rights. It further rightly mandates that adoption law dictate the terms involved in relinquishing parental rights in surrogacy. Thus, the contract is unenforceable should a dispute arise.

Indiana[68]

Indiana law renders the surrogacy contract void and unenforceable, in all its provisions. It is against public policy to enforce any of the following provisions of the agreement: providing a gamete for conception, becoming pregnant, consenting to undergoing an abortion, undergoing medical or psychological treatment or examination, waiving parental rights or duties to a child, terminating care, custody, or control of a child, and consenting to stepparent adoption. In addition, evidence of a surrogacy contract cannot be considered by any court in making custody decisions. There is nothing in the law about payment of fees to a surrogate. Apparently this is legitimate, though a significant risk to the contracting party, since the contract cannot be enforced.

The drawback in this law is that it does not clearly prohibit fees to the surrogate beyond reasonable medical expenses. In leaving that area unaddressed, it leaves the door open for commercial surrogacy, even with brokers involved, but with the contract being unenforceable. The features that the law does address are consistent with this work's moral framework, that the surrogate cannot be forced to give up her child against her will. Though a definition of motherhood is not given, the unenforceability of the contract suggests that the normal presumption of motherhood applies, that the mother is the woman who gives birth to the child.

Kentucky[69]

In contrast to Indiana, Kentucky law is aimed at prohibiting commercial surrogacy, with little comment about the enforceability of non-paid agreements. It prohibits both individuals and agencies/brokers from receiving compensation for artificial insemination and the subsequent termination of parental rights. Clearly the legislature disagreed with the Kentucky Supreme Court in its evaluation of surrogacy as the equivalent of baby selling. In *Surrogate Parenting Associates, Inc. v. Kentucky*,[70] the Kentucky Supreme Court denied that surrogacy constituted baby selling, holding that there was a fundamental difference between surrogacy and the clear sale of children in black market adoptions. The legislature, however, rejected the court's assessment of surrogacy by prohibiting its commercial practice. In addition, no one is allowed to advertise adoption services, either for procurement or placement of children. The law places surrogacy squarely in the context of existing adoption law in denying any fee beyond reasonable expenses, including those paid to licensed adoption agencies for their services in placing a child.

The final statement of KRS 199.590 (3) reads, "Contracts or agreements entered into in violation of this subsection shall be void." Though the focus of this law is different from that in Indiana, this statement makes it clear that even non-commercial agreements are not enforceable. There is nothing in the law concerning any penalties for violation.

This law, too, is quite consistent with the moral analysis in chapters two and three. The fee to the surrogate, which constitutes baby selling, is prohibited and the fundamental maternal rights of the surrogate are protected. This is done by the contract being clearly unenforceable and by the explicit statements that any transfer of parental rights must be done in accordance with existing adoption law. The definition of motherhood is not specified, but it is likely that the normal maternal presumption applies here since no exception is made for surrogacy.

Louisiana[71]

In the briefest of the state surrogacy laws currently on the books, the Louisiana law treats the surrogacy contract as null, void, and contrary to public policy, whether it includes compensation or not. There is nothing in the law that expressly prohibits paying of a fee; the law provides only that if there is a dispute, the contract cannot be enforced. There are no criminal sanctions or other penalties for violation.

This law could be made more consistent with the preceding moral analysis by clearly prohibiting the fee to the surrogate and more clearly defining motherhood, particularly in the context of genetic and gestational surrogacy. In the absence of a change in the existing presumption of motherhood, it is likely that maternal rights would reside with the surrogate, and the unenforceability of the contract rightly protects her fundamental right to associate with and raise her child.

Michigan[72]

Michigan was one of the first states to criminalize surrogate arrangements, and the associated penalties are the most stringent of all the state surrogacy laws. The parties to the agreement are guilty of a misdemeanor, punishable by a $10,000 fine and/or one year imprisonment. Brokering a surrogacy arrangement is a felony, with penalties up to a $50,000 fine and/or five years imprisonment, particularly if the surrogate is a minor or in some way mentally disabled. Should a dispute arise among the parties, the one who has physical custody of the child shall retain it until a court orders otherwise, but the court is directed to use the best interests standard for final custody decisions.

As soon as the law was passed, the ACLU challenged its constitutionality, seeking to overturn the part of the law that banned payment to surrogates.[73] In response, the Michigan attorney general suggested that the law only sought to prohibit agreements that contained an irrevocable waiver of parental rights prior to conception or birth. In the same way, third party involvement in brokering these contracts that did not contain the above provision would be within the law. The Michigan Circuit Court accepted that interpretation of the law. Though the attorney general's position on enforcement of the law settled the controversy, it appears that this interpretation is not consistent with the original intent of the law's framers. Surrogacy brokers can get around the law by simply not mentioning any waiver of parental rights in the contract, indicating that the couple pays for gestational services only and not the transfer of the child. The law, which was intended to criminalize paid surrogacy, now permits it as long as the parties acknowledge that the contract is not enforceable, since both elements of the agreement, the fee and the waiver of parental rights, must be expressed in order for the law to be violated.

However, it should be clear that the primary intent of the surrogacy agreement is to effect the waiver of parental rights. Thus, in early 1989, the original author of the 1988 law introduced an amendment in the legislature. It contained a crucial statement that acknowledged a presumption that surrogacy contracts contain a provision for parental rights to be transferred: "It is presumed that a contract, agreement or arrangement in which a female agrees to conceive a child. . ., by a person other than her husband, or agrees to surrogate gestation, includes a provision, whether or not express, that the female will relinquish her parental or custodial rights to the child."[74] Thus the law would again be consistent with the Michigan judicial precedent set in *Doe v. Kelley.*

As the law stands interpreted at present, it partially conflicts and partially adheres to the preceding moral analysis. The loophole in the law that allows for a fee to the surrogate is out of harmony with earlier court decisions in Michigan, which clearly labeled surrogacy for a fee as the sale of children. However, the strong language on the unenforceability of the contract does not conflict with the rights of the surrogate. Though a full definition of motherhood in the context of surrogacy is not given, it is assumed throughout the statute that the surrogate is the mother, and if maternal rights are to be relinquished, they are hers to give up.

Nebraska[75]

This is a very brief statement, similar to the Louisiana law. It makes any commercial surrogacy contract void and unenforceable. There is no maternal custody presumption here since the natural father of the child will have all the rights under existing law as any other natural father. The normal presumption of paternity thus does not apply in surrogacy. It is assumed that custody disputes will be settled based on a best interests standard. There is no mention of any penalties for violation. It would appear that even commercial surrogacy is lawful, but the contract is not enforceable in the case of any dispute.

In terms of the key elements of the moral analysis, the law only addresses one of them clearly. The rights of the surrogate are protected by the contract not being enforceable. In so protecting her rights, the normal presumption of motherhood is assumed. The fee to the surrogate, though not addressed, can apparently be legal, since the arrangement itself is not illegal, only void and unenforceable. Thus the door seems to be open to commercial surrogacy, but with significant risks involved since the contract is not enforceable.

Nevada[76]

Nevada makes surrogacy an exception to adoption laws and appears, at least on the surface, to be the most permissive state in regard to surrogacy arrangements. The law affirms that payment of consideration in connection with adoption is illegal, but makes an exception for surrogacy. Section 5 of the statute states, "The provisions of this section [Section 127.303] do not apply if a woman enters into a lawful contract to act as a surrogate, be inseminated and give birth to the child of a man who is not her husband." What constitutes a lawful surrogacy contract is not clear, and the courts have not been asked as yet to interpret the statute. It would appear that both payment to surrogates and intermediaries is allowed.

However, it is not clear that Nevada law supports the enforceability of the contract.[77] In the same legislative session as the one in which the current law was passed, the legislature amended Revised Statute 127.070.1, which provided that, "All releases to consent to adoption executed in this state by a mother before the birth of a child *or within 72 hours after the birth of a child* (part in italics added in the amendment) are invalid." Since the state addressed surrogacy under the heading of adoption, excepting it from baby selling laws, this amendment would likely apply to surrogacy-related adoptions. Thus, the birth mother would have up to seventy-two hours to change her mind and keep the child. Any contract that would force her to waive her parental rights irrevocably prior to conception would be void.

In apparently allowing for commercial surrogacy, Nevada law conflicts with the rights of a child not to be the object of barter. However, the law does properly protect the interests of the surrogate by making the contract unenforceable and allowing a recision period in which she can change her mind and keep the child. Since the law addressed surrogacy within the adoption statutes, it may be assumed that the normal maternal presumption applies here. The mother is the one who bears the child and she cannot be forced to waive parental rights under force of contract.

New Hampshire[78]

In the most extensive of the laws regulating surrogacy, New Hampshire passed legislation in April 1990, effective in January 1991, to permit non-commercial surrogacy. No fee is to be paid to the surrogate; however, she may receive pregnancy-related medical expenses, lost wages from pregnancy-related absence from work, insurance up to six weeks after the delivery, attorney's fees, court costs, and counseling fees related to her pregnancy.

The surrogate and her husband are presumed to be the parents under the law, although it may be rebutted by clear evidence to the contrary. Proof of artificial insemination or in vitro fertilization is not sufficient to rebut. Only a court decree establishing paternity by another man can rebut the presumption.

The surrogate has the right to change her mind and claim the child as her own up to seventy-two hours after birth. It appears from the language of the law that if she chooses to keep the child, it may not be contested, and a custody hearing would not be held. In the event that she does wish to keep the child, after the seventy-two hour waiting period, the birth certificate shall name her and her husband as the legal parents. The birth certificate is not to be completed until the waiting period has passed. Should the surrogate and her husband not claim the child, the intending parents are to be named as the legal parents on the birth certificate. If the surrogate and her husband desire to waive parental rights after the seventy-two hour waiting period, parental rights are transferred without the need to formalize such a transfer by adoption proceedings. However, specific performance of the contract cannot force the surrogate to give up the child against her will. There is no difference whether the surrogate is genetically related to the child or is simply the gestational mother. The mother is presumed to be the one who bears the child. Neither can she be forced under the contract to become impregnated if she changes her mind, or to have an abortion against her will, or forbidden to terminate the pregnancy if she so chooses. There is a section in the law concerning damages, but interestingly, only for the surrogate to recover if the intending parents breach the contract. In that case, the surrogate is entitled to health care expenses that the couple would have paid under the contract, and any other "fees" that the surrogate would have received. If the intending parents refuse to accept the child, then they are liable for child support as well.

This law bears strong similarity to the legislative proposal outlined in the conclusion and is consistent with the moral analysis of chapters two and three. No fee to the surrogate is allowed, the surrogate is presumed to be the child's mother, and the contract cannot be enforced if she desires to keep the child and expresses that desire within the recision period. Though there is considerable risk to the intending parents in becoming involved in surrogacy, the rights of the child and the surrogate are properly protected.

New York[79]

In the most recently enacted surrogacy law, the New York legislature prohibited compensation to the surrogate beyond reasonable medical expenses and adoption expenses already allowed by law, and made surrogacy contracts void and unenforceable. This new law went into effect in July 1993 and the legislature followed the recommendation of the State Task Force on Life and the Law.

Surrogacy contracts are declared contrary to public policy and and violation of the law is a felony. Penalties for arranging or participating in a commercial surrogacy arrangement involve a fine of up to $10,000 and forfeiture of any illegal compensation received by the parties involved.

North Dakota[80]

North Dakota became the first state to adopt the Uniform Status of Assisted Conception Act proposed by the National Conference of Commissioners on Uniform State Laws.[81] The law defines the mother as the one who gives birth to the child, and makes surrogacy agreements that contain an irrevocable parental rights waiver void. In the event that the surrogate changes her mind, she is the legal mother, and her husband is presumed to be the legal father, assuming he was a party to the agreement. The law does not address custody disputes, and it would appear that the contracting couple does not have a right to challenge for custody if the surrogate breaches the contract.

An important part of the law is the specific amendment to Section 12.1-31-05 of the N.D. Century Code, in which surrogacy is exempted from the child selling laws of the state. This would appear to open the door to payment of a fee to the surrogate beyond reasonable expenses. However, the law does not contain any provision for damages or for recovery of the fee should the surrogate decide to keep the child.

Though the sections of the law that make the contract unenforceable and confer maternal rights on the surrogate are consistent with this work's moral analysis, the opening in the law for payment of a fee to the surrogate is not. Thus, in the exemption of surrogacy from child selling laws, legislators have failed to see that the fee to the surrogate is for much more than simply gestational services. It is, in part, for the transfer of parental rights, which constitutes the sale and purchase of children.

Utah[82]

Here commercial surrogacy is outlawed, and the prohibition applies both to individuals and intermediaries. In addition, non-commercial surrogacy contracts are unenforceable, though no sanctions are prescribed for these arrangements. The surrogate and her husband are presumed to be the legal parents, but the law does allow for custody decisions to be made on a best interests standard. This is only a temporary law that expired in July 1991. A more permanent law will be formulated pending completion of a study by the Legislative Interim Social Services Committee.

Should the updated law be similar to the interim one that has recently expired, it will be in harmony with the key moral concepts underlying the discussion of surrogacy presented here. A fee to the surrogate is not allowed, and even brokers are prohibited from arranging surrogacy contracts. The surrogate is defined as the mother and her rights are properly protected, with the contract being unenforceable in the event of a dispute.

Virginia[83]

Effective in July 1993, surrogacy law in Virginia is part of an entire law encompassing all methods of assisted reproduction. The law allows for altruistic surrogacy but prohibits payment of a fee to the surrogate and the activities of surrogacy brokers. The law distinguishes between contracts that are approved by the court and those which are not. The law requires that all surrogacy arrangments be subject to court approval, but makes allowance for those which proceed without such approval. In order to insure that the parties to the agreement, particularly the child, are adequately protected, there are elaborate precautions taken before any surrogacy arrangement can be approved by the court.

In arrangements approved by the court, the intending parents are recognized as the legal parents of the child. But in those arrangments that proceed without court approval, the legal parents are the surrogate and her husband. In these cases, the intending parents can gain parental rights only by following the state's adoption laws.

In general, the prohibition of the commercial element in surrogacy is consistent with the thesis of this work. But the treatment of parental rights in which the court, in court approved arrangements, may allow the intending parents to be named the legal parents violates the fundamental right of the surrogate, as the mother, to associate and raise her child.

Washington[84]

Persons who enter into or arrange commercial surrogacy contracts are guilty of a gross misdemeanor. Similar to the Michigan law, this law awards temporary custody to the party who has physical custody of the child at the time of the dispute, until a court decides otherwise. The court will make the custody decision on a best interests standard. In another similarity to the Michigan law, this act makes it illegal to induce a minor female or a woman with a mental illness or developmental disability from entering into any surrogacy agreement, whether paid or not.

By prohibiting the fee and not allowing the contract to be enforced, the Washington law embraces the key elements of this work's moral analysis. The definition of motherhood is left unaddressed, but since the contract cannot be enforced against her will, it is likely that the normal maternal presumption applies, and the woman who bears the child is considered the mother.

Other State Laws

In addition to the laws enacted in the above states, several other states have bills pending or have established study commissions to make recommendations to the legislature. One example of pending state policy, which I favor, is that of California. A Joint Legislative Committee on Surrogate Parenting, chaired by Alexander M. Capron, former executive director of the President's Commission on Ethical Problems in Biomedical and Behavioral Research, issued its report in November 1990. The majority report recommended that the surrogacy law should:[85]

1. Prohibit payment to a surrogate mother for other than expenses allowed in adoption proceedings. Violation of this by an individual or intermediary would be a misdemeanor.

2. Prohibit commercial surrogacy agencies.

3. Prohibit advertising for surrogacy.

4. Designate the natural father as the one who donates the sperm for artificial insemination.

5. Designate the gestating woman as the mother of the child when the egg or embryo comes from someone other than the woman who gives birth.

6. Make surrogate contracts void and unenforceable.

In sum, unpaid voluntary surrogacy should be allowed in California, and it should be handled in a way consistent with the existing state adoption practices.

The Minority Report[86] would not criminalize commercial surrogacy, since the minority does not consider receipt of payment for surrogacy services to be child selling. It holds that the circumstances surrounding adoption are significantly different from surrogacy, so that the concerns related to commercialization of adoption do not exist in surrogacy. However, with the majority, it does recommend that the legal status of the contracts be clarified, specifically that they be considered void. In the rare cases of dispute when the surrogate does not fulfill the contract, they suggest that custody should be decided on the best interests standard.

The bill recently passed by the California legislature (Alternative Reproduction Act of 1991; SB 937) reflects neither the majority nor minority positions of the Joint Legislative Commission, though it does have some similarities, such as the prohibition on advertising. The law would "specify that upon birth of the child the infertile couple assumes parental responsibility and custody for the child; [and] provide that in any dispute between the parties to the surrogate agreement, custody of the child shall be awarded in the best interests of the child."[87] It appears that the current California bill would consider the contract void in the event the surrogate breaches it. The bill allows compensation to the surrogate for services rendered, exempting surrogacy from child selling adoption laws.[88] The bill also contains provisions relating to counseling of the parties involved, medical evaluation of the surrogate and the natural father, and payment of medical expenses, including medical and life insurance, for both the surrogate and the intending parents.[89] As of February 1993, the bill had been approved by the state Senate and Assembly but was vetoed by the governor, since he felt that surrogacy arrangements could be adequately handled by present state law.[90]

The great majority of states that have enacted legislation as of July 1993 have evaluated surrogacy negatively and sought to discourage it. With respect to the major issues addressed in this work (commercialization, definition of mother and parental rights, and enforceability of the contract), most states have prohibited a fee to surrogates (and some have expressly prohibited brokers of the agreements), defined the mother as the surrogate, and refused to enforce the contract in cases of custody disputes.

There are exceptions to this general trend, however. For example, Arkansas, Indiana, Louisiana, Nebraska, Nevada, and North Dakota do not specifically prohibit payment of a fee to the surrogate, though these states generally view the contract as void. Only Arkansas grants parental rights to the contracting couple instead of the surrogate, yet it must be inferred from the statute that a court proceeding would normally follow the birth of a child in surrogacy in order to effect the transfer of parental rights, since the name of the surrogate and her husband are placed on the child's birth certificate. No state that has passed a surrogacy law has attempted to redefine motherhood, and, as a result, it can be reasonably assumed that current state laws accept the normal presumption of maternity. No state definitively allows for enforcement of the contract, though the language of the statutes in both Arkansas and Nevada is ambiguous on this point. These are the only two states that have passed laws on surrogacy so far where the law can be interpreted as allowing commercial surrogacy. These states view it through the lens of contract rather than adoption law. However, it remains to be seen whether the courts in these states will interpret the law in this way, and approve commercial, contractual surrogacy.

Thus, the thrust of state law is consistent with the moral analysis attempted in this work. The fee to the surrogate is prohibited in the majority of states, though not in all of them. Except for Arkansas, the mother is assumed to be the surrogate with full maternal rights upon birth of the child, and there is no distinction made between a gestational and genetic surrogate. Finally, with the exception of Arkansas and Nevada, states view the surrogacy contract as void and unenforceable.

SURVEY OF INTERNATIONAL LAW

There has been strong public opposition to surrogacy from Europe, Australia, Canada, and Israel. Commercial surrogacy has been banned in France, Germany, Great Britain, and Israel. Most states in Australia, the Netherlands, and Spain have issued study commission reports that as yet have not been enacted into law. These commissions have generally recommended against commercial surrogacy, with the exception of the Ontario Law Reform Commission in Canada; and the Dutch Health Council Committee. For most study commissions, however, both commercial and non-commercial surrogacy have been disapproved.

Germany recently passed the strictest surrogacy law anywhere in the world, not only addressing commercial surrogacy, but also genetic engineering and in vitro fertilization.[91] The law bans women from being used as surrogates, and in vitro fertilization is allowed only when the egg comes from the woman who will bear the child. Thus, egg donation is prohibited. There are no criminal sanctions for the surrogate mothers, but physicians who are involved could face up to three years in prison.

Commercial surrogacy is also prohibited in Great Britain. The Surrogacy Arrangements Act of 1985 essentially followed the recommendations of the

Warnock Report, issued in 1984.[92] The law prohibits both individuals and intermediaries from arranging commercial surrogacy contracts, and declares such contracts them void and unenforceable. The principal reason for this was that the danger of exploitation outweighed any positive benefits. There are no criminal sanctions on private individuals entering such an agreement, in order to prevent children born under surrogacy arrangements from any taint of criminality.

In Australia, three states have received reports from study commissions, and one has passed legislation dealing with surrogacy. The most extensive of these reports came out of Victoria, where the Waller Committee published four reports between 1982 and 1984,[93] culminating in the 1984 Infertility (Medical Procedures) Act, which prohibited both non-commercial and commercial surrogacy. It declared the contracts void and attached criminal penalties for surrogate procurement services by third parties.

In Queensland, a 1984 report recommended that surrogacy be prohibited on the grounds of baby selling.[94] No criminal penalties were proposed. Rather, the contract was considered void, unenforceable, and illegal. Penalties were reserved for those who advertised to recruit women as surrogates or facilitate the arrangements.

In South Australia, a report issued in 1983 recommended that surrogacy not be practiced in that region, and that the law be drafted in accord with existing adoption statutes to prevent surrogacy from taking place.[95] This is similar to the reports issued by the states of Tasmania[96] and Western Australia.[97]

In Canada, the province of Ontario is the only one to date to have issued guidelines for legislators.[98] The report is one of the few to endorse surrogacy, though it issued detailed guidelines for its regulation. It recommended that payment of a fee beyond expenses be allowed, but be subject to court approval. The commission suggested that should the surrogate change her mind and decide to keep the child, the court could order seizure of the child if necessary to effect the transfer of custody to the contracting couple. Since the service of the surrogate was largely completed by birth, they reasoned that forcing specific performance of the remainder of the contractual obligation was reasonable. Though they admitted that there was no clear evidence concerning the child's best interests (whether to stay with the surrogate or be transferred to the contracting couple), they recommended that the child be immediately surrendered at birth, regardless of the desires of the mother, thus favoring contract law over adoption law.

The Dutch Reports also affirmed commercial surrogacy.[99] They recommended allowing it for a fee and suggested a non-profit government-supervised agency to supervise all arrangements, and even to recruit suitable women to serve as surrogates.

France[100], Spain,[101] Germany, Greece, Norway, Switzerland, Great Britain, and Israel, by contrast, all deny the legality of surrogacy, with or without the fee.and have passed laws prohibiting it.[102]

Thus, the way in which surrogacy is treated internationally is generally consistent with both the moral analysis of this work and with the general thrust of the laws that have been passed in the United States. Some, such as Victoria, Australia, have extended the prohibition of the fee to the surrogate to include non-commercial surrogacy as well. In most countries that have addressed the issue, the contract is void and unenforceable, and the normal presumption of maternity is followed in defining the mother. At least in the official public policy-making bodies in the countries that have dealt with surrogacy, there appears to be a widespread consensus that commercial surrogacy should be unlawful and surrogacy contracts should not be enforced.

SURROGACY AND AID/ADOPTION LAWS

Any attempt to write laws that encourage surrogate parenting will have to address existing laws on adoption and artificial insemination by a donor. Four specific obstacles are posed by these laws: the prohibition against child selling, the recission period prior to an irrevocable termination of parental rights, and the prohibition against private placement adoptions, all from adoption law, and the presumption of paternity from artificial insemination law. There are significant hindrances to commercial surrogacy presented by adoption laws, but the barriers presented by AID laws are not insurmountable.

Many states have enacted laws preventing exchange of consideration from adoptive parents to the natural mother for the waiver of parental rights.[103] These laws were clearly intended to prevent black market adoptions when financial coercion replaces the best interests of the children. However, such laws were also aimed at preventing something inherently problematic, irrespective of the surrounding circumstances: the sale of children.[104]

In addition, most adoption laws allow for a time period, some up to fifteen days after the birth of the child,[105] in which the natural mother may change her mind and reclaim her child.[106] This is different from the waiting period that the courts require between the time an adoption petition is filed and final approval is given.[107] These laws recognize the ambivalence that surrounds an unplanned pregnancy and the strength of the bond between mother and child. There is little doubt that giving up one's child for adoption is one of the most difficult things imaginable, and the law protects a mother's right to associate with the child she has borne, even though the process of coming to that decision may be confusing and may involve repeated changes of mind. As with the laws against payment of a fee, the laws that provide a recission period are designed to insure that the woman's consent to adoption is freely given.

A final obstacle to deriving surrogacy legislation from adoption laws is these laws in many states prohibit private placement of an adopted child. Nineteen states and the District of Columbia have no laws prohibiting private placement.[108] However, most states require that placement of adoptive children take place through the state or a state-licensed adoption agency,[109] making the private placement of a child born to a surrogate illegal. One exception to this occurs when a stepparent is the adoptive parent; many states exempt stepparent adoptions from private placement laws, and some states permit parents to place the child privately with the couple that adopts the child.[110] The states that absolutely prohibit private placement would not allow the transfer of parental rights necessary to complete a surrogacy arrangement. Though this is not an insurmountable obstacle nationwide, laws that would recognize surrogacy will need to exempt the contracting couple from conflicting private placement laws.

Laws regulating artificial insemination have a bearing on the surrogacy contract as well. In order to provide for children born from AID and to legitimize their birth, most states have laws that are in accord with the Uniform Parentage Act, which states, "The donor of semen for use in artificial insemination of a married woman other than the donor's wife is treated in law as if he were not the natural father of a child conceived thereby."[111] In some states this presumption is rebuttable, again consistent with the Uniform Parentage Act,[112] but the courts have been hesitant to recognize the natural father as the legal father, except for purposes of determining support.[113]

In the states that have enacted surrogacy laws, the obstacle presented by AID laws has not been difficult to overcome. Surrogacy arrangements are exempt from AID laws (originally designed to prevent anonymous donors from later claiming parental rights) in that the presumption of paternity is rebuttable by clear evidence of paternity. This is usually accomplished through blood or DNA testing, resulting in the establishment of the sperm donor as the natural and legal father. Should there be a disagreement over custody of the child, it is handled as a normal custody dispute, with the rights of the natural father fully recognized, though his rights are subordinate to the child's best interests. Admission of artificial insemination by the surrogate is not considered sufficient to rebut the presumption.

Adoption laws have been a more difficult obstacle. Most states, with the exception of Arkansas and Nevada, have applied adoption law to surrogacy, prohibiting a fee and allowing a recission period. Surrogacy appears to be exempt from private placement laws.

CONCLUSION

One is struck by the degree of consistency in the approaches taken to surrogacy by various courts, state legislatures, and international policy-making bodies. With some notable exceptions, among the states and countries that have addressed the issue of surrogacy, the majority have generally followed the moral analysis presented in this work. Most have viewed the commercialization of third party reproduction in a negative light by proscribing a fee for the surrogate. Many have also prohibited brokers from arranging surrogacy contracts. Most consider the contract either void or voidable, and thus the waiver of parental rights is not enforceable should the surrogate change her mind.

The moral principles that underlie the above judicial precedent, state and national laws, and commission reports, have been brought out in chapters one through three of this work. Except for France, Spain, Israel, and some states in Australia, which have banned all surrogacy, most judicial and legislative bodies have seen no harm in permitting non-commercial surrogacy, thereby allowing latitude for the exercise of procreative liberty. The commercial element and enforcing the contract are the aspects of the practice that are objectionable to these bodies. The moral principle that children are not to be objects of barter is undoubtedly a major factor that has driven these legislative groups to place restrictions on the fee paid to the surrogate, and for some, to restrict the activity of brokers in arranging surrogacy contracts. It is a widely held maxim that is foundational to the Constitution's Thirteenth Amendment that human beings, and particularly children, are not to be bought and sold as commodities, and thus any payment to the surrogate that purchases parental rights is rightly prohibited, in keeping with adoption laws in many states and countries. In addition, respecting the rights of the mother, when motherhood is defined either directly or by implication, most legislation has attempted to take seriously the fundamental right of a mother to raise and associate with the child to whom she has given birth. In all likelihood, this is the central moral principle that underlies the widespread legislative consensus that the contract should be considered either inherently void or voidable should the surrogate decide to retain her maternal rights. The overall thrust of surrogacy legislation is consistent with these important moral principles, and it appears that deontological moral reasoning, in the form of these principles, has played an important role in formulating state and international policy on surrogacy.

The one important area to which further legislation can give more detailed attention is the definition of motherhood in surrogacy, should states and nations choose to allow some form of surrogacy. The majority of laws and court decisions that have dealt with surrogacy have either not addressed the difference between gestational and genetic surrogacy, or have concluded that the two types of surrogate arrangements should not be distinguished. Most of the statutes and court cases have not attempted a detailed definition of the mother, since it was not really necessary until *Johnson v. Calvert*.

It would appear that the future for commercial surrogacy, in which the contract is enforced and the initiating couple receives parental rights at the time of the child's birth, is not bright. Without the fee, there is insufficient incentive for most surrogates to undertake that role. Without the ability to enforce the contract, there is significant risk to the initiating couple that they will have to share custody of the child with the surrogate. In general, a couple contemplating surrogacy under present legal conditions should be aware of the possibility that the surrogate will be involved in their lives for the indefinite future.

Should some states allow the fee and the brokers to arrange the contracts, but not enforce the contract, this would make more potential surrogates available, but would not substantially decrease the risk to the contracting couple. With the general legal climate averse to commercial surrogacy, this compromise scenario is not likely, since the focus of most laws passed to this point has been to discourage the commercial element in third party reproduction.

NOTES

1. John Stuart Mill, *On Liberty*, cited in H. L. A. Hart, *Law, Liberty and Morality*, (London: Oxford University Press, 1963): 4.

2. Ibid.

3. Wolfenden Committee, *Report of the Committee on Homosexual Offenses and Prostitution*, Cmd. no. 247 (1957), cited in Ronald A. Dworkin, *Taking Rights Seriously* (Cambridge, Mass.: Harvard University Press, 1978), 240.

4. Lord Devlin, *The Enforcement of Morals* (London: Oxford University Press, 1965), cited in Hart, *Law, Liberty and Morality*, 16.

5. Ibid., 7-25.

6. Ibid., chapters. 5-7.

7. H. L. A. Hart, "Positivism and the Separation of Law and Morals," *Harvard Law Review* 71 (February 1958): 593-629; Lon L. Fuller, "Positivism and Fidelity to Law: A Response to Professor Hart," *Harvard Law Review* 71 (February 1958): 630-72.

8. Hart, "Positivism and the Separation of Law and Morals," 598-99.

9. Fuller, "Positivism and Fidelity to Law," 644.

10. Ibid., 645.

11. Ibid., 641. Professor Hart appears to accept this notion of an internal morality of law when, in rejecting a command theory of law, he insists that the foundation of a system of law is not coercion but "fundamental accepted rules specifying the essential lawmaking procedures." Fuller then presses the issue by questioning whether these rules are rules not of law but of morality, which are accepted based on a general perception that they are necessary and right. Thus, there is a merger, not simply an intersection, of law and morality at this point. Ibid., 639.

12. For example, adultery is considered by most moral traditions to be immoral, yet it is not illegal, and should not be, primarily due to the difficulty involved in enforcing it. To effectively police such a law would involve intolerable invasions of privacy, and would likely discredit the moral or religious social vision that prompted its enactment.

13. Fuller, "Positivism and Fidelity to Law," 659.

14. Ibid., 659.

15. Ibid., 656.

16. For further discussion of this objection to positivism, see Dworkin, *Taking Rights Seriously*, 81-130, and Dworkin, "Natural Law Revisited," *University of Florida Law Review* 34 (Winter 1982): 165-88.

17. See Fuller, "Positivism and Fidelity to Law," 662-64.

18. 106 Mich. App. 169, 307 N. W. 2d 438 (1981).

19. 431 U.S. 678 (1972).

20. 381 U.S. 479 (1965). For further discussion of these and other cases relating to procreative liberty, see chapter one.

21. 307 N. W. 2d 438, at 441.

22. 122 Mich. App. 506, 333 N. W. 2d 90 (1983).

23. The original law stated, "Statutes are to be construed as they were intended to be understood when they were passed. Courts have a duty to enforce unambiguous statutes as written." 333 N. W. 2d at 93.

24. 333 N. W. 2d at 94.

25. *In re Baby Girl,* Ky Cir. Ct. Jefferson City, March 8, 1983, 9 *Family Law Reporter* 2348.

26. Ky. R. S. Section 199.600.

27. Ibid.

28. Ibid.

29. Ibid.

30. Ibid.

31. This feature of surrogacy has prompted some to suggest that adoption law, not contract law is the appropriate vehicle with which to regulate surrogacy. See for instance, Martha Field, *Surrogate Motherhood: The Legal and Human Issues* (Cambridge, Mass.: Harvard University Press, 1988), 84-96, and Alexander Morgan Capron and Margaret J. Radin, "Choosing Family Law over Contract Law as a Paradigm for Surrogate Motherhood," *Law, Medicine and Health Care* 16 nos. 1-2, (1988): 34-43.

32. 144 Mich. App. 12, 373 N. W. 2d 228 (1985).

33. Michigan Adoption Code, M.C.L. Section 710.41; M.S.A. Section 2.7.3178(555.41).

34. 373 N. W. 2d at 232.

35. Ky., 704 S. W. 2d 209 (1986).

36. Ibid., 210.

37. Ibid., 211.

38. Ibid., 211-12.

39. They state, "The Attorney General contends that by including this in vitro fertilization procedure in the statute while leaving out the surrogate parenting procedure presently under consideration, the legislature was legislating against surrogate parenting. We do not divine any such hidden meaning. All we can derive from this language is that

the legislature has expressed itself about one procedure for medically assisted conception while remaining silent on the others" (Ibid., 212).

40. Ibid.

41. It seems that the parental rights aspect of surrogacy fits well within the framework of adoption, and the court followed adoption law closely in this area. By contrast, it rejected the adoption framework in the earlier discussion of the fee for the surrogate. Ibid., 212-13.

42. He states, "I view the subsequent delivery of the child together with an agreed judgment terminating the parental rights of the natural mother in exchange for a monetary consideration to be no less than the sale of a child" (Ibid., 214).

43. Ibid., 215.

44. Ibid.

45. 109 N.J. 396, 537 A. 2d 1227 (1988). For examples of the voluminous contrasting commentary on this case, see Richard E. Brennan, "In re Baby M: The Structure of the Opinion," *Seton Hall Law Review* 18 (1988): 885-89, and Gary N. Skoloff and Edward J. O'Donnell, "Baby M: A Disquieting Decision," *Seton Hall Law Review* 18 (1988): 827-30.

46. 217 N.J. Super. 313, 525 A. 2d 1128 (1987).

47. *In the Matter of Baby M*, 537 A. 2d., 1238.

48. Ibid., 1241.

49. Ibid., 1245.

50. Ibid., 1257.

51. See discussion below of *Moschetta v. Moschetta*.

52. Calif. Super. Ct., AD 57638, 22 October, 1990, cited in Joint Legislative Committee on Surrogate Parenting, *Commercial and Non-commercial Surrogate Parenting*, (Sacramento: Joint Publications Office, November 1990): 101-25.

53. Ibid., 103.

54. Ibid., 105, 107.

55. Ibid., 111.

56. Ibid., 121.

57. Ibid., 116-19.

58. Calif. Super. Ct., , AD 59584, 11 January, 1991. For further reference, see Sonni Efron, "Three Parents Fight Over Custody in Surrogate Case," *Los Angeles Times* 3 March 1991, A1, 30.

59. Sonni Efron and Maria Newman, "Surrogate Mother Gets Rights of Legal Parent," *Los Angeles Times*, 19 April 1981, A1.

60. Matt Lait and Carla Rivera, "Father Ordered to Share Custody with Surrogate," *Los Angeles Times*, 27 September 1991, A1,30.

61. Field, *Surrogate Motherhood*, 155-56.

62. See further discussion of this and other international laws on surrogacy later in this chapter.

63. 1989 Ariz. Sess. Laws 14. The law amended Arizona Revised Statutes Title 25, Chap. 2, Art. 2 by adding Section 25-218, and by amending Section 36-322. This survey of state laws is taken from the NCSL State Legislative Report, pp. 1-5, cited in Joint Legislative Committee on Surrogate Parenting, *Commercial and Non-commercial Surrogate Parenting*, pp. 23-73.

64. 1989 Ariz. Sess. Laws 14, p. 1.

65. 1989 Ark. Acts 647, amending Arkansas Code 9-10-201.

66. Field, *Surrogate Motherhood*, 166.

67. Fla. Stat. Sec. 63.212 (1) (1988).

68. Indiana Code Sec. 31-8-2-1 to 31-8-2-3 (1988).

69. Ky. Rev. Stat. Sec. 199.590 (amended 1988).

70. 704 S. W. 2d 209 (1986).

71. La. Rev. Stat. Ann. Sec. 9:2713 (1987).

72. Mich. Comp. Laws, Sec. 722.851-722.863 (1988)

73. Field, *Surrogate Motherhood*, 162. This challenge took place on August 4, 1988, and the decision was handed down on November 9, 1988.

74. Senate Bill 100, 1989, cited in Field, *Surrogate Motherhood,* 224, n.35.

75. Ne. Rev. Stat., Sec. 674 (1988).

76. Nev. Rev. Stat., Sec. 127.303.5 (1988).

77. Field, *Surrogate Motherhood*, 159.

78. N.H. Rev. Stat. Ann. 168-B (1990).

79. Amendment of the New York Domestic Relations Law, (s 1906), by adding Article 8, Surrogate Parenting Contracts, 1992.

80. 1989 N.D. Sess. Laws 184, amending Sec. 12.1-31-05 of the North Dakota Century Code.

81. Text of the act is reprinted in *Family Law Reporter* 15 (February 21, 1989): 2009-2010. North Dakota adopted the more restrictive Alternative B, which allows the surrogate to change her mind after birth, as opposed to Alternative A, in which the surrogate has 180 days after insemination to terminate the agreement if she so chooses. The act was endorsed by the ABA House of Delegates in 1988. See Robert D. Arenstein, "Is Surrogacy Against the Public Policy? The Answer is Yes." *Seton Hall Law Review* 18 (1988): 831-38.

82. 1989 Utah Laws 140.

83. Va. Stat. Ann. 20-156-20-165, 1993.

84. 1989 Wash. Laws 404.

85. Ibid., 22.

86. See Joint Legislative Committee on Surrogate Parenting, *Commercial and Noncommercial Surrogate Parenting*, M1-26. For a summary of the minority position, see p. M-3.

87. Taken from the legislative counsel's digest of SB 937, 1. See also section 7317 (a) of the Alternative Reproduction Act of 1991 (SB 937).

88. Ibid., Sec. 7306, 7319 (e). There is a cap of $15,000 set on the fee paid to a surrogate mother over and above pregnancy-related expenses.

89. Ibid., Sec. 7319 (j), 7320 (c), 7319 (c-d).

90. "California may sanction paid surrogate pregnancies," *Medical Ethics Advisor* 8 no. 5, (May 1992): 56-58.

91. See Rolf Soderlind, "Germany Bans Surrogate Mothers," *Orange County Register*, 25 October 1990, A1.

92. United Kingdom, Department of Health and Social Security. 1984. *Report of the Committee of Inquiry into Human Fertilization and Embryology*. Hereafter referred to as the *Warnock Report*.

93. Victoria, Committee to Consider the Social, Ethical and Legal Issues Arising from In Vitro Fertilization, *Interim Report* (1982). See also, *Issues Paper on Donor Gametes* (1983), *Report on Donor Gametes and In Vitro Fertilization* (1983) and *Report on the Disposition of Embryos Produced by In Vitro Fertilization* (1984). When citing the *Waller Report,* the final report is the one to which commentators are referring.

94. Queensland, Australia. *Report of the Special Committee Appointed by the Queensland Government to Enquire into the Laws Relating to Artificial Insemination, In Vitro Fertilization and Other Related Matters* (1984).

95. South Australia, *Report of the Working Party on In Vitro Fertilization and Artificial Insemination by Donor* (1984).

96. Tasmania, Australia. Committee to Investigate Artificial Conception and Related Matters. *Interim Report* (1984); *Final Report* (1985).

97. Western Australia. Committee to Enquire into the Social, Legal and Ethical Issues Relating to In Vitro Fertilization and Its Supervision. *Interim Report* (1984); *Report* (1985).

98. Ontario, Law Reform Commission. *Report on Human Artificial Reproduction and Related Matters* (1985).

99. Netherlands, Health Council, Committee on In Vitro Fertilization and Artificial Insemination by Donor. *Interim Report on In Vitro Fertilization* (1984); *Report on Artificial Reproduction, with Special Reference to In Vitro Fertilization, Artificial Insemination with Donor Sperm, and Surrogate Motherhood* (1986).

100. France, National Consultative Committee on Ethics. *Report on Ethical Problems Related to Techniques of Artificial Reproduction* (1984); *Report on Research Involving Human Embryos In Vitro and Their Use for Medical and Scientific Purposes* (1986).

101. Spain, Congress of Deputies, General Secretariat, Special Commission for the Study of Human In Vitro Fertilization and Artificial Insemination. *Report* (1986). To date, in July 1993, no law has been passed in Spain.

102. Adler, "Baby M Revisited," *New Jersey Law Journal* 123 (1989): 421, 436. See also New York State Department of Health, *The Business of Surrogate Parenting*, (Albany: State of New York Department of Health, 1992): 12.

103. Barbara Cohen, "Surrogate Mothers: Whose Baby Is It?" *American Journal of Law and Medicine* 10 (Fall 1984): 247, n. 30.

104. For more extended discussion of this point, see chapter two.

105. For example, this fifteen-day recission period is a part of the law in Rhode Island. R.I. Gen. Laws Sec. 15-7-6 (1981), cited in Shireen Taylor, "Conceiving for Cash: Is It Legal?" *Human Rights Annual* 4 (1987): 430, n. 79.

106. Ibid., 430-31.

107. Ibid., 429, n. 73.

108. Ibid., 419, n. 23.

109. Ibid., 419.

110. Ibid., 420, n. 25.

111. Uniform Parentage Act, section 5(b). States that have adopted this include California (Cal. Civ. Code 7005, West 1983), Colorado (Colo. Rev. Stat. 19-6-106, 1978), Minnesota (Minn. Stat. Ann. 257.56, West 1982), Montana (Mont. Code Ann. 40-6-106, 1982), Washington (Wash. Rev. Code Ann. 26.26.050, Supp. 1983) and Wyoming

(Wyo. Stat. 14-2-103, 1978). Other states that have AID laws that would seem to present an obstacle to surrogacy are Alaska (Alaska Stat. 25.20.045, 1983), Arkansas (Ark. Stat. Ann. 61 1-141(c), 1971), Connecticut (Conn. Gen. Stat. 45-69f-45-69n, 1981), Florida (Fla. Stat. 742.11, Supp. 1983), Kansas (Kan. Stat. Ann. 23-128-23-130, 1981), Louisiana (La. Civ. Code Ann. Art. 188, West Supp. 1984), New York (N.Y. Dom. Rel. Law 73, McKinney 1977), North Carolina (N.C. Gen. Stat. 49 A-1, 1976), Oklahoma (Okla. Sat. Ann. Title 10 551-553, West Supp. 1983), Oregon (Or. Rev. Stat. 109.239, 1983), Texas (Tex. Fam. Code Ann. Title 2, 12.30, Vernon 1975), and Virginia (Va. Code 64.1-7.1, 1980); cited in Cohen, "Surrogate Mothers: Whose Child Is It?" 255, n. 92.

112. Taylor, "Conceiving for Cash: Is It Legal?," 435.

113. See the previous discussion of *Syrkowski v. Appleyard*, 122 Mich. App. 506, 333 N.W. 2d 90 (1983), and *Czajak v. Varonese*, 428 N.Y.S. 2d 986 (1980). In this latter case, a New York man claimed to be the natural father of a child conceived by AID. The child was being supported by the husband of the mother, and the court held that there was no basis for any decision of paternity under paternity laws, since the paternity laws only concerned child support and not paternity status. Cited in Taylor, "Conceiving for Cash: Is It Legal?," 434.

CONCLUSION: LEGISLATIVE PROPOSAL FOR SURROGATE MOTHERHOOD

INTRODUCTION

Given the complexities of surrogacy arrangements, and the potential for complications and prolonged custody contests, there is a pressing need for states to define their positions on surrogacy by passing legislation. The matter of surrogacy properly belongs in the legislatures, not the courts, and the courts have asked repeatedly for legislative direction for future cases.

The *Johnson v. Calvert* case is a good example of this need. The California Supreme Court recently decided this case. At the time the case was decided, the child was three years old, and it is difficult to see how any change in his home environment at this stage in his life can be in his best interest. Of course, the Court could have made a decision about Anna Johnson's parental rights, yet refuse to make a custody change, similar to the *Baby M* decision. Yet clearly the best interests of the children born of surrogacy arrangements mandate that the issue of surrogacy be treated before they are brought into existence, so that after birth, they have their home environment and legal parents settled. Advocates of a contract approach to surrogacy will insist that this is precisely what the contract provides, and that enforcing the contract is in the child's best interests. In cases of a breach of the agreement, it may be that a custody arrangement with the child place with the intending couple may be best for the child, again similar to the *Baby M* decision. But that is very different from enforcing a contract that involuntarily divests the mother of her parental rights to the child, with whom she has a fundamental right to associate. Though custody should be decided on the best interests standard, and often results in the child being awarded to the intending parents, it does not follow that the child's best interests also authorize enforcing a contract to relinquish parental rights prior to the child's birth.

There are two different approaches taken to drafting legislation to deal with surrogacy. The first is to enact a statute that deals exclusively with surrogacy.

This has been the method used by the majority of states that have passed surrogacy laws.[1] A second approach is to amend existing state adoption laws, expanding their scope to include surrogacy, thereby subsuming surrogacy under current adoption statutes.[2] In this approach, commercial surrogacy is banned and the contract is not enforceable, consistent with long-standing adoption law. This proposal will take the first approach, even though the moral analysis of surrogacy undertaken in this work indicates that surrogacy should be treated similarly to state-sanctioned adoption.   Were the focus of this work on California law only, for example, there would be no problem fitting surrogacy into existing adoption law.   Since the focus is beyond any one state, the proposed law will be drafted to stand on its own. It could serve as a basis for amending any state's current adoption laws, but could also stand as a statute on its own.

Some of the legislation that has already been enacted is very brief, stating essentially that surrogacy contracts are void and unenforceable.   For example, the laws in Nebraska and Louisiana contain just two sections each, one stating that the contract is void, and the other defining what a surrogacy contract is. Other legislative proposals are quite long, covering every conceivable contingency in surrogacy.   The New Hampshire law is quite thorough, for example, and some of the sample drafts of legislation are even more thorough.[3] The approach taken in this proposal will be to focus on the areas of commercial surrogacy and parental rights, and to show how the moral analysis and conclusions might be enacted into law.

SURROGATE MOTHERHOOD STATUTE

Purpose: An act to declare surrogate motherhood contracts as void and unenforceable; to prohibit surrogate motherhood contracts for compensation; to provide for children born through a surrogate motherhood contract; and to specify sanctions for violation.[4]

Section 1. Definitions.

As used in this statute:

A. "Compensation" means any valuable consideration paid to a surrogate mother in excess of medical expenses associated with her pregnancy and lost wages due to work missed for reasons directly related to the pregnancy.
B.   "Intended Parents" means the people who enter into a surrogate motherhood agreement by which they intend to become the legal parents of the resulting child.

C. "Surrogate" means a woman who agrees to bear a child for the intending parents, becoming pregnant either by sexual intercourse, artificial insemination, or embryo transfer.

D. "Participating Parties" includes the intended parents and the surrogate.

E. "Commercial Surrogacy Contract" means a contract, arrangement, or agreement by which a surrogate agrees to conceive and bear a child for the intending parents for compensation and voluntarily agrees to relinquish her parental rights to the child.[5]

F. "Non-Commercial Surrogacy Contract" means an agreement for a surrogate to bear a child for intended parents without compensation.

G. "Genetic Surrogacy" means that the surrogate has provided the egg and is thus genetically related to the child she is carrying.

H. "Gestational Surrogacy" means that the surrogate is not genetically related to the child she is carrying.

Section 2. Commercial Surrogacy Contracts.

No person may enter a commercial surrogacy contract, nor may any person, agency, institution, or intermediary procure or otherwise arrange a commercial surrogacy contract. Nothing in this section shall be construed to prohibit non-commercial surrogacy contracts.

Section 3. Parental Rights.

A. The woman who gives birth to the child in a surrogacy arrangement is the mother of the child. Her husband is presumed to be the child's father. This presumption is rebuttable by blood test or acknowledgment of the surrogate's husband that he is not the father.

B. Should the surrogate so desire, she may relinquish her parental rights to the child in accordance with existing adoption statutes.

C. Any surrogacy contract that requires a surrogate to relinquish parental rights or requires consent to stepparent adoption prior to conception or before the end of any recision period provided by state adoption law, is void and unenforceable. Once custody is transferred to the intending parents after the recision period, parental rights are irrevocably relinquished.

D. Should the surrogate desire to retain parental rights to the child, custody shall be decided based, first, on the child's best interests. If the best interests standard does not indicate a clear preference for one parent, then the parent with the greater parental claim shall receive custody.[6] Visitation may be awarded based on the child's best interests.

E. Should the surrogate receive custody of the child, she will return all payments made to her that were made to reimburse her for medical expenses incurred as a result of the pregnancy. She shall also return any reimbursement for lost wages paid to her by the intending parents.

F. The person who receives custody of the child is solely responsible for the child's financial support.

G. Should the child be born with a physical deformity or should prenatal examination indicate physical deformity, the child will be the responsibility of the intending parents. If the surrogate desires to retain her parental rights, then custody will be decided according to section 3D.

Section 4. Privacy Rights of the Surrogate.

A. Any surrogacy arrangement that requires that the surrogate do any of the following is void and unenforceable:[7]

(1) Provide an egg to conceive a child.

(2) Consent to artificial insemination in order to become pregnant.

(3) Consent to undergo an abortion at the request of the intending parents.

(4) Continue the pregnancy should the surrogate desire to terminate it.

(5) Consent to amniocentesis to determine fetal abnormality.

(6) Consent to any medical or psychological examinations or treatment during the pregnancy.

(7) Waive parental rights, duties or custody of the child born to her.

(8) Forego the use of alcohol or tobacco during the pregnancy.

(9) Restrict her activity at the request of the intending parents.

B. All medical decisions concerning the pregnancy belong solely to the surrogate.

Section 5. Penalties.

A. Any person who arranges or participates in a commercial surrogacy contract shall be guilty of a misdemeanor, punishable by a fine of up to $5,000.

CONCLUSION

This proposed legislation is not as comprehensive as others that have been put forth and enacted. The reason for this is that instead of regulating commercial surrogacy, this statute aims to prohibit it. Therefore other aspects of a surrogacy contract such as eligibility of the surrogate, psychological testing of the surrogate, regulation of the intermediaries who assist in procuring a surrogate and drafting the contract, arrangements concerning the fee paid to the surrogate, and damages in the event of a breach, do not need to be addressed. Since this work's moral analysis of surrogacy led to a prohibition of both commercial surrogacy and enforcement of the arrangement, there is no need to address these issues in any legislative proposal.

NOTES

1. Florida, Indiana, Louisiana, Michigan, Nebraska, Nevada, New Hampshire, New York, North Dakota, Utah, and Washington have all followed this approach.

2. States that have taken this approach are Arkansas, Arizona and Kentucky. This is also the approach taken by the Joint Legislative Committee on Surrogate Parenting in California in the majority report to the legislature, which reflects the views of the advisory chairman, Alexander Capron. This report spells out, with specificity the more general recommendations on surrogacy he has made in his published writings on the subject. See for example, Alexander Morgan Capron and Margaret J. Radin, "Choosing Family Law over Contract Law as a Paradigm for Surrogate Motherhood," *Law, Medicine and Health Care* 16, nos. 1-2 (1988): 34-43.

3. See for example, Note, "Model Human Reproductive Technologies and Surrogacy Act," *Iowa Law Review* 72 (1987): 943-1013. Though this act also deals with other reproductive technologies, the principal focus is surrogacy.

4. This is adapted from the introductory purpose statement of Michigan Public Act 199 of 1988.

5. This is adapted from Michigan Public Act 199 of 1988, Sec. 3(i).

6. As indicated in chapter three, on the basis of both a biological contribution and bonding of relationship, the surrogate will usually have the greater parental claim at birth. Though this part of the statute does not automatically establish a presumption for the surrogate, in most cases, she will have the stronger parental claim.

7. This is adapted from the Indiana law, Indiana Code Annotated, Sec. 31-8-21-1 to 31-8-2-3 (1988).

BIBLIOGRAPHY

BOOKS AND JOURNAL ARTICLES

Adler, M. "Baby M Revisited," *New Jersey Law Journal* 123 (1989): 421-436.

American Civil Liberties Union. Policy on Surrogate Parenting. New York: ACLU, 1987.

American College of Obstetricians and Gynecologists, Committee on Ethics. "Statement on Surrogate Motherhood." Washington, D. C., 1990.

Anderson, Elizabeth A. "Is Women's Labor a Commodity?" *Philosophy and Public Affairs* 19 (Winter 1990): 71-92.

Andolsen, Barbara Hilkert. "Why a Surrogate Mother Should Have the Right to Change Her Mind: A Feminist Analysis of the Changes in Motherhood Today." In *On the Problem of Surrogate Motherhood: Analyzing the Baby M Case*, ed. Herbert Richardson, 41-55. Lewiston, Pa: Edwin Mellen Press, 1987.

Andrews, Lori. "The Aftermath of Baby M: Proposed State Laws on Surrogate Motherhood." *Hastings Center Report* 17 (October/November 1987): 31-40.

———. "Control and Compensation: Laws Governing Extracorporeal Generative Materials." *Journal of Medicine and Philosophy* 14 (October 1989): 541-60.

———. "Feminism Revisited: Fallacies and Policies in the Surrogacy Debate." *Logos (USA)* 9 (1988): 81-96.

———. *New Conceptions*. New York: Ballantine, 1985.

———. "The Stork Market: The Law of the New Reproduction Technologies." *American Bar Association Journal* 70 (August 1984): 50-56.

———. "Surrogate Motherhood: An Ethical Perspective," *Law, Medicine and Health Care* 16, nos. 1-2 (1988): 73-91.

———. "Surrogate Motherhood: The Challenge for Feminists," in *Surrogate Motherhood: Politics and Privacy*, ed. Larry Gostin, 171-76. Bloomington: Indiana University Press, 1990.

Annas, George J. "Baby M: Babies (and Justice) for Sale." *Hastings Center Report* 17 (June 1987): 13-15.

———. "Death Without Dignity for Commercial Surrogacy: The Case of Baby M." *Hastings Center Report* 18 (April/May 1988): 21-24.

_____ . "Redefining Parenthood and Protecting Embryos: Why We Need New Laws." *Hastings Center Report* 14 (October 1984): 50-52.

Annas, George J., and Sherman Elias, "Noncoital Reproduction," *Journal of the American Medical Association* 255 (3 January 1986).

_____ . "In Vitro Fertilization and Embryo Transfer: Medicolegal Aspects of a New Technique to Create a Family," *Family Law Quarterly* 17 (1983).

Appelton, Susan French. "Surrogacy Arrangements and the Conflict of Laws." *Wisconsin Law Review* 1990 no. 2 (1990): 399-482.

Arenstein, Robert D. "Is Surrogacy Against the Public Policy? The Answer is Yes." *Seton Hall Law Review* 18 (1988): 831-38.

Arms, Suzanne. *To Love and Let Go.* New York: Alfred Knopf, 1986.

Armstrong, Paul W., and T. Patrick Hill. "Baby M: New Beginnings and Ancient Mileposts." *Seton Hall Law Review* 18 (1988): 848-54.

Arrow, Kenneth. "Gifts and Exchanges," *Philosophy and Public Affairs* 4 (1972): 343-362.

Baber. H.E. "For the Legitimacy of Surrogacy Contracts." In *On the Problem of Surrogate Parenting: Analyzing the Baby M Case*, ed. Herbert Richardson, 31-40. Lewiston, Pa: Edwin Mellen Press, 1987.

Bach, Kathleen K. *Research Guide: Surrogate Motherhood.* Buffalo, N. Y.: William S. Hein, 1987.

Bartels, Dianne, ed. *Beyond Baby M.* New York: Humana Press, 1988.

Bettenhausen, Elizabeth. "Hagar Revisited." *Christianity in Crisis* (4 May 1987): 714-716.

Bhimji, Shabir. "Womb for Rent: Ethical Aspects of Surrogate Motherhood." *Canadian Medical Association Journal* 137 (15 December 1987): 1132-35.

Bitner, Lizabeth A. "Wombs for Rent: A Call for Pennsylvania Legislation Legalizing and Regulating Surrogate Parenting Agreements." *Dickinson Law Review* 90 (Fall 1985): 227-59.

Black, Robert C. "Legal Problems of Surrogate Motherhood." *New England Law Review* 16 (1981): 373-95.

Blank, Robert H. *Regulating Reproduction.* New York: Columbia University Press, 1990.

Blodgett, Nancy. "Who is Mother: Genetic Donor, Not Surrogate," *American Bar Association Journal* 1 June 1986

Boskey, James B. "Adoption, the Termination of Parental Rights and Baby M." *Seton Hall Law Review* 18 (1988): 866-76.

Bradley, Thomas. "Prohibiting Payments to Surrogate Mothers: Love's Labor Lost and the Constitutional Right to Privacy." *John Marshall Law Review* 20 (1987): 715-45.

Brennan, Richard E. "In Re Baby M: The Structure of the Opinion." *Seton Hall Law Review* 18 (1988): 885-89.

Brody, Eugene. "Reproduction without Sex--But with the Doctor." *Daily Journal Report* 88, no.6 (1 April 1988): 26-29.

Cahill, Lisa Sowle. "The Ethics of Surrogate Motherhood: Biology, Freedom and Moral Obligation." *Law, Medicine and Health Care* 16, nos. 1-2 (1988): 65-71.

_____ . "Women, Marriage, Parenthood: What Are Their Natures?" *Logos (USA)* 9 (1988): 11-35.

"California May Sanction Paid Surrogate Pregnancies," *Medical Ethics Advisor* 8, no. 5 (May 1992): 56-58.

Callahan, Sidney. "The Ethical Challenge of the New Reproductive Technology," in *Medical Ethics: A Guide for Health Care Professionals*, ed. John F. Monagle and David C. Thomasma. Frederick, Md.: Aspen Publishers, 1987.

_____ . "Lovemaking and Babymaking: Ethics and the New Reproductive Technology." *Commonweal*, 24 April 1987, 233-39.

Capron, Alexander Morgan. Alternative Birth Technologies: Legal Challenges." *U.C. Davis Law Review* 20 (1987): 679-704.

_____ . "The New Reproductive Possibilities: Seeking a Moral Basis for Concerted Action in a Pluralistic Society." *Law, Medicine and Health Care* 12 (October 1984): 192-98.

_____ . "Surrogate Contracts: A Danger Zone." *Los Angeles Times*, 7 April 1987, B5.

Capron, Alexander Morgan and Margaret J. Radin. "Choosing Family Law over Contract Law as a Paradigm for Surrogate Motherhood." *Law, Medicine and Health Care* 16, nos.1-2 (1988): 34-43.

Caraballo, Wilfredo. "Baby M: A Non-Contract Contract Case." *Seton Hall Law Review* 18 (1988): 855-65.

Carbone, June. "The Limits of Contract in Family Law: An Analysis of Surrogate Motherhood." *Logos (USA)* 9 (1988): 147-60.

Cohen, Barbara. "Surrogate Mothers: Whose Baby Is It?" *American Journal of Law and Medicine* 10 (Fall 1984): 241-85.

Coleman, Phyllis. "Surrogate Motherhood: Analysis of the Problems and Suggestions for a Solution," *Tennessee Law Review* 50 (1982): 71-118.

Corea, Gina. *The Mother Machine: Reproductive Technologies from Artificial Insemination to Artificial Wombs*. New York: Harper and Row, 1985.

Corea, Gina, Genate Duelli Klein, Jalna Hanmer, Helen B. Holmes, Betty Hoskins, Madhu Kishwar, Janice Raymond, Robyn Rowland, and Roberta Steinbacher. *Man Made Woman*. London: Hutchinson and Co., 1985.

Crow, Carol A. "The Surrogate Child: Legal Issues and Implications for the Future." *Journal of Juvenile Law* 7 (1983): 80-92.

DeMarco, Donald. *Biotechnology and the Assault on Parenthood* San Francisco: Ignatius Press, 1991.

Dodds, Susan, and Karen Jones. "A Response to Purdy's Surrogate Motherhood." *Bioethics* 3 (January 1989): 35-39.

Dolgin, Janet L. "Status and Contract in Surrogate Motherhood: An Illumination of the Surrogacy Debate." *Daily Journal Report* 90, no. 12 (28 December 1990): 2-18.

Eaton, Thomas A. "Comparative Responses to Surrogate Motherhood." *Nebraska Law Review* 65 (1986): 686-727.

Ellin, Joseph. "Reproductive Technology, Catholicism, Feminism and the Thesis of Bootstrap Pessimism." *Logos (USA)* 9 (1988): 37-49.

Evans, Debra. *Without Moral Limits: Women, Reproduction and the New Medical Technology*. Westchester, Ill.: Crossway Books, 1989.

Field, Martha. *Surrogate Motherhood: The Legal and Human Issues.* Cambridge, Mass.: Harvard University Press, 1988.

Fleck, Leonard M. "Surrogate Motherhood: Is It Morally Equivalent to Selling Babies?" *Logos (USA)* 9 (1988): 135-45.

Gaffney, James. "Hagar and Her Sisters: Precedent for Conduct." *Commonweal*, 24 April 1987, 240-42.

Garrison, Marsha. "Why Terminate Parental Rights?" *Stanford Law Review* 35 (February 1983): 423-96.

Garvey, John. "Contracting Anguish: Sara, Melissa or Baby M?" *Commonweal*, 24 April 1987, 232.

Gatens-Robinson, Eugenie, "Selling Spare Parts and Renting Useful Spaces." *Journal of Social Philosophy* 18 (Winter 1987): 28-37.

Gilliam, Rene R.. "When a Surrogate Mother Breaks a Promise: The Inappropriateness of the Traditional `Best Interests of the Child' Standard." *Memphis State University Law Review* 18 (Spring 1988): 514-539.

Gilligan, Carol. "The 1984 James McCormick Mitchell Lecture: Feminist Discourse, Moral Values and the Law--A Conversation," *Buffalo Law Review* 34 (1985): 11-64.

Gordis, Daniel H. *Give Me Progeny: Jewish Ethics and the Economics of Surrogate Motherhood.* Los Angeles: University of Judaism, 1988.

Gostin, Larry. "A Civil Liberties Analysis of Surrogacy Arrangements." *Law, Medicine and Health Care* 16, nos.1-2 (1988): 7-15.

_____ . *Surrogate Motherhood: Politics and Privacy.* Bloomington: Indiana University Press, 1990.

Graham, M. Louise. "Surrogate Gestation and the Protection of Choice." *Santa Clara Law Review* 22 (1982): 291-323.

Handel, William. "An Argument for Surrogate Parenting." *Daily Journal Report* 88, no. 6 (1 April 1988): 9-16.

Hepper, Peter. "Foetal Learning: Implications for Psychiatry." *British Journal of Psychiatry* 155 (1989): 289-293.

Holder, Angela R. "Surrogate Motherhood: Babies for Fun and Profit." *Law, Medicine and Health Care* 12 (June 1984): 115-17.

Hollinger, Joan Heifetz. "From Coitus to Commerce: Legal and Social Consequences of Noncoital Reproduction." *University of Michigan Journal of Law Reform* 18 (Summer 1985): 865-932.

Houlgate, Laurence D. "Whose Child: In re Baby M and the Biological Preference Principle." *Logos (USA)* 9 (1988): 161-177.

Hull, Richard T., ed. *Ethical Issues in the New Reproductive Technologies.* Belmont, Calif.: Wadsworth Publishing Co., 1990.

Joint Legislative Committee on Surrogate Parenting. *Commercial and Noncommercial Surrogate Parenting.* Sacramento, Calif.: Joint Publications Office, November 1990.

Jonsen, Albert R. "Ethics of Reproductive Technology: The Deconstruction of a Paradigm." *Logos (USA)* 9 (1988): 3-9.

Kane, Elizabeth. *Birthmother.* New York: Harcourt Brace Jovanovich, 1988.

Katz, Avi. "Surrogate Motherhood and the Baby Selling Laws." *Columbia Journal of Law and Social Problems* 20 (1986): 1-53.

Katz, Katheryn D. "The Public Response to Surrogate Motherhood Agreements: Why They Should Be Illegal and Unenforceable." *New York State Bar Journal* (May 1988): 21-36.

Keane, Noel. "The Baby M Decision: Facts and Fictions, Before and Beyond." *Seton Hall Law Review* 18 (1988): 839-47.

————. "Legal Problems of Surrogate Motherhood," *Southern Illinois Law Journal* (1980): 147, 153.

Keane, Noel, and Dennis Breo. *The Surrogate Mother.* New York: Everest House, 1981.

Ketchum, Sara Ann. "Selling Babies and Selling Bodies." *Hypatia* 4 (Fall 1989): 116-27.

Kopytoff, Barbara K. "Surrogate Motherhood: Questions of Law and Values." *University of San Francisco Law Review* 22 (Winter/Spring 1988): 205-49.

Kornegay, R. Jo. "Is Commercial Surrogacy Babyselling?" *Journal of Applied Philosophy* 7 (March 1990): 45-50.

Krauthammer, Charles. "Ethics of Human Manufacture." *New Republic* 4 May 1987, 17-19.

Krimmel, Herbert T. "The Case Against Surrogate Parenting." *Hastings Center Report* 13 (October 1983): 35-39."

————. "Statement Regarding the Proposed Surrrogate Parent Act, Assembly Bill 3771." Statement in Hearings before the California Assembly Committee on the Judiciary, Los Angeles, Calif.. 19 November 1982.

————. "Surrogate Motherhood Arrangements from the Perspective of the Child." *Logos (USA)* 9 (1988): 97-112.

Kuo, Lenore. "The Morality of Surrogate Mothering." *Southern Journal of Philosophy* 27 (Fall 1989): 361-80.

Landes, Elisabeth M., and Richard A. Posner, "The Economics of the Baby Shortage," *Journal of Legal Studies* 7 (June 1978): 323-48.

Laufer, William M. "Can Surrogacy Co-Exist with New Jersey's Adoption Laws?" *Seton Hall Law Review* 18 (1988): 890-95.

Lee, Robert, and Derek Morgan, eds. *Birthrights: Law and Ethics at the Beginnings of Life.* London: Routledge, 1989.

Logan, Brent. "Teaching the Unborn: Precept and Practice," *Pre- and Peri-Natal Psychology* 2 no.1 (Fall 1987):

London, Harriet Johnson. "Baby M: The Real Loser." *Seton Hall Law Review* 18 (1988): 877-84.

Lukesch, Monika. "Psychologie Faktoren der Schwangerschaft." Ph.D. dissertation, University of Salzburg, 1975.

Macklin, Ruth. "Artificial Means of Reproduction and Our Understanding of the Family." *Hastings Center Report* 21 (January/February 1991): 5-11.

————. "Is There Anything Wrong with Surrogate Motherhood?: An Ethical Analysis." *Law, Medicine and Health Care* 16, nos. 1-2 (1988): 57-64.

McCormick, Richard A. "Theology and Bioethics." *Hastings Center Report* 19 (March/April 1989): 5-10.

McNeil, Maureen, Ian Varcoe, and Steven Yearley. *The New Reproductive Technologies.* London: MacMillan Press, 1990.

Mady, Theresa. "Surrogate Mothers: The Legal Issues." *American Journal of Law and Medicine* 7 (1981): 323-52.

Malm, H. M. "Commodification or Compensation: A Reply to Sara Ketchum." *Hypatia* 4 (Fall 1989): 128-35.

Malm, Heidi. "Paid Surrogacy: Arguments and Responses." *Public Affairs Quarterly* 3 (April 1989): 59-60.

Mandler, John J. "Developing a Concept of the Modern Family: A Proposed Uniform Surrogate Parenthood Act." *Georgetown Law Journal* 73 (1985): 1283-1329.

Martin, David K. "Surrogate Motherhood: Contractual Issues and Remedies under Legislative Proposals." *Washburn Law Journal* 23 (1984): 601-37.

May, William F. "Surrogate Motherhood and the Marketplace." *Second Opinion* 9 (1987): 132-40.

Mellown, Mary Ruth. "An Incomplete Picture: The Debate About Surrogate Motherhood." *Harvard Women's Law Journal* 8 (1985): 231-46.

Michel, Vicki. "Legislating Surrogate Mothering." *Ethical Currents* (1989): 4-5, 7.

Miller, Frances H. "Surrogate Fatherhood." (Review of *Surrogate Motherhood*, by Martha A. Field.) *Boston University Law Review* 70, no. 1 (January 1990): 169-83.

Miller, Robert H. "Surrogate Parenting: An Infant Industry Presents Society with Legal, Ethical Questions," *Ob/Gyn News* 18 (1983): 1-4.

Moraczewski, Albert S. "Surrogate Mother or Surrogate Wife?" *Ethics and Medics* 13 (June 1988): 1-2.

Morgan, Derek. *Surrogacy and the Moral Economy* . New York: Gower Publishing, 1990.

———, ed. *Birthrights: Law and Ethics at the Beginning of Life.* London and New York: Routledge, 1989.

Neale, Ann. "Responsible Stewardship Requires Not Cooperating with Surrogacy." *Health Progress* (March 1987): 39, 42-43.

Nelson, Hilde, and James L. Nelson. "Cutting Motherhood in Two: Some Suspicions Concerning Surrogacy." *Hypatia* 4 (Fall 1989): 85-94.

Newton, Lisa. "Surrogate Motherhood and the Limits of Rational Ethics." *Logos (USA)* 9 (1988): 113-34.

Note. "Developing a Concept of the Modern "Family": A Proposed Uniform Surrogate Parenthood Act," *Georgetown Law Journal* 73 (1985): 1291-1293

Note. "Model Reproductive Technologies and Surrogacy Act." *Iowa Law Review* 72 (1987): 943-1013.

Note. "Reproductive Technology and the Procreative Rights of the Unmarried." *Harvard Law Review* 98 (January 1985): 669-85.

Note. "Rumplestiltskin Revisited: The Inalienable Rights of Surrogate Mothers." *Harvard Law Review* 99 (June 1986): 1936-55.

Note. "Surrogate Parenthood--An Analysis of the Problems and a Solution: Representation for the Child." *William Mitchell Law Review* 12 (1985): 143-82.

O'Donovan, Oliver. *Begotten or Made?* . Oxford: Clarendon Press. 1984.

Oliver, Kelly. "Marxism and Surrogacy." *Hypatia* 4 (Fall 1989): 95-115.

O'Neill, Onora, and William Ruddick, eds. *Having Children: Philosophical and Legal Reflections*. New York: Oxford University Press, 1979.

Overall, Christine. *Ethics and Human Reproduction: A Feminist Analysis.* Winchester, Mass.: Allen and Unwin, Inc., 1987.

Page, Edgar. "Donation, Adoption, and Surrogacy." *Journal of Applied Philosophy* 2 (October 1985): 161-72.

Parker, Philip J. "Motivation of Surrogate Mothers: Initial Findings," *American Journal of Psychiatry* 140 (January 1983): 117-18.

Patterson, Suzanne M. "Parenthood by Proxy: Legal Implications of Surrogate Birth." *Iowa Law Review* 67 (1982): 385-99.

Phillips, John W., and Susan D. Phillips. "In Defense of Surrogate Parenting: A Critical Analysis of the Recent Kentucky Experience." *Kentucky Law Journal* 69 (1980/81): 877-931.

Prettyman, W. Marshall. "The Next Baby M Case: The Need for a Surrogacy Statute." *Seton Hall Law Review* 18 (1988): 896-929.

Pritchard, J. Robert S. "A Market for Babies?" *University of Toronto Law Journal* 34 (1984): 341-57.

Purdy, Laura. "A Response to Dodds and Jones." *Bioethics* 3 (January 1989): 40-44.

_____. "Surrogate Motherhood: Exploitation or Empowerment?" *Bioethics* 3 (January 1989): 18-34.

Rachels, James. "Baby M." *Bioethics* 1 (October 1987): 357-65.

Radin, Margaret J. "Market-Inalienability." *Harvard Law Review* 100 (June 1987): 1849-1937.

Raymond, Janice G. "Reproductive Gifts and Gift Giving: The Altruistic Woman" *Hastings Center Report* 20 (November/December 1990): 7-11.

Richardson, Herbert. "God Is the Creator of Human Life: A Calvinist Defense of Surrogate Parenthood." In *On the Problem of Surrogate Motherhood: Analyzing the Baby M Case*, ed. Herbert Richardson, 111-34. Lewiston, Pa.: The Edwin Mellen Press, 1987.

_____, ed. *On the Problem of Surrogate Motherhood: Analyzing the Baby M Case.* Lewiston, Pa.: Edwin Mellen Press, 1987.

Robertson, John A. "Embryos, Families and Procreative Liberty: The Legal Structure of the New Reproduction." *Southern California Law Review* 59, no. 5 (July 1986): 939-1041.

_____. "Procreative Liberty and the Control of Conception, Pregnancy and Childbirth." *Virginia Law Review* 69 (April 1983): 405-64.

_____. "Surrogate Mothers: Not So Novel After All." *Hastings Center Report* 13 (October 1983): 28-34.

Ross, Judith Wilson. "Considering the Other Edge of Life." (Review of *Recreating Motherhood: Ideology and Technology in Patriarchal Society*, by Barbara Katz Rothman, and *Surrogate Motherhood: The Legal and Human Issues*, by Martha A. Field.) *Hastings Center Report* 20 (September/October 1990): 46-48.

Rothman, Barbara Katz. *Recreating Motherhood: Ideology and Technology in Patriarchal Society.* New York: W. W. Norton, 1989.

_____. "Surrogacy Contracts: A Misconception." *Daily Journal Report* 88, no. 6 (1 April 1988): 17-21.

Rust, Mark. "Whose Baby Is It?: Surrogate Motherhood After Baby M." *ABA Journal*, 1 June 1987, 52-56.

Ryan, Michael D. "Sorting Out Motivations: Personal Integrity as the First Criterion of Moral Action." In *On the Problem of Surrogate Motherhood: Analyzing the Baby M Case*, ed. Herbert Richardson, 107-10. Lewiston, Pa.: Edwin Mellen Press, 1987.

Schultz, Majorie Maguire. "Reproductive Technology and Intent-Based Parenthood: An Opportunity for Gender Neutrality." *Wisconsin Law Review* 1990, no. 2 (1990): 297-398.

Shalev, Carmel. *Birth Power: The Case for Surrogacy*. New Haven: Yale University Press, 1989.

Shannon, Thomas A. *Surrogate Motherhood: The Ethics of Using Human Beings*. New York: Crossroad, 1988.

Sherman, Roxie. "Three Lawyers and a Baby M." *Daily Journal Report* 88, no. 6 (1 April 1988): 30-31.

Singer Peter, and Deane Wells. *Making Babies: The New Science and Ethics of Conception*. New York: Charles Scribner's Sons, 1985.

Singer, Peter. "Altruism and Commerce: A Defense of Titmuss against Arrow." *Philosophy and Public Affairs* 5 (1973): 312-20.

Sistare, Christine. "Reproductive Freedom and Women's Freedom: Surrogacy and Autonomy." *Philosophical Forum* 19 (Summer 1988): 227-40.

Skoloff, Gary N., and Edward J. O'Donnell. "Baby M: A Disquieting Decision." *Seton Hall Law Review* 18 (1988): 827-30.

Sloan, Irving J. *The Law of Adoption and Surrogate Parenting*. London: Oceana Publications, 1988.

Sly, Karen Marie. "Baby-Sitting Consideration: Surrogate Mother's Right to `Rent Her Womb' for a Fee." *Gonzaga Law Review* 18 (1982/83): 539-65.

Smith, George P., II. "The Razor's Edge of Human Bonding: Artificial Fathers and Surrogate Mothers." *Western New England Law Review* 5 (1983): 639-66.

Sontag, L. W. "Parental Determinants of Postnatal Behavior," in *Fetal Growth and Development*, ed. Harry A. Weisman and George R. Kerr. New York: McGraw Hill, 1970.

―――――― . "Somatopsychics of Personality and Body Function." *Vita Humana* 6 (1963): 11-24.

Stanton, Elizabeth Rose. "The Rights of the Biological Father: From Adoption and Custody to Surrogate Motherhood." *Vermont Law Review* 12 (1987): 120.

Stanworth, Michelle, ed. *Reproductive Technologies: Gender, Motherhood and Medicine*. Cambridge, U.K.: Polity Press, 1987.

Steinbock, Bonnie. "Surrogate Motherhood as Prenatal Adoption." *Law, Medicine and Health Care* 16, nos. 1-2 (1988): 44-50.

Stott, Dennis. "Children in the Womb: The Effects of Stress." *New Society* (19 May 1977): 329-31.

―――――― . "Follow-up Study from Birth of the Effects of Prenatal Stresses." *Developmental Medicine and Child Neurology* 15 (1973): 770-87.

Stumpf, Andrea. "Redefining Mother: A Legal Matrix for the New Reproductive Technologies." *Yale Law Journal* 96 (1986): 187-208.

"Surrogate Mothers." *Fertility and Sterility* 46 (September 1986): 62S-68S.

"Surrogate Parenthood." *ABA Journal* 1 June 1987, 38-39.

Taub, Nadine. "Surrogacy: Sorting Through the Alternatives." *Daily Journal Report* 90, no. 12 (28 December 1990): 19-27.

Taylor, Shireen. "Conceiving for Cash: Is it Legal?: A Survey of the Laws Applicable to Surrogate Motherhood." *Human Rights Annual* 4 (1987): 413-44.

Titmuss, Richard. *The Gift Relationship: From Human Blood to Social Policy*. New York: Pantheon Press, 1971.

Townsend, Margaret. "Surrogate Mother Agreements: Contemporary Legal Aspects of a Biblical Notion." *University of Richmond Law Review* 16 (1982): 467-83.

Van den Bergh, B. R. H. "The Influence of Maternal Emotions During Pregnancy on Fetal and Neonatal Behavior." *Pre- and Peri-Natal Psychology* 5 (Winter 1990): 127.

Verny, Thomas, M.D., and John Kelly. *The Secret Life of the Unborn Child*. New York: Dell Publishing, 1981

Walters, LeRoy. "Ethics and New Reproductive Technologies: An International Review of Committee Statements." *Hastings Center Report* 17 (1987): 3-9.

Walzer, Michael. *Spheres of Justice*. New York: Basic Books, 1983.

Weber, Leonard J. "Social Responsibility Demands Treating All in Need." *Health Progress* (March 1987): 38, 40-42.

Werhane, Patricia. "Against the Legitimacy of Surrogacy Contracts." In *On the Problem of Surrogate Motherhood: Analyzing the Baby M Case*, ed. Herbert Richardson, 21-30. Lewiston, Pa.: Edwin Mellen Press, 1987.

Winkler, Robin, and Margaret van Keppel, *Relinquishing Mothers in Adoption*. Melbourne, Australia: Institute of Family Studies, 1984.

Wolf, Susan M.. "Enforcing Surrogate Motherhood Agreements: The Trouble with Specific Performance." *New York Law School Human Rights Annual* 4 no. 2 (Spring 1987): 403-8.

Women's Rights Committee, American Civil Liberties Union. "Statement of the Women's Rights Committee in Support of the Proposed Policy on Surrogate Parenting." New York: ACLU, 1987.

Zax, Melvin, et al., "Birth Outcomes in the Offspring of Mentally Disordered Women." *American Journal of Orthopsychiatry* (April 1977): 218-30.

Zax et al., "Perinatal Characteristics in the Offspring of Schizophrenic Women." *Journal of Nervous and Mental Disorders* 157 (1973): 191-99.

COURT CASES

In re Baby Girl, Ky. Cir. Ct., Jefferson City, March 8, 1983, 9 *Family Law Reporter* 2348 (1983).

In re Baby M, 525 A. 2d 1128, 1164 (1987).

In the Matter of Baby M, 109 N.J. 396, 537 A. 2d 1227 (1988).

Caban v. Muhammed, 441 U.S. 380 (1979).

Carey v. Population Services International, 431 U.S. 678 (1977).

Czajak v. Varonese, 428 N.Y.S. 2d 986 (1980).

Doe v. Bolton, 410 U.S. 179 (1973).

Doe v. Kelley, 106 Mich. App. 169, 307 N.W. 2d 438 (1981).

Eisenstadt v. Baird, 405 U.S. 438 (1972).

Grissom v. Dade County, Fla., 293 So. 2d 59 (1974)

Griswold v. Connecticut, 381 U.S. 479 (1965).

Johnson v. Calvert, Calif. Super. Ct. AD 57638, 22 October, 1990.

Lehr v. Robertson, 463 U.S. 248 (1982).

Meyer v. Nebraska, 262 U.S. 390 (1923).

Michelle Marie W. v. Ronald W, 139 Cal. App. 3d 24, 188 Cal. Rptr. 413 (1983).

Moore v. City of East Cleveland, 431 U.S. 494 (1977).

Moschetta v. Moschetta, AD 59584, 11 January, 1991.

People v. Keane, 144 Mich. App. 12, 373 N.W. 2d 228 (1985).

People v. Sorenson, 437 P. 2d 495.

Pierce v. Society of Sisters, 268 U.S. 510 (1925).

Planned Parenthood of Central Missouri v. Danforth, 428 U.S. 52 (1976).

Quilloin v. Walcott, 434 U.S. 246 (1978).

Reimche v. First National Bank of Nevada, 512 F.2d 187 (1975).

Santowsky v. Kramer, 455 U.S. 745 (1981).

In re Shirk's Estate, 186 Kan. 311, 350 P.2d 1 (Kan. 1960).

Skinner v. Oklahoma, 316 U.S. 535 (1942).

Smith v. Jones, no. 85-53201402 (Mich. Cir. Ct., Wayne County), 14 March 1986.

Stanley v. Illinois, 405 U.S. 645 (1972).

Surrogate Parenting Associates, Inc. v. Kentucky, Ky., 704 S.W. 2d 209 (1986).

Syrkowski v. Appleyard, 122 Mich. App. 506, 333 N.W. 2d 90 (1983).

Willey v. Lawton, 8 Ill. App. 2d 344, 132 N.E. 2d 34 (1956).

NEWSPAPER AND MAGAZINE ARTICLES

Brennan, Pat. "Surrogate to Share in Custody of Child." *Orange County Register,* 27 September 1991, A1, 12.

Callahan, Daniel. "Surrogate Motherhood: A Bad Idea." *New York Times,* 20 January 1987, B11.

Efron, Sonni. "Attempt to Deceive Surrogate Is Alleged." *Los Angeles Times*, 11 April 1991, B1, 12.

———. "Estranged Wife Is Denied Custody of Surogate Baby." *Los Angeles Times,* 9 April 1991, B1, 10.

———. "Father Gets Custody in Surrogate Case." *Los Angeles Times,* 15 January 1991, B1, 5.

———. "Surrogacy Custody Battle Has New Twist." *Los Angeles Times*, 14 January 1991, B1, 9.

———. "Surrogate Mother Gets Rights of Legal Parent." *Los Angeles Times*, 19 April 1991, A1, 30.

———. "Surrogate Mother Says That Couple Deceived Her." *Los Angeles Times*, 10 April 1991, B1, 6.

———. "Three "Parents" Fight Over Custody in Surrogate Case." *Los Angeles Times,* 3 March 1991, A1, 30.

Efron, Sonni, and Kevin Johnson. "Decision Hailed as Proper, Criticized as Outrageous." *Los Angeles Times,* 23 October 1990, A1, 26.

Efron, Sonni, and Maria Newman, "Surrogate Mother Gets Rights of Legal Parent," *Los Angeles Times*, 19 April 1981, A1.

Gewertz, Catherine. "Genetic Parents Win Sole Custody in Surrogate Case." *Los Angeles Times*, 23 October 1990, A1, 26.

_____ . "Judge May Rule on Surrogate Case Monday." *Los Angeles Times* 18 October 1990, A1, 30.

Hager, Philip. "State High Court to Rule in O.C. Surrogacy Case." *Los Angeles Times,* 24 January 1992, A1, 12.

Kantrowitz, Barbara. "Who Keeps Baby M?" *Newsweek*, 19 January 1987, 44-51.

Kelleher, Susan, and Pat Brennan. "Experts Agree Johnson surrogacy Ruling Establishes Strong Precedent." *Orange County Register,* 9 October 1991, A18.

Kevies, Betty Ann. "Mom and Dad and Mom: Surrogacy's New Family." *Los Angeles Times*, 22 March 1987, B12.

Lacayo, Richard. "Whose Child Is This?" *Time*, 19 January 1987, 56-58.

Lait, Matt, and Carla Rivera. "Father Ordered to Share Custody with Surrogate." *Los Angeles Times*, 27 September 1991, A1, 30.

Lichtblau, Eric. "Appellate Court Rules Against O.C. Surrogate." *Los Angeles Times*, 9 October 1991, A1, 18.

Lifsher, Marc. "Surrogacy Bill in Legislature Aims to Avert Conflict." *Orange County Register,* 9 October 1991, A18.

Parsons, Dana. "Surrogate Equation Didn't Require a King Solomon." *Los Angeles Times*, 23 October 1990, B1.

Petersen, Susan, and Susan Kelleher. "Court Upholds Ruling Against O.C. Surrogate." *Orange County Register* 9 October 1991, A1,18.

Rohrlich, Ted. "Ruling Gives Surrogation Legal Boost." *Los Angeles Times*, 23 October 1990, A26.

Soderlind, Rolf. "Germany Bans Surrogate Mothers." *Orange County Register*, 25 October 1990, A1.

"Surrogate Parenting: The Bioethical Issue." *Los Angeles Times* (20 August 1990): B10.

Voegler, William. "Scholar Assails Legislative Plan to Outlaw Surrogacy Contracts." *Los Angeles Daily Journal,* 15 January 1990, Section II, 1.

INDEX

About the Author

SCOTT B. RAE is an Associate Professor of Biblical Studies and Christian Ethics at Talbot School of Theology, Biola University, La Mirada, California. He is the author of several books and many articles on ethics in medicine, the workplace, and in biblical studies. He is also Ethics Consultant for Holy Cross Medical Center in Mission Hills, California.

ISBN 0-275-94679-7

90000>

EAN

9 780275 946791

HARDCOVER BAR CODE